Brian J. Robb is a writer and biographer whose previous books have included a *New York Times* and *Sunday Times* best-selling biography of *Titanic* star Leonardo DiCaprio; *Screams & Nightmares*, the definitive book on horror director Wes Craven; *Counterfeit Worlds*, exploring the life and work of Philip K. Dick; and a series of acclaimed film star biographies. For over ten years he was the managing editor of *The Official Star Trek Magazine*.

A BRIEF GUIDE TO

STAR WARS

The Unauthorised Inside Story Of George Lucas's Epic

BRIAN J. ROBB

ROBINSON

RUNNING PRESS
PHILADELPHIA · LONDON

Constable & Robinson Ltd
55-56 Russell Square
London WC1B 4HP
www.constablerobinson.com

First published in the UK by Robinson,
an imprint of Constable & Robinson Ltd., 2012

A copy of the British Library Cataloguing in
Publication data is available from the British Library.

ISBN 978-1-78033-399-1 (paperback)
ISBN 978-1-78033-583-4 (ebook)

1 3 5 7 9 10 8 6 4 2

First published in the United States in 2012 by Running Press Book Publishers,
a member of the Perseus Books Group.

Books published by Running Press are available at special discounts for bulk purchases in the
United States by corporations, institutions, and other organizations. For more information,
please contact the Special Markets Department at the Perseus Books Group, 2300 Chestnut
Street, Suite 200, Philadelphia, PA 19103, or call (800) 810-4145, ext. 5000, or email special.
markets@perseusbooks.com.

US ISBN 978-0-7624-4627-8
US Library of Congress Control Number: 2011942357

9   8   7   6   5   4   3   2   1
Digit on the right indicates the number of this printing

Running Press Book Publishers
2300 Chestnut Street
Philadelphia, PA 19103-4371

Visit us on the web!
www.runningpress.com

Printed and bound in the EU

For Cameron, my very own space cadet . . .

Contents

Chapter 1

A Long Time Ago . . .

When I decided I wanted to be a filmmaker, all my friends thought I was crazy. Nobody went into film; the girls all gave a wide berth to film students because they were supposed to be weird.

George Lucas

George Lucas was born into a time of rebellion. The post-war years through to the 1960s saw many social conventions challenged and overthrown, as society and its tastes changed. For most of his teenage years in the late 1950s, Lucas was himself a rebel. This rebellious, anti-authoritarian streak continued as he entered professional filmmaking in the late 1960s, refusing to make movies in the style of the dying studio system, but instead adopting his own approach. However, with the unimaginable success of *Star Wars* in 1977 – and all that came after it – George Lucas became a rebel who built an empire. He became the very personification of the establishment he had set out to fight against. This is the story of how it all happened.

As a ten-year-old growing up in Modesto, California, the biggest thing in the life of young George Lucas was television. After several years of resisting, his father had finally purchased a set for the family. It opened up a window on a whole new world for George Jr as he no longer had to visit friends' houses to see what was on TV. His favourite show quickly became *Adventure Theater*, screened nightly on San Francisco's Channel 4 KRON-TV. The programme was a compilation of old movie serials from two decades before, including the black-and-white adventures of *Tailspin Tommy*, *Lash La Rue* and *Spy Smasher*. 'It was a twenty-minute serial chapter, and the left over minutes of the half hour were filled with [the cartoon] *Crusader Rabbit*. I loved it.'

There was one serial hero in particular that caught Lucas's imagination. 'I used to love the *Flash Gordon* serials,' Lucas recalled in later years. 'They were a profound influence on me. The way I see things, the way I interpret things, is influenced by television. Visual conception, fast pace, quick cuts. I can't help it. I'm a product of the television age.'

Buster Crabbe had played Alex Raymond's space-faring hero in three chapter-play movie serials made between 1936 and 1940. The character started life in newspaper comic strips in January 1934, following the adventures of polo player Flash Gordon after he and friend Dale Arden are kidnapped by scientist Dr Hans Zarkov. They journey to the planet Mongo, where the evil Emperor Ming attacks Earth with flaming meteorites. The popular strip was rapidly adapted into a movie serial by Universal Studios, spanning thirteen cliff-hanging instalments.

It would be twenty years after they were made before Lucas saw these three serials on television, but they were to have a profound effect on his creativity as a filmmaker and on his future. At the time, the adventures of Flash Gordon were an escape into adventure for a young boy who felt his everyday life was very dull indeed.

As suggested by its name, Modesto in northern California is a very modest town. The town might have been geographically close to San Francisco, but in terms of atmosphere and feel, Modesto was more like a Midwestern American town than one near either of the more socially progressive coasts. Modesto had a long history of nothing much happening at all. The flat land-scape was dotted with farms, where every vehicle was worked hard. It was a town where ambitions were neither born nor fulfilled, where little of note ever happened.

It was here that George Lucas Sr ran L. M. Morris, a stationery store. The son of a Californian oilfield worker, Lucas Sr had come from a family that had never seen wealth. However, after years of working there, he'd managed to buy the stationery store from its founder and was determined to make a success of it. As a young man he had lived through the Great Depression of the early 1930s, and he was determined that his own family would not suffer in the same way or want for anything.

Lucas Sr had moved with his widowed mother, Maud, to Modesto in 1929, where he met the frail Dorothy Bomberger at high school. She was the daughter of a local businessman, Paul S. Bomberger. He had turned his father's property interests into a widely diversified business that took in a car dealership and a seed company, among others. By 1933, the twenty-year-old Lucas had married the eighteen-year-old Dorothy, abandoned his planned law degree and taken up employment in the Modesto stationery business of LeRoy Morris.

The newly married couple swiftly started a family, with a daughter named Ann born in 1934, followed two years later by Katherine (always known in the family as Kate). Following her first two pregnancies, Dorothy's always-frail health took a turn for the worse. With Lucas prospering in the stationery business, the family moved into a new home on Ramona Avenue in Modesto. After a few years, and despite a doctor's advice against it, Dorothy became pregnant again. The family's only son – George Walton Lucas Jr – was born on 14 May 1944. A third and final daughter – Wendy – followed within a year.

The childhood of the young George Lucas was largely unremarkable. While his father was doing well in business, his was a frugal family where waste and extravagance were frowned upon: everyone was expected to live within limited means and to earn money before they could spend it. Young Lucas spent his money on comic books, including *Batman* and *Superman*, and science-fiction story magazines like *Amazing Stories*. The 'pulps' (so-called as they were printed on cheap wood-pulp paper) contained truly amazing stories of space adventure, in which heroes would fly off in sleek, silver rocket ships, battle evildoers and win the hand of intergalactic princesses. They sparked the imagination of young Lucas to the extent that he spent much of his time drawing his own versions of the stories he read rather than studying.

Lucas had never liked school. He was a small, shy boy who often found himself a target for bullies. He lived in fear of being attacked on his way home by a group of bigger, older kids who would steal his shoes or his precious comic books. 'I was as normal as you can get,' said Lucas of those years. 'I wanted a car and hated school. I was a poor student. I lived for summer vacations, and got into trouble a lot shooting out windows with my BB gun.'

Lucas had a way of attracting some kids as friends, thanks to his father's store. Rechristened The Lucas Company and relocated to new premises, the burgeoning store was one of the first in town to stock the latest toys and games, and young George always had first pick. His favourite toy – and the one that attracted the most admirers from among the neighbourhood kids – was a three-engine Lionel Santa Fe train set, one of the biggest and most impressive available in the mid-1950s. Another attraction was the young boy's extensive comic book collection: he would eventually have over 500. His father had been forced to install shelves in the garden shed to store them all. The collection was nearly thrown out as Lucas grew up and lost interest in it, but it was saved by one of his sisters and returned to him many years later.

At school Lucas was withdrawn and uninvolved. He wasn't making as much progress in literacy as would be expected at his age, and his younger sister Wendy would often have to help him with his spelling when he was doing homework assignments. 'I was never very enthusiastic,' said Lucas of his school days. 'I always wanted to learn something other than what I was being taught [so] I was bored.' Lucas increasingly withdrew into his own world, reading comics, watching TV, creating his own comic strips and constructing elaborate models. 'He was hard to understand,' said his father of George Lucas as a young boy. 'He was always dreaming things up.' At school one day, Lucas ignored the assigned art project and spent his time instead drawing a pair of armoured space soldiers.

George Lucas's rebellion began when he discovered rock 'n' roll. It was 1958 and he was fourteen, and had already reached his full adult height of five feet and six inches. He habitually dressed simply in sneakers, blue jeans, checked shirts and colourful sweaters. It was to become his uniform for life.

Comic books and adventure stories had given way to music. Now he rushed home from school to play his growing collection of records, featuring artists such as Chuck Berry, Jerry Lee Lewis and Elvis Presley. He grew his hair longer, much to his father's disapproval. 'I was very much aware that growing up wasn't pleasant,' Lucas recalled. 'I was unhappy a lot of the time – I guess all kids feel depressed and intimidated. My strongest impression was that I was always on the lookout for the monster that lurked around the corner.'

The Lucas family moved into a new ranch-style house built on a one-time walnut ranch in Modesto when George was fifteen. The property was on the outskirts of town, cutting the young man off from his teenage peer group. He would have to return home from school by bus or bike, and then stay home all evening, listening to his records or watching TV. He had developed an interest in photography, encouraged by his father who could get the necessary supplies through the stationery store, but there was one thing the fifteen-year-old George Lucas longed for more than any other: a car.

In the United States in the 1950s and 1960s, teenage car-ownership was a badge of maturity, as well as a guarantee of mobility away from parents. American-made cars were cheap and widely available, and owning one was seen as a social necessity in the later years of high school. The long, straight country roads of Modesto were ideal for racing, and young George Lucas couldn't wait to get his hands on his own car. 'When I was ten years old, I wanted to drive in Le Mans,

Monte Carlo and Indianapolis,' said Lucas, establishing a life-long interest in speed.

The speeds Lucas might achieve would be limited thanks to his father's safety-first choice of his first car. It was a Fiat Bianchina, with a tiny, two-cylinder engine (disparagingly called a 'sewing machine') that made a terrible noise and was less powerful than a modest motorbike. However, it was a car and it provided an avenue of escape and a sense of teen identity for Lucas. He spent so much time working on the engine in an attempt to get it to go faster that his father thought he was destined to become a motor mechanic and so 'wasn't going to amount to anything!'

The car may have been small and low-key, like its driver, but it allowed Lucas to join the crowds of teenagers 'cruising' the streets of Modesto on Friday and Saturday nights. 'I had this intense love relationship with cars and motorcycles; it was really all-consuming,' he recalled. The roots of the film *American Graffiti* (1973) can be found in Lucas's teenage exploits on the roads of Modesto in the late 1950s and early 1960s. Kids would customize their cars and belonged to rival factions who would race against one another to the amusement and thrill of those watching. Lucas was keen to join the Faros (rechristened the Pharaos [*sic*] in the movie), a gang of would-be juvenile delinquents who would hang out at a burger bar called the Round Table (depicted as Mel's Drive-In for the movie). The Faros were more about posing and making noise than any actual criminal activity, but the group had great allure for the newly mobile teen Lucas.

His big problem was the car, which his father had also insisted should be used by Lucas Jr to make delivery runs for the store. 'It was a dumb little car,' recalled the filmmaker of his first set of wheels. 'What could I do with that? It was practically a motor scooter!' While waiting for his licence, Lucas was restricted to driving on his father's ranch property, where he promptly crashed into a walnut tree. It took two attempts to get his driver's licence as he had trouble remembering all the rules of the road. Once he was able to hit the streets of Modesto, he quickly put the small car into the garage after he rolled it over trying to reach 70 mph.

Lucas had a friend who worked at Modesto's Foreign Car Service garage, and the pair spent several weeks souping up the tiny Fiat, removing the roof and adding rollbars while beefing up the engine and adding an exhaust that made the car sound fiercer than it really was. Lucas was finally ready to make his mark amid Modesto's rebellious racing teens.

Hanging out on Modesto's main drag and occasionally taking part in unspectacular races became the focus for Lucas. It took up all his time out of school, so much so that his other hobbies – like photography – fell by the wayside. His grades continued to be a problem, threatening his chances of graduating. However, the young Lucas didn't much care.

Feeling his son would never amount to much, Lucas Sr set his sights on bringing him into the family stationery business when he completed his schooling. It was a prospect the younger Lucas came to dread. He was just sixteen and felt that his father's view of his future didn't match his own aspirations. 'I swore when I was a kid I would never do what he did,' Lucas said of his father. 'He wanted me to go into the business and I refused. I told him, "There are two things I know for sure. One is that I will end up doing something with cars . . . and two, that I will never be president of a company!"'

The world that would be reflected in *American Graffiti* was the one Lucas lived in for the first few years of the 1960s. He'd spend a huge amount of time at local races and demolition derbies, when he wasn't appearing in court on parking and speeding tickets, accompanied by his disappointed father. He would hang around older, prize-winning racers, unable officially to race competitively himself until he reached the age of twenty-one. His last year at high school was much like all those previously: Lucas knew he had little chance of getting to college and so began to turn his thoughts to life beyond Modesto.

There was one course that Lucas discovered when

checking out college prospectuses: a film class at the University of California. Lucas thought that he might be able to get on to a 'creative' course like that with his poor grades by presenting a portfolio of his drawings and photography. Graduating school had to be his first priority, though, which would be a struggle with a D-grade average and three incomplete course papers to deliver.

It's likely that this was where the thoughts of George Lucas were focused on Tuesday, 12 June 1962, as he drove back home from the school library after another day of frustrating study. Arriving outside the driveway to his home just before 5 p.m., he failed to see a Chevrolet Impala attempting to overtake him from behind. The heavy Chevy hit the side of the flimsy Fiat as it made the turn into the driveway. The smaller car rolled over and over, crushed like a child's toy. Entering a third roll, the seatbelt holding Lucas in place snapped, throwing him clear of the vehicle. He landed with considerable force on his chest as his car hit a nearby walnut tree at around 60 mph. It was just three days before he had to sit his final high school exams.

Eighteen-year-old George Lucas was rushed to Modesto hospital in critical condition. The driver of the Impala, seventeen-year-old Frank Ferreira, had escaped with barely a scratch. Lucas was suffering from serious internal bleeding and was immediately put on an emergency oxygen supply. A neighbour had called for an ambulance after he witnessed the crash, while his mother and sister inside the house had heard nothing and remained oblivious. They didn't find out what had happened until young George's father came to fetch them, having been called by a doctor, and took them to the hospital. Once there, they discovered Lucas hooked up to various medical machines, while doctors examined him for major damage.

Lucas awoke the next morning, only to be reassured by an attending nurse that he would survive the accident more-or-less intact. 'She said, "You're okay. All your arms and legs are okay." It was very reassuring to hear that, as I didn't know what parts of me were there or not. The fact that I was alive was a miracle.'

That day's *Modesto Bee* led with a front-page report of the crash, complete with a photo of the crushed Fiat and the tree that had been moved forward two feet by the impact of the tiny – but fast-moving – Italian car.

The crash came to be the defining moment of the life of young George Lucas, and probably contributed to the creation of the 'more machine than man' tragic, scarred figure of Darth Vader. Prior to the crash he was on course to becoming an underachieving drifter, with no particular ambition or goal, except not to become his father. Afterwards, once he'd taken four months to recover, he had a different outlook on things. 'I realized I'd been living my life so close to the edge for so long,' he admitted. 'That's when I decided to go straight, to be a better student, to try to do something with myself.'

Lucas had described his survival as a miracle. If his seatbelt had not failed and had instead done the job it was designed to do, he would not have escaped the Fiat before it hit the tree. The impact would almost certainly have killed him outright. Despite that, the authorities felt that Lucas had to accept some blame for the crash: while he was in hospital they issued him with a ticket for making an illegal left turn.

Lucas's injuries looked worse than they actually were and, following some basic medical treatment and respite care, he was free to return home after two weeks. His worries about graduating high school disappeared when on the Friday of the week of the crash – the day he was expected to graduate if he had passed the course work – his school sent his graduation diploma to the hospital, excusing his non-delivery of his final papers due to the accident. Lucas was severely bruised and spent the four months of the late summer and early autumn of 1962 mainly confined to bed at home.

'Before the accident, I never used to think,' said Lucas. 'When you go through something like that, it puts a little more perspective on things, like maybe you were here for a reason.' It is during this summer of enforced contemplation that the myth of George Lucas and the story of *Star Wars* really began.

During his convalescence, Lucas watched more television and read more comic books than ever before. Racing cars and hanging out with other teens in Modesto was simply not an option any longer. 'After my accident, I knew I couldn't continue with that,' remembered Lucas. 'I was sort of floundering for something [to do]. When I finally discovered film, I really fell madly in love with it. There was no going back after that.'

Confined to home, he watched episodes of *The Twilight Zone*, then in its third year on air, and animated future-set show *The Jetsons*. When he wasn't watching TV, he was listening to radio, catching the raucous broadcasts of Wolfman Jack, the alter-ego of Shreveport disc jockey Robert Weston Smith. Broadcasting from the border of Texas and Mexico, Smith's noisy, howl-filled presentation of rhythm-and-blues tracks kept Lucas entertained late into the night, and was another influence on his coming-of-age movie, *American Graffiti*.

George Lucas Sr took the aftermath of his son's near-fatal crash to be the ideal time to once more attempt to persuade him to join the family firm. However, Lucas was still as set against that as he had been previously: ever the rebel, he simply did not want to become like his father before him. Lucas was looking for another option, an escape from the sleepy, backward small town of Modesto. One downside of graduating school despite the crash was the possibility that he would now be drafted into the US Army to serve in Vietnam (as happens to the Lucas-surrogate character of Toad in *American Graffiti*). Although he would later be deemed unfit to serve, Lucas's first action to escape the draft was to enrol in junior college. It was also a way of taking his post-crash 'second chance' to apply himself to learning in a more positive frame of mind. A two-year arts major at Modesto Junior College, encompassing art history, speech, sociology and astronomy, was his next step – much to his father's continuing exasperation.

In 1964, Lucas graduated with an Associate in Arts degree having achieved his rather modest aims. He had done well in astronomy, but by his own estimation he was 'terrible' in speech class and failed to improve his rather poor communication skills. His grades were just enough to get him into the fee-free San Francisco State University to study art. He spent his spare time hanging out at racetracks once more, but he no longer drove the cars. 'I was still interested in racing, so I started doing a lot of photography at the races, rather than driving or being in the pit crew. I had always been interested in art, and I'd been very good at it. My father didn't see much of a career in being an artist, so he discouraged me from that whole thing,' admitted Lucas. Making his first steps in creating his own movies, Lucas used an 8 mm film camera his father had bought him to film the weekend races and the drivers, capturing much of the atmosphere, excitement and speed of racing that had thrilled him in the first place.

After just one term at San Francisco State, George Lucas was persuaded to transfer to the University of Southern California (USC) in Los Angeles, or 'sin city' as his ever-disapproving father dubbed the place. Despite his misgivings, Lucas Sr agreed to support his son through university, offering him $200 a month for as long as he was there. However, if he were to drop out, he would have to fend for himself financially.

It was documentary film cameraman Haskell Wexler (then aged thirty-six) who had persuaded Lucas to take up a proper film course. Lucas had worked on Wexler's racing car, and the older man became aware of his amateur filmmaking efforts around the racetracks. Wexler, who had worked with Roger Corman and Irvin Kershner on 1958's semi-documentary drug thriller *Stakeout on Dope Street*, was credited with spotting the potential in Lucas and would become something of a mentor to the young filmmaker. Another incentive was the fact that Lucas's school friend, John Plummer, was travelling to Los Angeles to take the admission test to become a business major: here was an opportunity to go on a road trip with a pal and take a chance on applying for USC while he was there. The outcome surprised Lucas: 'I went, I took the test, and I passed. I got accepted!'

Enrolling at film school had never been a particular ambition for George Lucas, and his father doubted the outcome would be much more than his son becoming a ticket-taker at a theatre or at nearby Disneyland. However, Lucas found himself among a like-minded group of people, all of whom, like him, didn't quite fit into mainstream society. He was among a group of young and driven rebels. For them all, film was a form of creative expression that played to their individual, unique strengths and gave them a direction in life beyond taking up whatever low-level jobs their home towns had to offer. Lucas's father told his son he expected him to return home within a few years, little better off. Lucas, full of defiance, replied: 'I'm never coming back! I'm going to be a millionaire before I'm thirty.'

Even when learning the basics of filmmaking, Lucas had trouble containing his rebellious streak. USC set its students assignments with limitations: movies made as student exercises were to be shot in black-and-white and kept very short. Lucas's classmate Howard Kazanjian recalled the newcomer's reaction. 'I'm gonna shoot my film in colour,' declared Lucas. 'I'm not gonna be limited to the footage I'm given or limited to the length of my completed film.'

Some of the earliest filmmaking efforts of George Lucas reflected his still strong interest in cars. Although he was no longer racing, he was still fascinated by that world. However, it wasn't the people, the drivers themselves, that he chose to make his student films about, but the vehicles. His dynamic film of a race was titled after the lap time, *1:42:08*, while another, called *Herbie* (long before Disney's *The Love Bug* movie of 1968), consisted of extreme close-ups of the gleaming bodywork of a Volkswagen, scored with the music of Herbie Hancock. These films immediately marked Lucas out from his contemporaries as a director who had a unique eye. Even a seemingly more conventional topic, like his documentary, *The Emperor* – about local disc jockey Emperor Hudson – was innovative, with its titles coming halfway through the short, and the film peppered with adverts.

As 1964 became 1965, this group of USC students came to know each other and their ambitions a little better. As well as Kazanjian (later executive producer on *Raiders of the Lost Ark* and *Return of the Jedi*, as well as a President of Lucasfilm), Lucas was classmates with Walter Murch (sound editor on *The Conversation* and *Apocalypse Now* for Francis Ford Coppola), John Milius (screenwriter for *Apocalypse Now* and director of surfing movie *Big Wednesday*), Hal Barwood and Matthew Robbins (respectively director and writer of *Dragonslayer*) and Lawrence Kasdan (writer, *The Empire Strikes Back*). Others who Lucas encountered were Don Glut (novelist, *The Empire Strikes Back*), Randal Kleiser (*More American Graffiti*), Basil Poledouris (composer, *Conan the Barbarian*), and Willard Huck and his wife Gloria Katz (writers, *American Graffiti*). Lucas was also a friend of Charles Lippincott, later credited with the smart, awareness-raising pre-publicity campaign for *Star Wars*.

These budding 'new Hollywood' filmmakers were among the first formally to be taught 'cinema'. They came to prominence just as the much vaunted studio system that had produced classic Hollywood's biggest successes since the 1930s was drawing to a close, thanks to corporate takeovers and the rise of rebellious youth culture. There was no guarantee any of them would actually get to make movies or take up any other role within Hollywood, given the changes that were underway. Perhaps, as Lucas's father feared, he might amount to nothing more than a cinema ticket-taker after all. One thing was sure: if he was to succeed George Lucas would have to create his own future.

George Lucas made the most of the opportunities afforded him on the USC campus in the mid-1960s. Film history was studied, with many movies watched and discussed. Screenwriting was taught, an art Lucas never really adequately mastered, reflecting the poor literacy that had dogged him since high school. Lucas would later describe the process of writing for him as being 'terrible; it's painful, atrocious'. Editing was his forte, but he also had an interest in animation. Many a long night was spent in front of the Moviola machine, reviewing and editing material for his student films. Lucas became so caught up in his work during this period that he neglected his health, a tendency he had inherited from his mother. Laid low with a variation of glandular fever, he was diagnosed as diabetic, probably connected with his seemingly non-stop student diet of Hershey chocolate bars. His commitment to education and his health status resulted in an exemption from military service in Vietnam, which is ironic considering he had initially planned to direct the military-focused, Vietnam-set drama *Apocalypse Now*.

Lucas's student short films displayed a command of style and pace, thanks to his editing skills and tight control of his material. His second-year directing project was *Freiheit* (German for 'freedom'), billed as 'A film by LUCAS'. It featured fellow student Randal Kleiser as an unnamed fugitive attempting to cross a frontier, only to be shot down. The soundtrack featured distant gunfire and concluded with various abstract voices discussing aspects of freedom and the sacrifices necessary to maintain it. This short movie was in stark contrast to the work of others, like Don Glut, who were turning out genre pastiches based on their love of 1950s monster movies.

Lucas often helped out on others' movies, especially when it came to editing. Many of the student projects produced during this period were cooperative efforts, with everyone lending their growing expertise to achieve the finished results. He edited an animated film made by John Milius (*Marcello, I'm So Bored*), and he learned some of the subtleties of sound manipulation for film from Walter Murch. Many of the people he met and worked with at USC became lifelong friends and would find themselves involved in various capacities in his future empire-building.

Lucas graduated from USC in 1966, and he now faced some serious choices about his future direction. He thought of re-enlisting at USC as a graduate student, but missed the deadline for the 1967 intake. He did, however, secure part-time employment at USC running a refresher course for Navy cameramen. It was not quite what he wanted to be doing, but it kept him attached to the film school and put off any bigger moves into employment. With his re-entry to USC to complete a Master of Fine Arts degree confirmed for 1968, Lucas took a job early in 1967 editing a project for the United States Information Agency. The film was *Journey to the Pacific*, a chronicle of President Lyndon B. Johnson's tour of the Far East. He worked in the San Fernando Valley home of director Verna Fields, who had converted the basement of her home into an editing suite. While working there, he met Marcia Griffin, another talented editor working with Fields. Although Lucas was generally shy with women, discovering Griffin had been born in Modesto broke the ice between the pair. Their common interest in movies formed the basis of the majority of their conversations while they both worked on Fields's project. Through their enforced proximity, they drifted into dating.

Lucas was looking to launch his own project with an idea for a short science-fiction film he thought he could shoot with the help of some of his friends, before returning to USC full time in 1968. While at film school he had attended a screening of *Alphaville* (1965) introduced by its director, Jean-Luc Godard. Lucas had been impressed by Godard's low-budget attempt at science fiction, presenting modern Paris as if it were a high-tech future. Lucas felt he could apply a similar minimalist approach to his idea about a fugitive escaping an oppressive underground civilization (echoing *Freiheit*). He worked with Walter Murch in coming up with a suitable story, but the pair got stuck and the film was put on hold.

In thinking up ideas for his science-fiction short, Lucas had returned to his teenage world of comics and fantasy fiction, something he had largely abandoned while at film school. In the United States in the 1960s, J. R. R. Tolkien's epic *The Lord of the Rings* had become very popular with the 'stoner' crowd, while Frank Herbert's *Dune* had been published as a novel following an early 1960s serialization in *Analog* magazine. Many of the specifics of these titles would feed into Lucas's creation of *Star Wars* a decade later.

Returning to USC as a graduate student, Lucas continued to teach his Navy refresher class while working on new short subjects. He made a film with Paul Golding with the unwieldy title of *anyone lived in a pretty little [how] town* (based on an e. e. cummings poem) using trained actors for the first time. He also moved in with Marcia, and attended a ramshackle and free-wheeling directing class given by Hollywood clown Jerry Lewis (the main attraction being that attendance got the students on to the Columbia lot, where Lewis was then making movies).

One day in class, Lucas met another young filmmaker who was presenting his twenty-four-minute short called *Amblin'*. The movie was Steven Spielberg's calling card to the industry, and it told the slight tale of a pair who meet and fall in love while hitchhiking. Spielberg had been rejected as a student by USC, instead attending University of California at Long Beach. He'd had a similar upbringing and had similar interests to Lucas. Admitting he didn't like *Amblin'* much, Lucas told Lippincott that he thought it was 'saccharine'. Spielberg, however, seemed to hit it off with other members of Lucas's USC group, and began attending their regular Thursday night movie screenings.

Lucas made another contact during his second stint at USC that was to be even more important in his immediate future. Francis Ford Coppola was slightly older and already working in Hollywood when Lucas met him. Lucas had won a student film scholarship awarded by Warner Bros. to USC's most promising student (he'd been in competition with Murch for the award). This involved a six-month work experience period on the Warner Bros. lot in Burbank, where Lucas could attach himself to one of the professional production departments to further his understanding of how Hollywood filmmaking worked. Lucas joined Warner Bros. just as the last of the founding brothers, Jack Warner, was leaving as a result of one of the many corporate takeovers that were happening in Hollywood in the 1960s and that would eventually see the end of the studio system.

Looking to work in the animation department (famous for

Bugs Bunny and *Daffy Duck*), Lucas found the foundering studio to be uncannily quiet. The cartoon production unit had been closed down many years before, and the crisis in studio film production meant that there was not much actually going on. There was only one film in active production on the lot: the musical *Finian's Rainbow*, directed by twenty-seven year-old newcomer Coppola. Sneaking on to the set, hoping to watch the production in action, he was soon spotted by the young director. Coppola had come to Hollywood through the practical-focused University of California, Los Angeles (UCLA) film course, seen as a rival to the more esoteric USC course. He had worked for exploitation filmmaker Roger Corman and had made the low-budget thriller *Dementia 13* (1963). As seemingly the only people on the lot under the age of forty, Lucas and Coppola quickly struck up a friendship. It was to become a master–apprentice relationship, with Lucas becoming Coppola's assistant during his time at Columbia.

Lucas continued his film education, discovering the work of Akira Kurosawa, especially his film *The Hidden Fortress* (1958) that followed the misadventures of two lowly peasants who escape a battle and rescue a princess from captivity. For his final student film, Lucas returned to his loosely worked out idea for a science-fiction film and co-opted his Navy students as an ad-hoc film crew. The result was *Electronic Labyrinth: THX 1138 4EB* (1967), a fifteen-minute tale of a fugitive (Navy man Dan Natchsheim) fleeing an oppressive society that puts its people under constant surveillance. Lucas commandeered an impressive amount of resources, drawing on Navy-supplied equipment, film stock and locations as well as USC material to make his film in just twelve weeks (while he was also editing the Lyndon Johnson documentary). Much of the important work was done in post-production, with clever editing and photo-graphic effects adding hugely to the impressive short's impact on the viewer. The use of screens and surveillance images gave the film an oppressive nature that reflected the society depicted, accompanied by a discordant and disruptive score and soundtrack (Lucas having learned much from Murch). Tightly edited, the film won the praise of one of Lucas's USC tutors, filmmaker Irvin Kershner. *THX 1138 4EB* was screened in a programme of student shorts at the Fairfax Theater in Hollywood, where eminent German director Fritz Lang (*Metropolis*, 1927) was in attendance. He acclaimed Lucas's movie as the best.

Lucas screened his film for Coppola, who saw the potential in it. He knew that Lucas had ambitions to become a director, but Coppola was convinced that the best way to achieve that was to write your own material. He suggested that the young, aspiring filmmaker should think of expanding his short film to feature length. Writing a full-length screenplay was going to be a challenge for Lucas, who did not find it easy to turn his visual ideas into coherent words on paper. When Coppola embarked upon production of his melodrama *The Rain People* in 1968, he brought Lucas along as his assistant cameraman, sound recordist and production manager. Despite this commitment, Lucas found time (and a spare camera and film) to make a surprisingly frank behind-the-scenes documentary about the making of *The Rain People*, called *Filmmaker*. He had suggested the idea to Coppola and it would be his first professional directorial credit. During the work on the documentary, Lucas and Coppola would shoot the breeze, developing a joint dream of setting up an independent filmmaking utopia away from Hollywood. These chats were to sow the seeds that would spring into life as American Zoetrope for Coppola and, later, Lucasfilm for Lucas, both eventually based in Northern California far away from Hollywood.

The work with Coppola had taken Lucas away from Marcia Griffin. Determined not to give up on their blossoming relationship that easily, Marcia made the trip out to where the movie's location shooting was taking place. While scouting locations in Garden City, Long Island, that February, Lucas took Marcia along with him and proposed marriage. By April 1968, Lucas had left Marcia behind once more as the Coppola caravan of film vehicles made its way across America to complete *The Rain People.* He made up for it later by having Coppola hire her as assistant editor on the film.

As the 1960s drew to a close – and just as youth rebellion was erupting across the nation – George Lucas had made the transition from teenager to adult, and from small-town dreamer to professional filmmaker. Now, all he needed was a project to call his own.

Chapter 2

A Galaxy Far, Far Away

[American Graffiti] is about change. It's about the change in a young person's life at eighteen, and it's also about the cultural change that took place when the 1950s turned into the 1960s.

George Lucas

The idea of an independent filmmaking outfit free from Hollywood, of which George Lucas and Francis Ford Coppola had dreamed in 1968, was to become a reality by 1969. Coppola took advantage of a seed fund for independent filmmakers set up by Warner Bros. and secured funding for his new company, American Zoetrope. Coppola had visited Lanterna Films in Denmark, a filmmaking company based in a rural country mansion, with complete production facilities. In the 1950s, Britain's Hammer Films had operated a similar set-up at a West London mansion house. For American Zoetrope, a street-front warehouse on Folsom Street in San Francisco would have to suffice. The loose association of talent that gravitated to American Zoetrope included many of Lucas's film-school friends, including John Milius, Walter Murch, Hal Barwood, Matthew Robbins and the married screenwriting couple of Gloria Katz and Willard Huyck.

Announcing the new company to the Hollywood trade press, Coppola outlined a statement of intent that was in keeping with the 'new Hollywood' that was beginning to take shape as the 1960s gave way to the 1970s: 'The essential objective of the company is to engage in the varied fields of filmmaking, collaborating with the most gifted and youthful talent, using the most contemporary techniques and equipment possible.'

Lucas and Marcia Griffin were now living in the small town of Mill Valley in Marin County in Northern California. They had built an editing room into the attic of their house to ensure that their professional work never took them away from home. Lucas was a key member of American Zoetrope in the early days. He worked with Haskell Wexler shooting material from a 1969 Rolling Stones rock concert at Altamont for the documentary *Gimme Shelter* (1969). John Milius claimed that Lucas shot the infamous footage of the killing of an audience member by Hell's Angels security during the event, but Lucas professed not to remember.

The set-up as it evolved at American Zoetrope did not always suit Lucas. The first two film projects planned were a feature length version of his own short, with the truncated title *THX 1138*, and a Vietnam War movie to be scripted by Milius (who had been rejected for the draft despite his strong desire to fight for his country). The deal regarding the seed funding with Warner Bros. had a 'claw back' clause built into it: if no finished movies emerged (or the movies that did emerge were not to Warner Bros.' liking), then American Zoetrope would have to pay back the funding.

At the end of 1969, Lucas embarked upon a forty-day shoot for his first feature film, with a budget of $777,000 (seven being Coppola's lucky number) from American Zoetrope. Lucas filmed his Orwellian epic in the San Francisco area, making creative use of the tunnels for the then unfinished Metro system. He cast Robert Duvall (who'd worked with Coppola on *The Rain People* and would do so again on *The Godfather* films and *Apocalypse Now*) as the title character, a bald-headed functionary clad all in white. Attempting escape with LUH 3417 (Maggie McOmie), the pair flee the state's robotic security officers. After a period trapped in an all-white limbo, THX once more escapes, emerging from the underworld into a sun-drenched, parched landscape above ground. Donald Pleasence played SEN, who monitors the 'misdeeds' of THX and LUH. A planned sequence in which THX gets trapped in a garbage compactor and encounters a deadly creature was cut at script stage, but revived later for *Star Wars*. The finished film would open with a black-and-white clip from a trailer from a classic *Buck Rogers'* movie serial (rather than Lucas's beloved *Flash Gordon*), prefiguring his interest in big-screen space fantasy.

Having already made the short version of the film, the then twenty-five year-old Lucas knew exactly what he wanted, but he found working with the actors rather difficult. His short films had rarely featured people at their centre, having been more often about machines (mainly cars) or abstract situations. Now he had to offer direction to up-and-coming acting talent like Duvall and Pleasence, who expected a high degree of engagement from their director. It was to be a flaw that would pursue Lucas for his entire professional life, one he was never able to overcome.

His strengths were in the technical aspects of the film, giving his relatively low-budget movie a glossy sheen, and making imaginative use of surveillance footage and omnipresent cameras (or observers) to create an oppressive atmosphere. Shy and reserved in his dealings with cast and crew, Lucas was in his element in post-production when he was editing the film and applying the optical effects. Despite his problems with the actors, he was very happy with the finished movie, believing it contained an important message for the modern world.

'With my first film, I wanted to show the mess we'd made of the world,' explained Lucas of *THX 1138* in a lengthy interview in *Starlog* magazine in 1981. '*THX* sort of got a following, but it wasn't a big, successful movie and it didn't move people very much. [The message was] wanting to change the world and trying to say, "Look, we've got to change the way we live." The film did not accomplish that at all.'

Having completed his edit of *THX 1138*, Lucas was keen to

get moving on his next project for American Zoetrope, the John Milius-scripted Vietnam War movie, now with the title *Apocalypse Now*. He had met Gary Kurtz when Coppola had sent him to chat to Lucas about working in Techniscope, used by Lucas on *THX 1138*. Now, Lucas called on Kurtz – who had attended USC several years before Lucas – to produce *Apocalypse Now*. Kurtz had been in the Marines in Vietnam (although as a closet conscientious objector, he had refused to handle weapons). Working as a military cameraman he had captured some striking footage of US helicopters in action, which Lucas had seen and hoped could be used in the film.

The final cut of *THX 1138*, along with seven scripts American Zoetrope had in development (including those for later Coppola movies *Apocalypse Now* and *The Conversation*), had been sent to Warner Bros. in the hopes of securing additional funding. However, the package had the opposite effect. The studio took one look at Lucas's *THX 1138* and rejected the film outright, then claimed back $300,000 in script development money that had been paid to American Zoetrope.

Warner Bros.' action caused the near-immediate collapse of the initial incarnation of American Zoetrope. To add insult to injury, the studio took it upon itself to re-edit Lucas's movie in the hope of salvaging something it deemed to be releasable (even if it was only put out to the drive-ins frequented by undiscriminating teens). Lucas said, 'I don't feel they had the right to do it, not after I had worked on that thing for three years with no money. When a studio hires you, that's different, but when a filmmaker develops a project himself, he has rights.'

In March 1971 Warner Bros. eventually released the compromised film to generally positive reviews, although it failed to set the box office alight, bringing in under $1 million in rentals. American Zoetrope had collapsed, Coppola had vanished off to Europe to 'rethink his life' and Lucas had no savings and no income. He was relying on Marcia to provide for them both. He had been offered a director-for-hire project, a crime thriller called *Lady Ice* (1973), scripted by one of the writers of the

Steve McQueen movie *Bullitt* (1968). Although the job paid a $100,000 directing fee, Lucas felt no empathy with the story and turned it down. However, he desperately needed a new project, so he turned back to the Milius idea that was part of the wreckage of American Zoetrope: *Apocalypse Now*.

Gary Kurtz signed on as producer and went to the Philippines to scout suitable locations to recreate the jungles of Vietnam. Although he had not served himself, Milius had spent years hanging around with Vietnam vets, compiling their stories of outrageous adventures in the jungle into what he considered to be a satirical script of America's ongoing misadventure in Southeast Asia. Lucas, for his part, was inspired by Robert Altman's *M*A*S*H* (1970), a comedy set in the Korean War of the early 1950s, but clearly making reference to the then-contemporary events in Vietnam.

Complications quickly arose on the project. Kurtz reported that filming on location would bust the planned budget, while attempting to recreate Vietnam in Northern California would be a pointless exercise. It also became clear that Coppola, through American Zoetrope, had a legal claim on the material that would complicate Lucas's plan to direct the film. As a result, Kurtz and Lucas changed gear dramatically.

Lucas had long been criticized by his former film-school friends for his detachment, which was actually how his personal shyness was expressed. It had come across in his films, especially the cold *THX 1138*. Coppola had hoped that in expanding the short to feature length, Lucas would have come up with a more human story, but it had not happened. 'I was getting a lot of razz from Francis and a bunch of friends who said that everyone thought I was cold and weird, and why didn't I do something warm and human,' said Lucas. 'I thought, "you want warm and human? I'll give you warm and human!"'

George Lucas eventually turned to his own adolescence for a movie idea that would be 'warm and human' and would answer his critics. His time cruising the streets of Modesto in his souped-up car was still fresh in his memory, almost a decade on. There was plenty of material there to draw upon to create a nostalgic piece looking back at teen life in the late 1950s and early 1960s. He could create a group of characters based upon himself, his friends and others he knew at the time (some only by reputation). The dramatic structure of the piece was clear, climaxing with various characters being drafted for Vietnam (or escaping that fate, as Lucas had done). As was the soundtrack: Lucas called the project his 'rock 'n' roll movie'.

There was, however, a second project that Kurtz and Lucas kicked around at the same time. Both were big fans of *Flash Gordon* and felt there had been nothing like that since *Forbidden Planet* (1956). *The Planet of the Apes* film series (1968–73) and Stanley Kubrick's *2001: A Space Odyssey* (1968) had not hit the note of nostalgia and fantasy that the pair were looking for in their modern 'space opera'. The very basic idea of the movie involved clear-cut heroes and villains, grand space battles, evil empires, plucky rebels and a damsel-in-distress. Kurtz's first thought was to option the *Flash Gordon* rights, but he found they were far too costly as other interest had been expressed in making a film from the cartoon strip.

Lucas recalled Kurosawa's *The Hidden Fortress* and saw potential in relocating some of that film's characters and story elements to outer space. Again, Kurtz sought out the remake rights only to run up against the problem of money once more. The 'space thing', as they had taken to referring to what would ultimately become *Star Wars*, was put on the shelf when United Artists showed some interest in Lucas's 'rock 'n' roll movie' instead.

It was May 1971 and *THX 1138* had been screened at the prestigious Cannes Film Festival in France, affording Lucas and Marcia the opportunity for their first trip abroad. The European audiences reacted far more favourably to his cold-edged surveillance state sci-fi than had the small American audience that had seen it. While in France, Lucas met United Artists' David Picker, who offered the director a multi-picture deal, primarily for the 'rock 'n' roll movie', but with the 'space thing' also attached as a possible supplemental project.

Lucas, very happy with the deal, quickly commissioned a screenplay and then extended his stay in Europe with Marcia into a proper holiday. Returning to the United States, Lucas received the first draft of the screenplay from writer Richard Walter, but hated it. Picker read the screenplay, too, and felt it hadn't achieved the potential he saw in the project. With the deal going south rapidly, Lucas offered to come up with a second screenplay – at no additional cost – and if that didn't work, then United Artists could kill the deal. He also had a back-up plan in mind: he could always take his 'youth' movie to American International Pictures, a low-budget exploitation producer that backed Roger Corman's cheap films and had a history with biker and juvenile-delinquent films. It would mean rewriting the film to increase the exploitable violence and sex angle, but it was a sacrifice he could be willing to make.

Lucas had never been a writer. It was a weakness that Francis Ford Coppola had pointed out to him, but there was no one more qualified than Lucas himself to get his own story of living it up as a youth in 1962 down on paper. Universal saw the project as a potentially successful low-budget teen movie, so they felt it was important to capture the tone and sense of authenticity. Lucas needed a script quick, so he co-opted his old film-school friends Gloria Katz and Willard Huyck to work with him in getting his memories into script form and in building a drama around Lucas's various disjointed anecdotes of his own adolescent years.

Universal liked the finished replacement script and picked up the original two-picture deal with the 'space thing' still attached as the second film. There was only one condition: Universal wanted a 'name' producer to supervise Lucas on the project. There was only one name that Lucas and Kurtz had in mind – Francis Ford Coppola. He had emerged from exile in Europe and reluctantly gone to work for Paramount on a film of an obviously cheesy 'airport' novel called *The Godfather*. The resulting film would become the sensational hit movie of 1972, so Coppola's star was on the rise once more, with the collapse of American Zoetrope long forgotten. Lucas had done some uncredited second-unit directing work on *The Godfather*, so although their friendship was still somewhat strained after the Zoetrope affair, Coppola agreed to meet Universal's demand for an experienced producer on Lucas's 'rock 'n' roll' picture. While his name would be on the film, it would be down to Kurtz to carry out the actual practical work of producing the movie.

Before production could begin on what would become *American Graffiti*, George Lucas's lawyer recommended he set up a legal corporate entity through which the production could be financed. Having set up an initial production office in his house in Mill Valley, Lucas first thought that Mill Valley Films would suffice. Gary Kurtz persuaded him otherwise, recommending he use Lucasfilm Ltd. 'He was a bit leery of it,' recalled Kurtz. 'He thought it was a kind of an ego thing. We thought we'd just call it that for the incorporation and worry about it later.' The name would stick and would grow to become a movie-making behemoth.

Casting on *Graffiti* (under the working title 'Another Slow Night in Modesto') was fairly quick, with the three central roles rapidly filled. Lucas saw aspects of himself in each of Terry 'the Toad' Fields (Charles Martin Smith), drag-racer Milner (Paul Le Mat) and would-be college boy Curt (Richard Dreyfuss). Ron Howard – a Corman veteran – rounded out the central core of four as Steve. Cindy Williams was Laurie the girlfriend, Candy Clarke the rebel Debbie, and Suzanne Somers the mysterious, seemingly unattainable blonde. Cast as the older, aloof racer Bob Falfa was a relatively unknown actor, Harrison Ford. Another actor who auditioned to play one of the leads in *American Graffiti* but was rejected was Mark Hamill, the future Luke Skywalker.

Approaching the new film, Lucas was aware that he had to create something more engaging than *THX 1138*. '[*THX 1138*] was about real things that were going on and the problems we're faced with,' Lucas said. 'I realized after making THX that those problems are so real that most of us have to face those things every day, so we're in a constant state of frustration. That just makes us more depressed than we were before. So I made a film where, essentially, we can get rid of some of those frustrations, the feeling that everything seems futile.'

In June 1972, Lucas prepared with his cast and crew to embark upon a month of gruelling night shoots in San Rafael (the director believed Modesto itself had changed too much since the early 1960s to play itself). Shooting there only lasted a few nights, as local businesses complained of disruption, a crew-member was arrested for possession of marijuana and problems had emerged in fixing the camera mounts to the cars, necessary if Lucas was to capture the dynamic driving scenes he envisaged.

Location work quickly switched to Petaluma, 20 miles from San Rafael, where the city offered more cooperation. Filming quickly on location kept the budget down, and Lucas approached the film as he would a low-budget exploitation movie, working in a manner that was both fast and intense. The $750,000 budget (less than that of *THX 1138*) didn't have much leeway in it for mistakes or extravagance. Additionally, Lucas wanted to keep some money in reserve so he could license the pop songs he intended to use on the soundtrack. Rather than score the film with traditional film music, Lucas had structured each scene to play out to one of seventy-five period songs he wanted to include. He had written and rewritten the script to the accompaniment of tracks from his large collection of classic rock 'n' roll records. Each song was chosen to complement the scene, whether it was an action scene or something more introspective, and to offer a commentary on the characters and their predicaments.

Although filming went relatively smoothly, the cast and crew of *American Graffiti* made sure they had a lot of fun away from the cameras. Their adventures were often led by Harrison Ford, notably older than most of the rest of the cast. Ford was arrested one night following a bar fight, while a fake fight tussle with Le Mat saw Dreyfuss tumble into the hotel pool, gashing his head the night before he was due to shoot a series of close-ups. Another unnamed actor – according to legend – set fire to Lucas's hotel room. More seriously, an incident during the shooting of the climatic race scene saw two camera-operators narrowly escape injury or even death. Filming wrapped – much to the director's relief – on 4 August 1972.

Now, Lucas could embark upon the part of filmmaking he enjoyed the most: editing and post-production. This more enjoyable process was all about shaping the movie, telling the story in the best way possible with the material available. Lucas roped in Marcia to help edit the film and many of her choices made a dramatic impact on the way the movie unfolded. By the turn of the year, Lucas had a film he was ready to show to the executives at Universal.

An argument about the title of the movie had preceded the screening, with Universal's Ned Tanen – a strong supporter of the project so far – not understanding the meaning of *American Graffiti*. Coppola came up with an alternative – 'Rock Around the Block' – that Kurtz thought worked well, but Lucas was determined to stick to his preferred title as it had special meaning for him. On 28 January 1973, the film was screened for Tanen at the Northpoint Theater in San Francisco.

The film unfolded in front of a seemingly appreciative audience that Sunday morning, with the pop song soundtrack – including 'Rock Around the Clock', 'Why Do Fools Fall in Love' and 'The Great Pretender' – underscoring the on-screen action, interspersed with the distinctive vocal styling of radio DJ Wolfman Jack. As the final image appeared – a title card outlining the various fates of the main characters – the credits rolled and the filmmakers felt they had a potentially strong success on their hands.

However, Tanen hated *American Graffiti*. He had allowed Lucas a huge amount of freedom to make the film, after approving the screenplay and the budget, but the finished product was 'not fit to show an audience' according to Tanen. The executive accused Lucas, Kurtz and Coppola of having failed him by making a film he could not release. While Lucas and Kurtz were stunned into silence, Coppola defended the movie and made Tanen an offer to buy the film outright from the studio if he felt that negatively about it. Tanen refused the offer, and left the trio standing in a stunned silence in the cinema's foyer.

To George Lucas it seemed as though history was repeating. His *THX 1138* had turned out to be a disappointment to those who'd given him the money to make it, and now his cherished 'warmer and more human' – and definitely more personal – project, *American Graffiti*, had received the same poor reception from Universal. It appeared likely that the studio would re-edit the film to its own prescription before releasing it, maybe directly to television as a TV 'movie of the week' presentation. This news depressed an already shaken Lucas even more.

It was word-of-mouth recommendation from within the studio that saved *American Graffiti* from that fate. Four minutes had been cut from the film, but it was relatively intact. Whenever the studio planned a test screening, Gary Kurtz ensured it was packed with younger members of the Universal staff, the target audience for the film. Their positive reactions spurred Universal into giving the film a try-out in a limited release in key cinemas in Los Angeles and New York. The positive critical praise that followed saw studio executives decide the film was worthy of a wider release after all, and Universal invested a further $500,000 in developing a marketing programme under the slogan 'Where were you in '62?' The wide release – from August 1973 – saw the now $1.27 million budgeted film reap in excess of $55 million at the box office. Critical reaction was largely positive, with many of those writing about the movie attracted to it by its nostalgic depiction of a time they could remember well from their own youth. The American cultural specificity of the film, however, meant that it didn't travel well in Europe, although it was appreciated by audiences in the UK and in France, where it became something of a cult movie.

The last laugh was to belong to George Lucas. For the 46th Academy Awards event, *American Graffiti* was nominated in five categories. Although the film did not win any Oscars, the nominations themselves were significant. It lost Best Picture to *The Sting* (1973), but Lucas had been nominated as Best Director and co-nominated with Katz and Huyck for Best Original Screenplay. His wife Marcia, alongside editor Verna Fields, who had also worked on the picture, was nominated for Best Film Editing. Never great with actors, Lucas had nonetheless somehow directed Candy Clark to an Oscar-nominated performance as Best Supporting Actress. Lucas had also been nominated as Best Director for the 31st Golden Globe Awards, and for the Directors Guild of America Award for Outstanding Direction (although he didn't win either). The nominations were enough to reassure him that he had made the right choices in making the movie and the studio had been wrong in its initial take on the film. It was a situation he was determined not to find himself in again.

The date 17 April 1973 isn't regarded as a national holiday or a day worthy of celebration, but for some *Star Wars* fans it could be. It was on that day, in the middle of the *American Graffiti* debacle, that George Lucas sat down at his desk with a yellow legal pad and began writing his *Flash Gordon*-inspired 'space thing' that would eventually – four long years later – become *Star Wars*.

There's no historic plaque on the modest Mill Valley house where Lucas drafted the words, 'A long time ago, in a galaxy far, far away'. Those words were Lucas's version of 'Once upon a time' and he and Gary Kurtz were clear that they wanted their space-opera movie to have something of the fairy tale about it. Lucas, however, had a problem. In writing *American Graffiti* he was able to adhere to the old writing adage of 'write what you know', but even then he had needed considerable help from Katz and Huyck to shape his material into a coherent screenplay. Now, he was attempting to get down on paper a blueprint for a film about aliens and monsters, an evil Empire, a beautiful princess, an innocent farm boy and a rogue smuggler who are all caught up in dramatic adventures amid events far larger than themselves. How could he possibly do it?

Lucas drew on the things he had liked as a child and some of the science fiction and fantasy he'd read since, mixed in some elements of *The Hidden Fortress* – the Kurosawa film, to which he had failed to secure the remake rights – and used Joseph Campbell's book on storytelling and mythology, *The Hero with a Thousand Faces*, for tips on structure, incident and character. He also had his frustrated attempt to make *Apocalypse Now* in mind. Walter Murch believed Lucas had transposed the Vietnam War epic to outer space instead, replacing helicopters with X-wing fighters. 'There was this great nation with all this technology which was losing a war to basically tribesmen,' said Lucas, sowing the seeds for the defeat of his evil Empire at the paws of the primitive Ewoks in *Return of the Jedi* (1983). Murch noted of Lucas that 'he took that situation and transposed it not only out of Vietnam, but to a galaxy far, far away'.

Five weeks later, on 20 May, Lucas had a thirteen-page story synopsis. It was a sprawling epic, purporting to be a 'found document' from the *Journal of the Whills* telling the story of Mace Windu and a group of chivalrous knights known as the Jedi Bendu. Set in the far future of the thirty-third century, the universe of the story was dominated by an evil Empire, while the core of the tale echoed Kurosawa's movie in that it had a General Luke Skywalker and his sidekick, Anakin Starkiller, escorting a feisty teenage rebel princess named Leia Aquilae across the galaxy. The group was evading the agents of the evil Empire, General Darth Vader and Valarium, known as the Black Knight. Featured in the story were two 'everyman' figures, essentially the peasants from *The Hidden Fortress*, but in this universe they were artificial robots dubbed Threepio and Artoo (having started out as human Imperial bureaucrats). Running from planet to planet – each of which seemed to have only one eco-system, either a jungle, a desert or a gas cloud – the rebel group hide out in an asteroid field and are helped by a gilled, green alien smuggler figure named Han Solo. Other incidental characters included a group of 'lost boys' (seemingly lifted from Peter Pan) and a large, hairy alien called Chewbacca. Elements of Frank Herbert's then-popular *Dune* novels featured in the valued 'aura spice', and the setting of the desert world of Ophiuchi. The climax of the story outline saw the rebels stage an attack on an Empire colony, freeing the captured princess, who then rewarded them all at an opulent ceremony.

Many who read through the material found it difficult to understand what the creator was trying to achieve, but one thing was certain: George Lucas intended 'The Star Wars', as it was then known, to be a project he would realize on his own terms.

Chapter 3

A New Hope

I thought, 'This'll be the last movie I direct.' I wanted to make a fairy tale epic, but I had this huge draft of a screenplay, like War and Peace*!*

George Lucas

Two men would become notorious in Hollywood as the studio executives who turned down *Star Wars*. David Picker at United Artists – a studio founded in 1919 by Charlie Chaplin, Mary Pickford, Douglas Fairbanks and D. W. Griffith to serve the vision of filmmaking artists – had supported George Lucas since he first pitched his *Flash Gordon*-inspired 'space thing' back in Cannes.

However, despite being the studio behind the James Bond spy-film phenomenon, Picker felt that the treatment Lucas had finally put together in 1973 would simply be far too expensive to realize on film (except perhaps as animation). He also feared that the scenes and locations described in the outline would be beyond special effects technicians' abilities. It showed a lack of imagination and forward thinking on Picker's part, given that movie special effects had not changed a whole lot since the 1950s. A willingness to invest in new technology – as Lucas himself would have to do to bring *Star Wars* to the screen – might have given United Artists a very different future than the one of decline it faced during the 1980s and 1990s.

The other unlucky executive was Ned Tanen, the man at Universal who thought that Lucas's *American Graffiti* was unreleasable, except perhaps on television. During the turmoil of the 1960s, Universal had enthusiastically embraced production for television as a replacement for the collapsing theatrical film business. Tanen simply couldn't get to grips with the new material Lucas presented, admitting later that he had 'a very tough time understanding' the thirteen-page storyline. Additionally, he was looking for material that had television potential, and this – whatever it was – certainly wasn't that. Tanen solicited the opinion of other Universal executives, none of whom could see any merit in the idea either. Despite all this negativity, Tanen does appear to have requested that Lucas draft a simpler telling of his story before passing a final verdict.

The famous memo in which Universal finally rejected *Star Wars* has been much studied, especially by later executives who hoped to avoid repeating such a catastrophic mistake. The memo suggested that the project would be like 'rolling dice', so uncertain was the outcome. The writer did concede that the revised outline was 'rather exciting', packed full of 'potential action'. Even so, the ideas would be 'difficult to translate visually', especially in realizing the robot 'heroes' of the piece, Threepio and Artoo. Even if everything came together perfectly, and the special effects and creature make-up problems envisaged were overcome, the memo still expressed some reservations about whether the epic story would appeal to audiences who might not 'completely understand the rights and wrongs involved' between the characters, so strange was the universe to be portrayed. The studio concluded that the decision of whether to proceed came down to 'how much faith we have in Lucas's ability to pull it all off'. In the end, the studio executives at Universal lacked the necessary faith and followed United Artists in rejecting *Star Wars*.

Unbowed by these rejections, Lucas had a new hope. He had been impressed by the way Twentieth Century Fox – another failing studio with a proud history right back to the beginnings of Hollywood – had handled the *Planet of the Apes* series of films. Since 1968, there had been four further films, with the last

– *Battle for the Planet of the Apes* – in cinemas during the summer of 1973 when Lucas was writing and rewriting his *Star Wars* story ideas. It would go on to become a one-year television series the following year, before being revived several times more in the twenty-first century. The *Apes* 'franchise' had supported an extravagant range of merchandise, and had proved that there was an audience for action-adventure science fiction, following the intellectual dead-end of Kubrick's *2001:A Space Odyssey* (1968).

The ownership of Hollywood studios had been changing from the end of the 1960s into the early 1970s, with corporate interests seeing off the last of the old-style Hollywood moguls who had run the business of movies since the 1930s. Las Vegas hotel and airline owner Kirk Kerkorian had taken control of the home of classic musicals, Metro-Goldwyn-Mayer (MGM), while United Artists had fallen under the sway of San Francisco insurance giant TransAmerica. New York moneymen controlled Columbia, waiting for truculent studio head Harry Cohn to see out his final days, while Paramount was owned by oil giant Gulf + Western. Fox had not escaped the purges and changes in ownership, with a new management backed by US bank Lehman Brothers taking control.

However, the man now running Twentieth Century Fox had impeccable Hollywood credentials. Alan Ladd Jr, known to all as 'Laddie', was the son of movie actor Alan Ladd, star of film noir *This Gun for Hire* (1942) and Western *Shane* (1953). After a difficult childhood, Ladd had started in Hollywood at talent agency CMA in the early 1960s. Just over a decade later he was a middle-ranking executive at Fox, having dabbled in film-making himself in Britain. Now he was running the studio and he had an appointment with an upstart moviemaker named George Lucas.

Lucas found a kindred spirit in Laddie. Both were quiet men who kept their thoughts close to their chests. They were both 'juniors', sons of overbearing fathers who shared their names. Ladd prided himself on opening his door to talent, and many directors and stars disenchanted with what was happening at other studios had come to make movies at Fox. He liked to take a chance on a maverick. Ladd had seen – and more importantly, liked – *THX 1138* and he was a fan of *American Graffiti*. He was also aware of the troubled time Lucas and Coppola had endured at Universal over the film's release.

In presenting his ideas for what would become *Star Wars* to Alan Ladd Jr, Lucas didn't simply rely on his written thirteen-page treatment, fearing that the negative feedback it had brought from both United Artists and Universal might be due to the poorly expressed concepts. This time, he pitched the story himself in person, a move that did not come easily to the still-shy Lucas. It wasn't so much the movie story that won Ladd over, but the enthusiasm expressed by its would-be director. The executive felt that if Lucas could be this excited by the mere idea of making his movie, then he would have enough energy and enthusiasm to carry him through what was bound to be a difficult and fraught filmmaking experience. 'It was a gamble, and I was betting on Lucas,' Ladd later admitted.

In creating *Star Wars*, George Lucas drew on a whole host of influences and inspirations. The writing of the screenplay would take over two years. It was a period Lucas often described as one of the worst of his life. As writing did not come naturally to him, sitting at his desk every morning attempting to turn his unwieldy, sprawling story treatment into a properly structured script, packed with incident and memorable dialogue, was something of a slog.

Lucas had several notebooks in which he had scribbled down ideas across the years, many relating to the growing story of his 'space thing'. Inspiration was all around him. While mixing the soundtrack for *American Graffiti* with Walter Murch, Lucas had been asked to fetch 'R2D2' from the shelf. Murch meant one of the recorded dialogue tracks, designated Reel 2, Dialogue 2, or R2D2 for short. Lucas had been struck by the alpha-numeric designation and felt it would make a great name for a robot. R2-D2: into the notebook it went.

Driving back and forward from his home to his office, Lucas was often accompanied by his dog, a huge black-and-white malamute called Indiana. Not only would this dog provide the inspiration for the name of Lucas's archaeological hero Indiana Jones in *Raiders of the Lost Ark* (1981), but his habit of riding up-front in the passenger seat was the inspiration behind Chewbacca, Han Solo's constant companion. Marcia, aware of Indiana's habits, had dubbed their dog his 'furry co-pilot'.

Another road trip gave Chewbacca his species. Lucas was driving with disc jockey Terry McGovern when their car hit a bump in the road. McGovern quickly quipped, 'Sorry George, must've run over a wookiee back there . . .' Ever alert for weird words and phrases for the unique galaxy he was creating, Lucas noted the oddball phrase and later applied it to Chewbacca, who would be a Wookiee. The phrase first turned up in the audio wild track on *THX 1138*, voiced by McGovern himself (although on the *THX 1138* director's cut DVD, Walter Murch apocryphally credits 'Wookiee' to McGovern having a dig at a Texan friend apparently named 'Ralph Wookie'). There's also a *Buck Rogers* comic strip from 1937–8 named 'Wokkie and the Novans', in which 'Wokkie' is Wilma Deering's pet midget elephant!

As he had poured much of his teenage self into several characters in *American Graffiti*, so the young hero of *Star Wars* – Luke Skywalker – was very much another George Lucas alter-ego. Trapped in a backwater environment (Tatooine is clearly the Modesto of this galaxy far, far away), Luke yearns for adventure, for bigger and better things, much as young Lucas had in refusing to follow in his father's footsteps and settle for a job running the local stationery store. 'You can't write a main character and not have him be part of you,' admitted Lucas. He also took inspiration from people around him at American Zoetrope, with much of Han Solo being drawn from the brash character of *Apocalypse Now* screenwriter John Milius.

Lucas was determined that his space fantasy should retain a fairy-tale feel. He felt that the success of *American Graffiti* and the increasing number of young people going to the cinema showed that American audiences were ready for something less cynical and fresher than recent entertainment had been (in the midst of the Watergate scandal and the end of the Vietnam War). He remembered his days watching old movie serials repackaged for television in the 1950s, the sense of unbridled adventure, of good guys versus bad guys. The space-opera of *Flash Gordon* had always been one thing above everything else: fun.

Yet, in writing the screenplay for *Star Wars*, Lucas was becoming bogged down in detail. He was, in effect, creating an entire universe, and the back-stories of his characters and galactic empires were threatening to overwhelm the forward motion of the action. For structure, Lucas was relying heavily on Joseph Campbell's *Hero with a Thousand Faces*. In particular, the saga of Arthurian legend, with its chivalrous knights and heroic quests, was proving useful. Elements of the Bible even came into play, with ideas of heroic redemption used as a transformative element for his characters. Lucas constantly changed the nature of his central characters, altering their names, changing their species and playing with their roles in the story, all with the aim of arriving at the perfect balance of action, adventure and character.

Even his personal history was not off-limits in the creation of this story. Lucas had issues with his own upbringing and his father, and those fed into his story. Luke would eventually discover he was the son of the film's main villain, Darth Vader (a corruption of a foreign-language version of 'dark father'), while he would be aided on his quest by an older mentor figure, representing the 'good father' and drawn from Lucas's interest in Japan and samurai movies, Obi-Wan Kenobi (possibly also an avatar for Francis Ford Coppola, the Jedi Master to Lucas's filmmaking padawan). Lucas was a big comic book fan and he was undoubtedly influenced by the work of Jack Kirby on *The New Gods*, launched in 1971. Kirby's hero Orion battles the evil

Darkseid, who is later revealed to be his father. It is a relationship that Lucas would subsequently use to link his villain Darth
Vader with his hero Luke Skywalker. John Morrow, editor of
The Kirby Collector, believed the debt was obvious: 'There are
just too many similarities for me to believe that Kirby wasn't
some kind of influence on Lucas.'

While he added new ideas and discarded others from his
core story, Lucas never threw anything away, accumulating a
huge amount of material surrounding the worlds of *Star Wars*.
Ever mindful of the budget, it was often down to Gary Kurtz
to persuade the writer-director that certain sequences were
simply not achievable. At one point, the script featured a visit
to Chewbacca's planet, the Wookiee homeworld, where the
heroes would meet many more of his species, including his
family. It was Kurtz who persuaded Lucas that it would be
difficult enough to create one believable Wookiee, never mind
hundreds. The idea was cut from the script, but not discarded,
and was eventually realized in various forms in the 1978 TV
Star Wars Holiday Special and in *Star Wars: Episode III – Revenge
of the Sith* in 2005.

'I had this huge draft of a screenplay,' recalled Lucas. 'I took
that script and cut it in half, put the first half aside [which would
become the loose basis for the *Star Wars* prequels, 1999–2005]
and decided to write the screenplay from the second half. I was
on page 170 and I thought, "Holy smokes, I need 100 pages not
500," but I had these great scenes. So I took that story and cut
it into three parts. I took the first part and said, "This will be my
script. But no matter what happens, I am going to get these
three movies made."'

Alan Ladd Jr and George Lucas had agreed on a 'deal memo'
for 'The Star Wars', outlining the areas the formal contract
would cover. The first draft script would earn Lucas $10,000,
with a further payment if the screenplay was accepted and an
additional $50,000 if the movie was put into production. For
directing the film, Lucas would be paid $100,000, with Gary
Kurtz set to pocket $50,000 for production duties. The budget

for the movie was set at $3.5 million, and a shooting schedule would be worked out once the whole production was given a formal green light.

By March 1975, the script and background material for 'The Star Wars' had grown to 500 pages, whereas a screenplay needed to be closer to 100 pages to produce a film of around 90–100 minutes in length. Early in the summer of 1975, George Lucas had worked at cutting back his material, reshaping the universe he had created on paper into one that could be realized on a cinema screen. The now familiar shape of *Star Wars* fell into place during this period, even if a lot of the details would only become concrete during the production process. The material that Lucas cut out – mainly the backstory to his universe – was put to one side, to be revived one day in the future. This allowed him to focus on the core of the tale he wanted to tell, without getting caught up in all the surrounding detail that he found so fascinating.

It was a simple tale, but so much material had been distilled down to tell it that it had a potent effect. Farm-boy 'Luke Starkiller' is keen to escape his dead-end existence working on his uncle's farm on the desert planet of Tatooine. Only his uncle Owen Lars knows he is the son of a famed warrior, 'Anakin Starkiller'. The larger universe lands on Luke's doorstep with the arrival of a pair of robots – 'droids' – called R2-D2 and C-3PO, who have a message from 'Princess Leia' who has been captured by agents of the evil Empire. Luke falls in with 'shabby old desert rat' Obi-Wan Kenobi, 'tough James Dean style starpilot' Han Solo and his sidekick, a seven-foot furry alien Wookiee called 'Chewbacca', in setting out to rescue the princess and destroy the Empire's space fortress, the 'Death Star'. It's all incredibly familiar now, but in the mid-1970s nothing quite like this story had ever been seen in film before.

In his own life Lucas had been searching for a faith he could believe in, but everything he had studied had come up short. Throughout the various drafts of his script he had incorporated various mystical elements that eventually became 'the Force', a mysterious power that 'binds the galaxy together'. This Force had positive and negative aspects, the light side (represented by Obi-Wan Kenobi and the ancient order of the Jedi Knights) and the dark side (represented by the Empire's Darth Vader and the 'dark Jedi', known as the Sith). These elements would form a backdrop to the adventure story that Lucas wanted to tell, but they were of equal importance to him as he felt these mystical aspects gave his otherwise slight tale some philosophical weight.

Alan Ladd Jr at Fox accepted this third draft script of *Star Wars*, and Lucas was paid in line with the agreement they had outlined. However, that alone didn't mean the film would be made. Until the film was given an official 'green light' by the studio – that is, put into actual production – nothing more could happen on it. At the time, *American Graffiti* was hugely successful after a faltering start, so Lucas felt confident in setting up a production company to handle the making of the movie: The Star Wars Corporation was born.

In one of the earliest interviews about his as yet unmade movie, Lucas told *Esquire* that *Star Wars* would be 'the first multi-million dollar *Flash Gordon* kind of movie, with *The Magnificent Seven* thrown in'. Aware that explaining the movie to the Fox board (who would ultimately decide whether it was to be made) or to anyone else he hoped to hire to work on it might be difficult on the basis of the rather strange script alone, Lucas decided to commission some visual aids. He turned to designer and artist Ralph McQuarrie to visualize some of the characters and concepts in the script: it was a cheap way of seeing what the resulting movie might look like. For a few thousand dollars (from Lucas's own funds), McQuarrie was tasked with creating paintings illustrating four key scenes in the movie: the robots arrival on Tatooine, the 'lightsaber' battle between Kenobi and Vader, the Imperial stormtroopers in action, and the make-or-break final attack on the 'hidden fortress' of the Death Star.

Based on the script and a few discussions with Lucas, these four images were key to the eventual look and feel of *Star Wars*. Lucas suggested one of the robots should be modelled after 'false Maria' from Fritz Lang's 1927 film *Metropolis*, while the other should be 'cute'. While his Chewbacca was a more frightening, feral creature than the one in the movie, McQuarrie's take on Han Solo seemed to have been based on the bearded George Lucas himself. Other iconic characters came about due to McQuarrie's practical considerations. The script opened with an assault on the ship carrying the princess, so feeling that the stormtroopers and Vader would be crossing a vacuum in space to board the vessel, he gave them all breathing masks. These specific looks stuck and, in the case of Vader, became key to the further development of the character.

Despite Alan Ladd Jr supporting Lucas and his new movie, Fox was wary of the then-huge investment it would require. It was the McQuarrie paintings – alongside a handful of model spaceships Lucas had *2001: A Space Odyssey* designer Colin Cantwell build – that persuaded the studio that this film was viable. They were prepared to spend $3.5 million, the cost of a 'cheap comedy' Lucas felt. The only way the film could be made with that budget was to approach it in the style of *THX 1138*, but Lucas hoped that as time went on things might change. It finally looked like George Lucas would realize his dream of getting to make his long-in-development 'space thing'.

Now that his project that had previously only largely existed on paper – as a lengthy script and a series of drawings – had the go-ahead, George Lucas was faced with the task of making his fantasy a reality. The biggest problem, he knew, would be how to bring to life the many special effects the film would require: after all, this was a movie featuring robots and aliens as main characters, spaceships engaged in dynamic battles, and an assault on an armoured space station. That was before he had even looked at how he would turn Earthbound locations into various exotic alien worlds.

There hadn't been a significant space-set movie since 1968's *2001: A Space Odyssey*, and most of the experienced special effects technicians who worked in Hollywood dated back to the 1950s heyday of movies like *This Island Earth* (1955) and *Forbidden Planet* (1956). Lucas knew that a new movie for the 1970s would require a new approach to special effects. To begin with, he looked at the people who had worked on *2001*, particularly Douglas Trumbull, who had gone on to direct the thoughtful, character-based, science-fiction movie *Silent Running* (1972), comparable to Lucas's own *THX 1138* in that it took a political view of the future. Despite the fact that they got on well, Lucas's need for control over the effects put Trumbull off from getting involved with *Star Wars*. Instead, he would go on to work with Steven Spielberg in realizing the alien mothership and other effects for *Close Encounters of the Third Kind* (1977). Understanding that no one working in Hollywood could offer him what he needed for the film, Lucas decided that he would have to build his own special-effects facility: at least that way he would have the control he felt he required.

Lucas turned to Trumbull's effects assistant, John Dykstra, to set up his special-effects facility, dubbed Industrial Light and Magic (ILM). Dykstra had worked on *Silent Running* and with Robert Wise on *The Andromeda Strain* (1971), but couldn't figure out from the script exactly what Lucas would need. The final sequence was one line in the screenplay: 'Then they attack the Death Star.' Lucas explained he wanted a much more dynamic approach to the spaceships in *Star Wars* than was evident in *Silent Running*, in which the huge, aircraft-carrier style ships had been largely static. Second World War dogfights and the climax of *The Dam Busters* (1955) were his touchstones for the feel he wanted for the space action.

Dykstra understood this could only be achieved by developing new technology. He had been working at college on a proposed 'motion control' camera, the theory being that the camera moved around the model (a spaceship, say) rather than have the model move, giving the illusion of dynamic movement in the final shot. Through George Lucas, ILM and *Star Wars*, he saw an opportunity to put into practice on a large-scale the technology he had only previously tried out in minor experiments. However, he knew it could give Lucas the kind of space dogfights he was looking for, if the money was available to develop, test and build the technology.

Combining several models with other film elements, such as matte paintings and animated inserts, would require multiple passes to be repeated with exacting precision. Such 'motion control' systems didn't yet exist, but Dykstra was confident he could create one. With Lucas funding the operation personally, ILM was up-and-running by November 1975 in an otherwise undistinguished warehouse in Van Nuys, California. Lucas was reinvesting his profits from *American Graffiti* in his next venture, giving him the control he craved after disappointment at the hands of the studios on his two previous films, but it would cost him almost $1 million without a single frame of film being shot.

When Fox came seriously to work out a production budget for *Star Wars*, the supervisor responsible assumed the film must be animated, so impossible were the scenes described in the script. It was only when he realized that this was, in fact, a live action movie that studio alarm bells started ringing. Far from being achievable on $3.5 million (as Lucas had known all along), Fox estimated that *Star Wars* would require around $5 million for the special effects alone. Even with cheap cast costs (Lucas was intent on hiring unknown actors), the studio reckoned that filming in Los Angeles studios would result in a final budget of over $13 million, and it was not prepared to fund the film at that level. It was down to producer Gary Kurtz to find savings. Between ILM producing hoped-for cheaper effects and filming in Europe rather than the US, Kurtz argued he could bring the film in for around $7 million, a figure Fox was far more comfortable with, although it was still far from ideal. The presentation to the studio board of McQuarrie's concept artwork sealed the deal, although Kurtz left the meeting knowing that $7 million would not be enough to complete the film the way he knew Lucas would want it.

A final element of the contract had to be negotiated, however. Neither Kurtz nor Lucas asked to increase their fees for writing, directing or producing *Star Wars*, despite the fact that the unexpected success of *American Graffiti* had given them greater bargaining power. Instead, they negotiated that 40 per cent of any profits on the movie would go to The Star Wars Corporation. Additionally, in a decision with incredible foresight – although it was simply an expression of Lucas's need for control – the rights to any merchandising, to the soundtrack and to any sequels were retained by Lucas. After two-and-a-half years of imagining, writing and deal-making, *Star Wars* was finally set for lift off.

While Gary Kurtz began to give some serious thought to how and where *Star Wars* would be shot, George Lucas turned his attention to the people who would populate his 'galaxy far, far away'. His budget meant that he could not afford to hire any 'film stars' for the movie, but that fitted with his preference for offering roles in his films to young, up-and-coming actors rather than established names. He also knew how important it would be to find three actors who could portray the trio at the centre of his story: the now renamed Luke Skywalker, Han Solo and Princess Leia.

Lucas hired an office to hold auditions for *Star Wars* at Goldwyn Studios in Hollywood, sharing the space with filmmaker Brian De Palma who was casting for *Carrie* (1976). This arrangement not only split the expense, but also allowed the two directors to see some of the same actors for both movies and allowed them to compare notes between auditions. Lucas was never very good at social skills and found dealing with actors to be problematic, so was not looking forward to the audition process.

Determined to avoid creating *American Graffiti* in space, Lucas decided not to cast anyone from his previous movie, despite several requests from cast members to be featured in his next film. *Star Wars* would instead boast an all-new roster of potential future movie stars. Despite that plan, Lucas did test *Graffiti*'s Cindy Williams for the role of Leia, only to decide he wanted a younger actress for the part. Having followed *American Graffiti* by starring in Spielberg's *Jaws* (1976), Richard Dreyfuss was keen to be seen for the part of intergalactic rogue Han Solo.

There was one *American Graffiti* actor that Lucas saw every day during the *Star Wars* auditions, although he was not up for a role in the new movie. Harrison Ford was working nearby as a carpenter on a door for the new offices of the slimmed down American Zoetrope, where Francis Ford Coppola was working on the pre-production for *Apocalypse Now*, which he had finally decided to direct himself. At thirty-three, Ford feared his film career might be behind him, after a small role in Coppola's *The Conversation* and a handful of other movie bit parts and television guest roles. He had fallen back on his carpentry skills as an alternative source of income.

Finally, Lucas came to realize that Han Solo was right before his eyes. 'Harrison was there, outside, working all the time, banging on things,' recalled Lucas. 'I just said at lunchtime or sometime, "Would you like to read some of these things, because I need somebody to read against all these characters?" And he said he would do it.' Through reading the role of Solo opposite actors up for the parts of Luke and Leia, Ford would eventually claim the character as his own, making his movie career and beating Christopher Walken to the part.

Lucas had a harder time filling the role of Princess Leia. He didn't want a standard 'Hollywood blonde', but an actress capable of conveying the rebel nature of the princess, while still being able to stand up against an actor like Ford. Among those he saw initially were Amy Irving (who would end up in *Carrie* and later became Steven Spielberg's wife) and Jodie Foster, the child star of Martin Scorsese's *Taxi Driver* (1976). At just thirteen years old, Foster was simply too young for the role, but Irving had the right look that Lucas was after. Terri Nunn (then famous as a *Penthouse* model, but later lead singer with punk pop band Berlin) was almost cast, but Lucas doubted she had the correct regal bearing for a princess. Instead, he turned to a genuine example of Hollywood 'royalty'.

Carrie Fisher was the daughter of actress Debbie Reynolds and crooner Eddie Fisher (who left Reynolds for movie star Liz Taylor). Although the then nineteen-year-old Fisher had the right look and attitude, Lucas felt she had too much 'puppy fat' to portray the character as he saw her. However, Fisher sparked well off Ford in the videotaped auditions, so she seemed like the best bet.

It was the addition of television actor Mark Hamill into the mix that secured the key parts for all three actors. His youthful good looks and optimism suited Luke Skywalker perfectly, and he lacked the cynical detachment shown by the other two. He had been talked into auditioning by his friend, actor Robert Englund (who would later become dream demon Freddy Kruger for Wes Craven in *A Nightmare on Elm Street*, 1984). Hamill was twenty-two, but looked younger, while Fisher looked older than she really was. He had been up for a role in *American Graffiti* four years before, but had made no impression on Lucas. This time things were different – Hamill completed the central trio cementing the relationships with Ford and Fisher. There was only one proviso: Fisher had to lose 10 lbs.

Concerned about so many unknowns in the movie, Fox's Alan Ladd Jr pressured Lucas to break his 'no stars' vow and cast a 'known name' in the grizzled mentor role of Obi-Wan Kenobi. Lucas had wanted to cast Japanese actor Toshiro Mifune, thereby laying plain the role's samurai origins. However, when the director learnt that veteran British actor Alec Guinness was in Hollywood wrapping up a movie, he saw an opportunity. Guinness had made his name in a series of classic Ealing Studios comedies in the 1950s and as Colonel Nicholson in David Lean's *The Bridge on the River Kwai* (1957), for which he won a Best Actor Oscar. By the 1970s, his theatre and screen career was in decline, with television guest roles and films he considered 'silly' the mainstay of his work. When he was sent the script for *Star Wars*, Guinness considered the film to be just as silly as any other he was invited to do at that time. Although he found the script baffling, he recognized a 'page turner' when he came across one. Although not much of it made sense to him, the film's sense of adventure – and his role in it – was clear enough.

After asking around about George Lucas, Guinness met with the director to discuss the role and the film. Although clearly a shy man, Guinness saw something in Lucas's enthusiasm for his tale. The older actor enjoyed the idea that Obi-Wan Kenobi was a combination of Doctor Dolittle and Merlin, with a dash of samurai thrown in. A while later, after considering the role, Guinness came back to Lucas with his own take on the part, something with a little more gravitas to it. However, the actor would not be a cheap option for the low-budget film. Not only did he require a five-figure fee, he also requested a 2 per cent share in the film's 'backend' profits. Guinness had been an actor for hire during the Ealing Studio days and was continually annoyed by their frequent screening on television for which he received no residual fees. Now aged sixty-three, he decided that *Star Wars* was the film he might be able to make a little money from if it were to be successful. Although Guinness drove a hard bargain, Lucas felt he had no choice but to give in to his demands, since it was getting close to the beginning of the shoot and it would please the studio executives who wanted a star name. Therefore, Alec Guinness would be Obi-Wan Kenobi.

Gary Kurtz had figured out that shooting *Star Wars* in Europe would be cheaper than working in the United States, so he toured studio facilities in Rome and London. He finally settled on Elstree Studios in Borehamwood, just outside London. Pinewood – famed for the James Bond movies – was too expensive, while the other two main facilities at Shepperton and Twickenham were deemed too small to meet the film's requirements. With filming set to take place in London, the remainder of the casting would be done there, too.

Matching Alec Guinness in the veteran actor stakes was sixty-three year-old Peter Cushing, famous for the 1950s Hammer horror films, cast as one of the Empire's functionaries, Grand Moff Tarkin. The casting of Phil Brown as Luke's Uncle Owen was interesting, as he was an American actor who had been living and working in London since the McCarthy anti-communist 'blacklist' era of the 1950s. The part of his screen wife, Luke's Aunt Beru, was taken by Shelagh Fraser, a British film and television actress.

Four of the most important roles remained unfilled as the start of shooting approached. Lucas needed distinctive and uniquely talented actors to take on the roles of the film's chief villain, Darth Vader, Han Solo's furry alien sidekick Chewbacca, and the two 'everyman' robot figures, the droids R2-D2 and C-3PO. The casting call was rather unusual, as it called for a 'little person' to play the smaller droid, a seven-foot giant for Chewbacca, a strongman to take on the black-suited Vader role and an effective mime artist to inhabit the gold casing of droid C-3PO. These were unusual requirements, even in the world of moviemaking.

At six feet and seven inches, bodybuilder and sometime actor David Prowse met at least some of Lucas's unusual requirements. Prowse ran his own gym, but had acting experience, often as a 'heavy'. He had played a hulking creature in the unofficial James Bond movie *Casino Royale* (1967), a circus strongman in Hammer's horror flick *Vampire Circus* (1972) and a bruiser in Stanley Kubrick's *A Clockwork Orange* (1971), which Lucas had seen. He wanted Prowse in the movie, and offered him the choice of two roles: Darth Vader or Chewbacca. Told that Chewbacca was a 'hairy gorilla'-type creature on the side of the good guys and that Darth Vader was the film's head villain, Prowse said, 'I'll take the bad guy: people will remember him.'

The role of Chewbacca fell to seven-foot two-inch hospital porter Peter Mayhew, who had come to fame thanks to a newspaper feature on men with huge feet. That had led to a role in the movie *Sinbad and the Eye of the Tiger* (1977) as the Minotaur. Several members of the *Sinbad* production team were being hired to work on *Star Wars* at Elstree, and word had reached Mayhew about the new film, so he had put himself forward for a part, little realizing that his unusual size would match Lucas's requirements exactly.

From casting a giant, Lucas turned his attention to Britain's smaller actors. Britain's smallest man – at three foot eight inches – was music hall and cabaret performer Kenny Baker, who started out performing in the circus. His casting was simplicity itself: he was the right size to fit into the cylindrical bodywork of R2-D2. Baker laid down a condition, though: the production would also have to take on his performing partner, four-foot two-inch Jack Purvis, as otherwise he would be out of work while Baker was committed to the movie. Lucas agreed and Purvis would play the Chief Jawa, one of Tatooine's short, hooded scavengers.

Filling the humanoid shell of the other robot was slightly trickier. As with R2-D2, it didn't matter what the actor sounded like as he would be dubbed over in post-production, with a series of bleeps and bloops for Artoo and the voice of a 'Bronx used car salesman' for Threepio. All Lucas was concerned about at this stage was the physical performance. Lucas felt that mimes and performance artists were the way to go for this role, so he auditioned Marcel Marceau, then the world's best-known mime artist. When Marceau was determined to be unsuitable for the role, Lucas turned his attention to a slightly built, British Shakespearean actor. Anthony Daniels won the role when he expressed strong admiration for Ralph McQuarrie's pre-production painting of C-3PO that was on display in the audition room. It was enough to convince Lucas, who was simply relieved that he had found someone willing to agree to wear the body-armour-style costume for the golden droid. Of all the cast members, Anthony Daniels would do the most to go on to make an entire career from *Star Wars*-related projects.

The *Star Wars* ensemble was now complete. A production

office was opened in Elstree Studios, and the cast and crew were assembled. Gary Kurtz had worked out a tightly scheduled production plan that had to be adhered to if the film was to remain within the strict budget set by Twentieth Century Fox. From ideas jotted down on a yellow legal pad several years before, George Lucas had created an entire enterprise: he and his team were about to embark upon an awfully big adventure together.

Chapter 4

Tatooine Troubles

I wanted to do a modern fairy tale, a myth. One of the criteria of the mythical fairy-tale situation is an exotic, faraway land, but we've lost all the fairy-tale lands on this planet. There is a bigger, mysterious world in space that is more interesting than anything around here.

George Lucas

The first shots of *Star Wars* were captured in March 1976, deep in the far-off, exotic desert of Tunisia. Gary Kurtz had chosen the location as the area offered everything needed for the alien world of Tatooine, all within manageable travelling distance. The exterior of the 'moisture farm' where Luke Skywalker lived, with his doomed aunt and uncle, was in Chott el-Djerid, a barren, dry desert. The interior would be filmed in the underground cave-like dwellings of the Hotel Sidi Driss in the town of Matama, 25 miles from the southern Tunisian oasis town of Gabès. The island of Djerba, in the Gulf of Gabès off the Tunisian coast, was to be the location of Mos Eisley, where Luke and Obi-Wan Kenobi would meet Han Solo in the white-domed cantina. The canyon in which R2-D2 would encounter some hostile Jawas was also located near Chott el-Djerid, while the sand dunes outside the city of Tozeur served as the location where R2-D2 and C-3PO first arrive on Tatooine.

These scenes with the two droids would be the first to be shot during the two-week period the filmmakers had scheduled for filming in Tunisia. The deadline was genuine, as Gary Kurtz had booked a huge Lockheed Hercules C-130 cargo plane to transport all the filmmaking equipment, props and sets to Elstree in London. Every hour the crew were late, the charter company would add a $10,000 surcharge for waiting on the airport tarmac. Given the tight budget, Lucas and Kurtz knew they would be under pressure to capture the location shots they needed quickly and efficiently. Unfortunately, everything seemed stacked against them right from the start.

Expecting to begin shooting on 26 March, the team was surprised to wake to discover an unexpected storm – the first in the region for fifty years – had drowned the desert landscape in rain water and virtually destroyed their ninety-foot mock-up for the lower half of the Jawas's sandcrawler transport vehicle (the upper section would be realized through a matte painting). The filmmakers had no option but to try to stretch the remaining working days left to their maximum, using all the daylight hours available.

First before the cameras was Anthony Daniels as C-3PO. Prior to coming out to Tunisia, a full body cast had been taken of the actor to allow for the construction of a fibreglass costume (as plastic might melt in the Tunisian heat) that would fit him perfectly. The process of putting on the various individual parts took at least two hours every morning. Once inside the suit, especially in the desert heat, Daniels would endure a long day of extreme discomfort. The distinctive gait of C-3PO was developed as it was the only way that Daniels found he could walk while encased in the heavy costume. By the end of the first day filming, he was having serious second thoughts about having committed to the movie.

His counterpart, Kenny Baker, was finding it equally difficult to operate R2-D2. Although the small actor fitted nicely within the barrel-shaped droid, he found it almost impossible to make the thing move properly. Attempts to put the whole shebang on wheels proved no more controllable. All Baker found he could do was rock the droid shell from side-to-side. In the finished movie, almost the only scenes used with Baker inside the costume are those in which Artoo rocks from side-to-side, giving him something approaching a personality (especially when combined with his bleep noise 'dialogue' added in post-production). After an attempt at electronic remote control failed the production resorted to the old-fashioned stand-by of pulling the empty droid casing along using a near-to-invisible wire, but only for long shots. The empty droid shell would often tumble over if pulled too suddenly.

It quickly became clear to Lucas that he would not be able to capture all the shots he wanted in the time available, due to the technical and weather problems. Within days of starting to shoot, the director was resigned to having to recreate shots or make additional pick-up shots in London or even back in California if he were to complete sequences the way he wanted them. In the meantime, he and the rest of the team had no option but to push on and complete as many of the Tatooine scenes on location as they could.

While many of the cast and crew were failing ill, due to the local food and water, veteran actor Alec Guinness struck up a good relationship with young newcomer Mark Hamill, reflecting the on-screen relationship between their characters. Hamill had little idea how to play Luke Skywalker and resorted to acting the role as he imagined his director George Lucas would do it, only to find that this strategy met with complete approval. Guinness had surprised everyone when it came to filming his first scene by throwing himself to the ground and rolling around in the sand. As he stood up and shook the sand off his Jedi robes, he explained that he felt the costume needed to be dirty and aged if his character had been living in the desert for many years rather than the pristine robe the costume department had just handed him.

Lucas's perennial need for filmic speed was included in the shape of Luke's 'landspeeder', an outer space hot-rod vehicle that the director's alter-ego would use to travel from his relatives' isolated farmstead to busy centres like Mos Eisley or to hang out with his pals at Anchorhead, just as the young Lucas had in Modesto. However, the pink, supposedly jet-powered floating landspeeder rarely worked, even when it was jerry-rigged in the style of a roundabout fairground ride that simply rotated around a fixed position. Mirrors were used to hide the wheels under the vehicle in the hope they would reflect the Tunisian sands and give the impression that the landspeeder was in fact floating. Much to the chagrin of Lucas, the vehicle couldn't move very fast either. It was just another scene he would have to work on in post-production in the hope that some primitive special effects might save it.

With malfunctioning droids, misbehaving weather, mechanical failure and disgruntled actors, location shooting on *Star Wars* wrapped in April 1976 on schedule, but the director was far from happy with what he had achieved. Lucas felt the production was slipping out of his control. None of the technology, mainly the radio-controlled droids, had worked as it was supposed to, while it had proved difficult to film in several locations. Lucas was worried that his epic space-opera was in danger of looking cheap and tacky, which was exactly what the majority of the cast and crew who worked on *Star Wars* felt about it. His faith in himself had been shaken by the Tunisian experience, and shooting the studio-based material back in London would take a toll on the director's health, too.

Returning to London, Lucas was demoralized by his *Star Wars* experience so far. While he was in Tunisia, the sound stages at Elstree had been filled with sets for the Mos Eisley spaceport and the hangar bay in which Han Solo's spaceship, the *Millennium Falcon*, is held on the Death Star. Around and between these two main sets were the corridors and rooms that made up the rest of the Death Star, where much of the film's action would unfold. While Gary Kurtz had felt that Shepperton Studios had been too small for the production's needs, he had booked one long, cavernous studio there for the final scene of the movie in which the heroes are awarded medals in a seemingly giant rebel hangar.

For many of the actors, the groundbreaking production techniques being used on *Star Wars* were totally new. While
blue-screen and green-screen shooting – in which exotic backgrounds are digitally dropped in later – is used extensively
today, back in the 1970s it was a technique little used in entertainment, except in often experimental British television shows
like *Top of the Pops* or *Doctor Who*. Many of the actors, whether
old hands like Guinness or relative newcomers like Ford and
Hamill, had trouble getting used to the idea that they had to act
and react to empty space (such as in the first view of the Death
Star space station from within the cockpit of the *Millennium
Falcon*, when Obi-Wan Kenobi declares, 'That's no moon!').
Guinness, Ford and Hamill found themselves looking out on a
plain blue screen, forced to use their imagination as to what it
was exactly their characters might be seeing. Lucas himself was
little help in his limited direction to his actors that often just
consisted of asking them to take a scene again, but this time to
be 'faster and more intense'.

It didn't help tempers that 1976 saw a heat wave sweep Britain,
resulting in one of the hottest summers of the century. The British
technicians working on the film were used to following strict
union rules, while the Americans had a more free-flowing attitude as to when they worked and how much got done. Conflicts
arose as Lucas appeared to put the needs of his film ahead of
those of his local crew. The cut-off point of 5.30 p.m. each week-
day had to be strictly observed, whereas Lucas would have been
happier to carry on filming into the slightly cooler evening in
order to get all his shots done. An official request to add an extra
two hours to the working day was roundly rejected by the union-
ized crew members. As in Tunisia, Lucas could feel himself falling
further and further behind his merciless schedule.

Here was another example of Lucas as the rebel, the outsider.
He had approached the making of *Star Wars* full of new ideas
about how to make a film, ideas that required throwing aside
many of the traditional, industrial methods that had been used
successfully for decades. While he had a vision in his head of

what the finished film could look like, he had great difficulty in communicating that to others: if he had, he might have found it easier to bring them along on the journey with him as willing partners and collaborators rather than as angry antagonists.

The most senior member of the crew to come into conflict with Lucas was cinematographer Gilbert 'Gil' Taylor, a late replacement for Geoffrey Unsworth who had worked with Stanley Kubrick on *2001: A Space Odyssey*. Taylor was a very traditional filmmaker, who got his start in the business in the 1930s as a camera assistant. In the post-war years he was a director of photography (or cinematographer) on a variety of films largely shot in Britain, including *Ice Cold in Alex* (1958), *Dr Strangelove* (1964), the Beatles' *A Hard Day's Night* (1964), Roman Polanski's *Repulsion* (1965) and *Cul-de-Sac* (1966), Alfred Hitchcock's *Frenzy* (1972) and *The Omen* (1976). He was also an old-fashioned man, used to the traditional ways of doing things in a British studio set-up.

A big taboo in British filmmaking was for a director to inter-fere with a cinematographer's lighting rig, but Lucas was so hands on and so often given to becoming carried way with the task at hand that he thought nothing of taking it upon himself to rearrange the lighting set-up if he felt it could enhance his shot. Lucas and Taylor were quickly at odds, even out in Tunisia when the cinematographer had questioned the lighting level requested by his director. Lucas wanted the film shot using a particular set of soft-focus lenses, something to which Taylor refused to accede. 'I was shooting for good portraiture,' said Taylor. 'You can see their faces; you can see their eyes. That's why *Star Wars'* popularity has lasted so long.' Where the younger members of the crew would express their low opinion of Lucas in private or among themselves in the pub after work, Taylor felt free to voice his disparaging opinions on set, rather loudly, in front of the cast and crew. Lucas knew he was already in deep water in his relations with the crew, so any thought of sacking Taylor was forgotten as he feared it might provoke a mutiny in the shape of industrial action among the rest of the British team.

The strain of making *Star Wars* took its toll on the health of the movie's director. Lucas took after his mother in not being the healthiest of people, and the long hours and constant stress of working on his film was causing him problems. At the studio from 7 a.m., he would work tirelessly preparing for the day's shooting and then directing the cast and crew, until the technicians downed tools at 5.30 p.m. His evenings would be spent in the production offices at Elstree planning the next day's work, as well as reviewing what had been achieved so far. A persistent cough made his state of health clear to all who were working with him, and the fact that he was feeling below par meant that he became even less communicative with those around him than he usually was.

Equally stressed out was Anthony Daniels. His troubles with the C-3PO costume in Tunisia had continued during the studio filming in Britain. In breaks between shots, he had little choice but to prop himself against a wall, or rest on special 'leaning boards' that had been created to allow him a break from standing on his feet. He was, however, occasionally mistaken for a movie prop by the British crew and manhandled off the set before he could protest. 'They'd strike matches on me and discuss their sex lives,' recalled Daniels of the film crew, 'quite unaware that I was inside the costume and could overhear every word.' The actor finally insisted that the golden droid's headpiece be removed between takes so that those around him could see the actor underneath and react to him accordingly. Daniels was further depressed the longer shooting went on. 'I was very, very unhappy in that suit,' he said. 'At times I thought, "Maybe I'm making a complete prat of myself."' The support of fellow British actor Alec Guinness helped Daniels endure.

The truculent British crew was convinced that not only Daniels, but the entire cast of *Star Wars*, were making 'prats' of themselves. None of them could get a handle on what this outer space movie was actually going to look like, and they were increasingly openly dismissive of the whole enterprise, joking that the movie looked like a particularly bad episode of the low budget TV show, *Doctor Who*.

Lucas's faith in his own work was shaken when his supporter from the studio, Alan Ladd Jr, visited London to view an assemblage of the footage shot so far. Ladd viewed what was planned as the opening sequence of the movie that saw Luke leaving the farm for a night on the town with some buddies (among them actress Koo Stark, later more famous for an affair with Prince Andrew than her acting credentials). Kurtz recalled that Ladd reacted to the sequence by declaring it to be just like '*American Graffiti* in space'. So negative was Ladd's feeling that the whole sequence was eventually cut from the movie (and was not made available to fans until a 1998 CD-ROM, *Star Wars: Behind the Magic*, and the 2011 release of the *Star Wars* saga on Blu-ray).

There were frequent jokes on set about the poor quality of the dialogue written for the characters by George Lucas. Harrison Ford famously complained, 'You can type this shit, George, but you sure can't say it' and ad-libbed much of his performance around the clumsily scripted dialogue. Of the dialogue, Mark Hamill admitted: 'It was not Noel Coward, let's face it.' These criticisms saw Lucas recruit his college friends and *American Graffiti* collaborators Willard Huyck and Gloria Katz to give the script a polish, halfway through the London studio shooting. Their task was to add some humour to the more straight-laced 'sci-fi' dialogue about warp speed and the Force, thereby lightening some of the characters and making others (especially the droids) more appealing. In some respects, Daniels was grateful his face was hidden behind a mask, reassured that if the film was to become a failure, at least none of his actor friends would know he was in it.

Script changes saw a major alteration to Alec Guinness's role as Obi-Wan Kenobi. The final part of the movie originally saw Kenobi injured in a lightsaber duel with Darth Vader, only for him to be carried around by the others for the rest of the film. Fearing that this would slow things down considerably, Lucas decided to kill off Kenobi in the fight with Vader, thereby upping the stakes. Guinness would only feature in the rest of the movie as a 'Force ghost', a mystical afterlife version of the character. Guinness only heard about his revised status second-hand through his agent and was so upset that he threatened to quit the production entirely. However, the veteran actor was persuaded that this more dramatic denouement for his character would make his role in the story more memorable. A placated Guinness returned to the set and saw the quirky production through to the end. He may not have bothered if he had realized how physical the duel with Vader would be, caused by the fact that actor Dave Prowse suffered from severely limited vision when encased in Vader's all-over black armour. Enthusiastically caught up in his sword-fighting actions, Prowse knocked Guinness flying, with the older actor landing in a crumpled heap on the studio floor.

With money running out and Fox keeping a watchful eye, the final week of filming at Elstree saw three camera units functioning simultaneously on three different sets. The frantic, ill director was having to rush from set to set (sometimes by bicycle) to give instructions to the actors and crew, before rushing back to the first set and starting all over again. Fox had dropped the guillotine on the production, giving Lucas a completion date beyond which it would cut off funding.

One of the final scenes to be shot was one of the first in the movie, as Darth Vader and his white armoured stormtroopers assault the rebel blockade runner with Princess Leia and the two droids aboard. More money had to be found when Lucas realized he simply didn't have enough stark white corridor set pieces to film the sequence the way he wanted. It was not to be the last budget crisis on *Star Wars*, just the final one of the London live-action shooting.

Gathering the material shot in Tunisia and all the studio work done at Elstree, Lucas prepared to return to California to see just what kind of film he had. Whether brought on by the ongoing pressure, or by the fact that he could now relax as shooting was finally over, Lucas's health once again took a serious turn for the worse. 'He was so exhausted,' noted Kurtz of the end of filming. 'He worried about all the details, afraid that if he let anything go it wouldn't be right. He almost had a breakdown because of that.'

At the end of the long, hot British summer of 1976, George Lucas was relieved to be returning to California. Back on his home turf, he felt he could take control of his movie once more. An extensive period of post-production lay ahead, but he knew that he could reshape *Star Wars* and hopefully make up for what he perceived as the deficiencies of the live action shoot. A brief break in Hawaii with his wife Marcia gave Lucas the chance to recover from the physical toll of shooting in Tunisia and London and to gather his thoughts before returning to Los Angeles, where the movie would be completed.

Star Wars was planned by Fox as a Christmas 1976 release, so the pressure was on for Lucas to complete the movie as quickly as possible. While the special effects wizards were working away at ILM, he put together an initial edit of the footage, partially to see how the film worked and partially to see where he would need to fill in scenes with model work and special effects. The resulting rough cut was a major disappointment: despite the length of the production time, the movie did not play at all well and even the writer-director could see it. Lucas needed help.

Luckily, such help was at hand in the shape of his wife Marcia. She, however, was extremely busy working on *Carrie* (the film that had shared casting facilities with *Star Wars*) for Brian De Palma, with Martin Scorsese's *New York, New York* lined up next. However, when her husband pleaded for her help in reshaping the material for *Star Wars*, she could hardly refuse. Neither, however, could she do the task alone. Two other editors – Richard Chew (Murch's assistant on Coppola's *The Conversation*) and Paul Hirsch (who was the main editor on *Carrie*) – were called on to help salvage *Star Wars*.

While the trio of editors tried to craft a coherent story from the footage Lucas had shot, the director decided to call on ILM and check on its progress in the months he had been away film-ing in Tunisia and London. There was another shock in store. Left in charge of the facility, John Dykstra had spent almost $1 million of Lucas's money developing the new motion control camera set-up and having all the starship models constructed, but very little finished work was available for viewing. 'They had spent a year and $1 million and had only come up with one acceptable shot,' claimed Lucas.

Dykstra had taken a loose approach to personnel manage-ment, knowing the kind of people who worked in special effects in the 1970s. They were more often to be found loung-ing in the hot tub or smoking relaxing herbal cigarettes than working inside the Van Nuys warehouse. Without air-condi-tioning the facility often reached temperatures of 115 or 120°F inside, making it impossible to work. Instead, the crew would work at night when it was a more acceptable 90°F. Filming on the model shots would wrap around 3 a.m. or 4 a.m., with an average week consisting of sixty working hours. Despite that, in Lucas's view, progress had been pitiful.

Lucas felt that Dykstra had got sidetracked into developing the new technology and had not concentrated on producing usable shots for the movie. The director had fully expected to return from London to find a complete set of special effects shots ready to be edited into the film. Instead, the only one that really worked was the opening escape pod sequence that results in C-3PO and R2-D2 crash-landing on Tatooine. There was simply no way the film could meet Fox's planned Christmas released date, but Lucas left it up to Kurtz – as producer – to inform the studio.

Dykstra and Lucas were opposites in terms of temperament and approach to work. The laid-back, hippie-ish special effects guru refused to be worried about things like deadlines or studio pressure, while the already frazzled, control-freak director was living in fear of having his film taken away from him as had already happened twice before. It did not make for a happy working relationship as work resumed on producing the special effects shots that the film needed, now under the stricter personal supervision of the director.

He took control of the scheduling at ILM, laying down a stricter regimen of discipline to ensure the work progressed at an acceptable rate. The stress of the situation once again hit Lucas hard, and he was admitted to hospital upon his return to San Francisco with chest pains. The diagnosis was hypertension and exhaustion, complicated by his diabetes, with a ruling from his doctor to simplify his life. There was not much prospect of that with his movie currently in pieces. The days of enforced relaxation in hospital, however, gave George Lucas time to pause and reflect, just as he had done after his crash in Modesto back in 1962. He came to an important conclusion: the stress was not worth it. After this, he decided, he would not direct a movie again.

Out of hospital, Lucas could not afford to relax and found himself a constant passenger on the one-hour flight between San Francisco and Los Angeles as he attempted to secure both a coherent edit of the film footage shot in London and a series of completed special effects shots to slot into it. A few nights each week, Lucas was to be found based in a cheap hotel in Van Nuys close to the ILM facility. He would spend his days in the warehouse, making sure that production of the shots he needed progressed in a sure and steady manner, rather than in the hit-and-miss fashion Dykstra had seemingly employed. The result was a tighter, less happy team, but at least Lucas was getting his shots.

Fox began to get cold feet over *Star Wars* and the release was rescheduled from Christmas 1976 to the summer of 1977. The best the studio felt a science-fiction film could earn at the US box office in the 1970s was around $15 million, based on previous experience. Cost overruns and other unexpected expenditure had seen the budget on *Star Wars* rise to around $9 million, with the additional cost of advertising promotion and release prints expected to bring the total to nearer $11 million overall. The executive board at the studio feared that if the film flopped, it stood to lose a fortune, perhaps even putting the future of the studio at risk. They contemplated selling the movie off to a group of German investors in the hope of divesting themselves of any more risk.

The unconventional production process had made things more difficult for the executives at Fox, who simply couldn't understand just what kind of film *Star Wars* was. The raw footage had looked terrible, with incomplete scenes, swathes of background blue screen and no completed special effects shots. They couldn't imagine how this would be turned into a finished movie and none of them understood the processes going on at ILM, despite repeated visits. The process of building shots up from a variety of elements was not entirely new, but had never been used in a film to this extent before. The success or failure of *Star Wars* would depend on whether Lucas could pull off this complicated production process.

In the middle of this, Lucas demanded additional funding so he could reshoot some sequences he was unhappy with from the London filming. The temporary edit of the movie put together by Marcia and her colleagues had shown up serious deficiencies in certain parts of the movie, and Lucas wanted to fix them. Kurtz had been protecting Lucas from many of the doubts emanating from Fox, but the director's request for an additional $100,000 for much-needed reshoots would make their lack of faith all too plain. Alan Ladd Jr came through once more for a film he believed in. While his fellow executives were questioning his sanity, Ladd would tell anyone who would listen that *Star Wars* would be 'the biggest grossing picture in the history of the industry'. He told the board point blank that this was 'possibly the greatest picture ever made'. He secured an extra $20,000 for the reshoots, far less than Lucas wanted, but better that than lose control of the picture.

Lucas used the extra money to reshoot elements for the alien and creature-populated cantina scene when Luke and Obi-Wan Kenobi first meet Han Solo and Chewbacca. Monkey make-up expert Rick Baker (who worked on the *King Kong* remake of

1976) was brought in to supervise a team making new creature masks. Some were created from scratch, while others were developed from masks Baker had on the shelf or could secure elsewhere, but all would become famous to *Star Wars* fans, acquiring names and personalities as the lore and characters of the movies expanded to fill a whole universe of spin-offs.

At the same time, Lucas hired aspiring filmmaker Dan O'Bannon to create the computer graphic readouts for the movie's spaceships, while young stop-motion animator Phil Tippett was put in charge of creating the holographic creatures featured in the chess game seen onboard the *Millennium Falcon*. Although almost throwaway background elements, these little touches did much to add to the 'lived in' feel of the universe in the movie.

That additional funding, however, would be the end of it: there was no more money and no more goodwill from Fox. The executives knew they had no alternative but to let Lucas finish his movie. All they had to do now was hope it was not only releasable but would also somehow find an audience willing to see it so it would cover its costs.

Lacking the final special effects shots, Lucas had filled out his new, revised rough edit of *Star Wars* with footage lifted from Second World War movies in place of the space dogfights he envisaged. Among the films used were *The Blue Max, 633 Squadron* and *Tora!, Tora!, Tora!* This served a dual purpose: it conveyed visually to anyone looking at the rough assembly the kind of shots they might expect to see, while it showed those at ILM working to compete the shots the level of dynamism and excitement the director wanted these sequences to convey. In doing so, Lucas had created a way of working that is now commonplace in movies, especially big-budget, special-effects heavy films. Known as 'pre-visualization', it's a technique that mixes found footage with storyboards or crude effects sequences to convey the impact that is required from the finished effects.

Several elements that contributed to the completion of the movie were still missing. Having worked with Walter Murch in the past and recognizing the importance of sound to movie, Lucas knew that if his film was truly to convey the idea that it was set in a galaxy far, far away, a whole host of unique sounds would be needed. To achieve this distinctive soundscape, he had hired sound engineer Ben Burtt, who used real-world sounds as the basis for all his *Star Wars* sound effects. Burtt spent months recording in a variety of locations, from Los Angeles airport, military bases and aircraft companies. Some of those sounds – of jet engines and aircraft flybys – were used for the in-flight noise of Han Solo's ship, the *Millennium Falcon*. Burtt recorded and slowed down the sound of the famous Goodyear airship, using it as the noise of the Imperial Cruisers. Most famous of all was the distinctive hum of the Jedi weapon of choice, the light-saber. Burtt had recorded film projectors at Lucas's old college, USC, and mixed it with the static from his TV's cathode ray tube at home to create the signature sound that would be imitated by an entire generation of children. He even recorded animals from the Los Angeles zoo, using a mix of a bear and lion sounds for Chewbacca's signature Wookiee growl.

Lucas also turned his attention to developing distinctive voices for some of his key characters. Although Dave Prowse has long maintained he had been promised his voice would be used for Darth Vader, his strong Cornish accent had been much mocked by the other actors in London, with Carrie Fisher dubbing him 'Darth Farmer'. Lucas toyed with the idea of asking filmmaker and actor Orson Welles, director of *Citizen Kane* (1941), to voice his villain (one of Welles's final roles would be the voice of Optimus Prime, the villain in the animated *Transformers* movie of 1985). Instead, the director went with Broadway actor James Earl Jones, whose lush, deep tones were exactly what he needed for Darth Vader. Jones would become inextricably linked with the role, even though he refused credit for the one-day vocal recording job as he feared the failure of the film might impact on his Broadway career.

Having long intended to replace the prissy voice of actor Anthony Daniels as C-3PO, Lucas hired comic Stan Freberg to record a variety of vocal approaches for the droid, including the caricature of a New York car salesman, as originally intended. Nothing worked, but Lucas realized that Daniels had inadvertently brought so much to the character. The actor's natural voice suited the role so well (or had become so attached to it during filming) that C-3PO was recast as an English butler.

Even more impactful than Burtt's sound effects or the various character voices was the music of John Williams. The composer had started out providing music and theme tunes for TV series and films in the 1960s, including a jaunty theme for Irwin Allen's *Lost in Space* (credited as Johnny Williams). Since the end of that decade, Williams had graduated to movie scores, starting with *The Reivers* (1969) starring Steve McQueen. Recognition had come Williams's way with an Oscar for his arrangement work on *Fiddler on the Roof* (1971), while he had returned to work for Allen again on mid-1970s disaster movies *Earthquake* (1974) and *The Towering Inferno* (1974). However, it was the brooding and menacing rhythmic score for Steven Spielberg's *Jaws* (1975) that brought Williams to the attention of Lucas. It was, in fact, Spielberg who put the two men together when he heard that Lucas was looking to score *Star Wars* with a classical music inspired sound, rather than the more expected electronic sounds associated with a science-fiction movie, like *Forbidden Planet*'s 'electronic tonalities'. Lucas was looking for something like the stirring and lush romantic scores of Erich Korngold who had provided the music for classic adventure movies like *Captain Blood* (1935), *The Adventures of Robin Hood* (1938) and *The Sea Hawk* (1940), all starring Errol Flynn.

Williams rose to the challenge set by Lucas, working to the rough cut of the movie, and composed a series of character-based themes. Each main character had a lyrical theme used in the film, with the overall theme music providing a stirring fanfare at the start. Working with the London Symphony Orchestra, Williams created and recorded a score that brought much human warmth to a film that may have otherwise lacked it. His distinctive themes heightened the emotional moments, such as Luke's yearning for escape before a twin sunset or his discovery of the deaths of his aunt and uncle at the hands of Imperial stormtroopers, while providing added excitement to action sequences, such as Luke and Leia's swing across a Death Star canyon or the climatic rebel attack on the seemingly impregnable space station.

Early in 1977, there was one final screening of the unfinished film for a group of friends of George Lucas before the general public got to see it. Supportive Fox executive Alan Ladd Jr flew up from Los Angeles, while among the others in attendance were Huyck and Katz, film directors Steven Spielberg and Brian De Palma and *Time* movie reviewer Jay Cocks. Martin Scorsese had also been invited, but didn't turn up, putting his non-appearance down to fog at the airport and his fear of flying. Some among the group, however, felt that Scorsese didn't want to be put in the position of criticizing the film.

The screening was not a success. 'When the film ended, people were aghast,' recalled Katz. While Ladd returned to Los Angeles, the others met up in a Chinese restaurant for a post-movie discussion. De Palma criticized Leia's weird Danish pastries-style hair, while others felt the notion of 'the Force' came across as some kind of weird sub-Eastern mysticism. Lucas appeared unconcerned, feeling that even if these criticisms were justified, his movie might succeed as a Walt Disney-style adventure screening at children's matinee performances. If the film broke even or made a modest profit, he would be happy enough.

There was one dissenter among the mocking crowd. 'This movie has a marvellous innocence and naïveté,' said Spielberg. 'That's all George – and people will love it. It's going to make $100 million!'

Chapter 5

Unleashing the Force

I like comics and toys. I have a particular affection for games and toys; there's no doubting that I haven't grown up. All this was a part of the film, the intention of launching toys, creating books ...

George Lucas

As Twentieth Century Fox feared it might have an expensive turkey on its hands with *Star Wars*, it was increasingly clear to those who had made the film that there would be little marketing and promotion support from the studio. Lucas had long realized how this aspect of moviemaking was becoming ever more important, especially when it came to movies that were something of an unknown quantity. He had hired Charles Lippincott, previously a publicist at MGM Studios, as marketing director for Lucasfilm and put him in charge of raising pre-release awareness of *Star Wars*. Lippincott had been at USC at the same time as Lucas and had been instrumental in bringing Gary Kurtz and Lucas together when Kurtz had expressed reservations about working with the seemingly very reserved director.

At MGM Lippincott was noted for his insight into the world of 'underground' magazines and he developed a knack for marketing movies to specialist, niche audiences and for reaching out to potential filmgoers that mainstream promotional media simply weren't reaching, especially teenagers. He had worked on a couple of science-fiction movies previously – Cornell Wilde's

No Blade of Grass (1970) and Michael Crichton's *Westworld* (1973) – and was a huge fan of comic books and *Flash Gordon*, just like Lucas. Lippincott had been working at Universal on Alfred Hitchcock's *Family Plot* (1976) when he ran into Lucas again, who was there to deal with projects he owed the studio after they rejected *Star Wars*, including a sequel to *American Graffiti* and another movie idea that pre-dated *Star Wars*, then called 'The Radioland Murders'. Chatting about future projects, Lucas mentioned *Star Wars* and promised to get a copy of the script to Lippincott. Once he had read it, the publicist couldn't wait to sign up to work on the project: this was something he just knew instinctively how to sell.

One of the earliest conversations Lippincott recalls having with Lucas was about the merchandise potential of the film. It was a subject Lucas was enthused about, but one that Lippincott saw as naive and fanciful. Some of Lucas's windfall from *American Graffiti* had been invested in a New York comic book-shop called Supersnipe. 'When I was writing [*Star Wars*],' said Lucas, 'I had visions of R2-D2 mugs and little wind-up robots, but I thought that would be the end of it.' Movie merchandise, with a few key exceptions, was virtually non-existent at the time, but it was something Lippincott was charged with looking into while Lucas was off making the actual film in Tunisia and London. He started with areas with which he was more familiar: comic books and paperback novels. He felt that *Star Wars*, based on his reading of the script, would benefit from having both, preferably released in advance of the movie to help drum up publicity for it. Rather than offer the properties to the high-est bidder, however, Lippincott decided that quality was paramount and he would approach publishers who were regarded as the best in the specialized field of science-fiction publishing in comics and books.

For comic books, there was only one stop: Marvel Comics. Founded in 1939 as Timely Comics, Marvel had become the home to a series of popular superheroes, notably the Fantastic Four and Spider-Man. Since the 1960s, Marvel had eclipsed

DC Comics, the home of Superman and Batman, with more youth-friendly heroes, many created by Stan Lee, who had risen to become editor-in-chief. Movie-related comics rarely lasted more than a few issues, but Lippincott was pitching a more ambitious publishing programme to Lee: he wanted three or four issues to appear before the film was even released, with the rest concluding the movie story in comic book form to follow afterwards. Lee was sceptical about *Star Wars*, so he made Lippincott a ludicrous offer – he would publish the *Star Wars* comic book, but Lucasfilm would receive no payment or royalties until the title had sold a whopping 100,000 copies. What Lee hadn't realized was that Lippincott was more interested in getting the *Star Wars* comic out there as a marketing tool associated with the Marvel assurance of quality than he was with making money, so he agreed to the deal. 'I was ridiculed at Twentieth Century Fox for that deal,' Lippincott told me in 2007, 'but I believed in the product. I wanted licences to go to the best companies that fans liked, rather than just to the highest bidders. The studios always thought that deals should be done for the most money.'

Lippincott's second title was a paperback novelization of the movie. Again, money was not the object. Lippincott persuaded science-fiction specialist Del Rey to publish the novel, but it would do so only if it could pay a very low advance, which its own staff described as 'embarrassing'. Alan Dean Foster was signed up to write the novel (after Lucas's film school chum Don Glut turned it down: he would novelize the sequel), and Lippincott was happy that he had secured yet another weapon in his publicity arsenal. The book – with Lucas credited as author – would be released at the end of 1976, well in advance of the movie, with a 100,000 copy print run.

Lippincott had learned about the power of science-fiction fans from the *Star Trek* TV show of the late 1960s: he had seen how the show had been saved from cancellation twice and how, through the 1970s when the series was endlessly rerun on TV, a dedicated *Star Trek* fandom had grown. 'Star Trek fans were the first ones to merchandise the TV show themselves, showing there was a market for that kind of thing,' said Lippincott. *Star Trek*'s creator Gene Roddenberry had visited science-fiction conventions before his show had even aired, building up a dedicated audience through word-of-mouth. Even after the show was cancelled, he had continued to cultivate fans, resulting in the series returning in animated form in the mid-1970s.

Inspired by Roddenberry's example, Lippincott put together a *Star Wars* presentation that he toured to fan events, including the 1976 San Diego Comic-Con (a far smaller affair than it is now), and the 1976 World Science Fiction Convention in Kansas City. 'I was the first one to go to the conventions. It was a process of building it up. There was peripheral interest, but it was a start. [San Diego] was very important,' Lippincott said. 'We'd had a very bad reaction from exhibitors to the film, but younger people loved it and were very enthusiastic about it. No one had done a film presentation at San Diego before. It was a real breakthrough and generated a lot of interest.' As well as images, artwork and models from the film, Lippincott took Luke Skywalker himself, Mark Hamill, to Kansas City where he and Kurtz introduced the film, its characters and concepts to a curious audience. This process built a sense of anticipation among science-fiction fans curious to find out more about these strange-sounding characters who inhabited a galaxy far, far away, like something from a science-fiction fairy tale.

Now it was time for the publicist and marketing manager to turn his attention to the toy world, a field in which he had no previous experience and little faith. Merchandise in the past had revolved around popular movie stars: Charlie Chaplin, Shirley Temple, Marilyn Monroe. In the mid-1970s, big American toy manufacturers like Mattel and Fisher Price were focused on producing items linked to TV shows, like *Star Trek* or *The Six Million Dollar Man*. Aurora had done very well from hobby kits that allowed fans to build models of Universal's classic monsters from the 1930s, like Frankenstein and Dracula. Disney had long made a success of marketing its films through Mickey

Mouse figures, but the best example that Lippincott had was the merchandise programme for the *Planet of the Apes* series: from action figures to spaceship models to lunchboxes, *Ape* merchandise had thrived. Fox, however, was concerned as its executives also recalled the 300 items of spin-off merchandise that had been produced to tie-in with the 1967 flop *Doctor Dolittle*. The expensive merchandise programme had crashed and burned, leaving stores with piles of unsold *Dolittle* stock. Fox wanted no part of any merchandising plans for another unknown quantity such as *Star Wars*.

Neither, however, did any of the major toy manufacturers Lippincott approached. With no indication of whether the film would be a success or not, manufacturers erred on the side of caution and said 'no' when Lippincott came calling with his extensive portfolio of *Star Wars* production art and a story outline. He toured company stands at the 1977 New York Toy Fair, only to be told by several company representatives to get lost and to stop wasting their time. The one company that did show some interest was Kenner, then a subsidiary of breakfast cereal company General Mills, and even it was lukewarm. 'Action figures and merchandise were associated with TV,' admitted Lippincott. 'Nobody thought a movie would have enough of an impact over time to sell merchandise. *Star Wars* is unique in that it still sells, long after the original movies.'

As a result there was not much *Star Wars* merchandise available until after the film had proven hugely successful. The material that was out there – the comic book and the novelization – gave Lippincott an early indication that the film might confound everyone's expectations and prove to be a hit. The novel had hit bookstores in November 1976 and was selling steadily, even before publicity had properly started for the film, so much so that Del Rey began to wonder if its original, seemingly extravagant 100,000 print run would be enough. By February 1977, the novel had all but sold out. In March, the first issue of Marvel's *Star Wars* comic hit newsstands and promptly sold out, too. The story was the same across the country, from Los Angeles, via Chicago to New York. 'That was the first real indication,' noted Lippincott. 'That's when we knew something was up . . .'

Despite a positive feeling within the *Star Wars* camp, Fox and cinema-owners felt differently. A team of Fox executives, including Alan Ladd Jr, viewed the completed film. Other than Ladd, the other executives felt the film was nothing special. However, they had some faith in Ladd's judgement, as he had backed Mel Brooks's offbeat comedy *Young Frankenstein* (1974) and horror picture *The Omen* (1976) against board advice. Both had proved to be hits. Maybe this *Star Wars* thing would be a winner, too, despite the failure of the executives to engage with it.

Feedback from early market research was proving to be negative, however, in direct contrast to the information Lippincott was receiving from the science-fiction fans to whom he was marketing the film. Many general filmgoers had little anticipation for the film. The title was apparently causing problems, with the 'Wars' part off-putting to women, while the 'Star' part suggested some kind of Hollywood biopic, like *A Star is Born* (made in 1937, and remade in 1954). The Fox marketing department suggested that another title be devised for the film, but it was a request that failed to get any traction within the studio or among the filmmakers.

Attempts to sell the film to cinema-owners had proved equally problematic, with little excitement surrounding *Star Wars* among exhibitors. It sounded like a low-budget, cheesy sci-fi movie to the cinema chains, nothing they wanted to put their promotional muscle behind. At presentations to cinema-owners, it was William Friedkin's remake of *The Wages of Fear* (1953), under the title *Sorcerer*, alongside Sidney Sheldon's Second World War melodrama *The Other Side of the Wind* that was generating all the excitement for 1977. They were seen as the sure-fire hits of the season. Other films thought of highly before release that year were *Jaws* follow-up *The Deep* (based on a Peter Benchley novel), starring Jacqueline Bisset, *The Exorcist* sequel *The Heretic*, and the Burt Reynolds comedy *Smokey and the Bandit*. Fox executives firmly believed that if their studio were to have a sci-fi hit in 1977, it would be *Damnation Alley*, starring Jan-Michael Vincent and George Peppard and based on a Roger Zelazny novel.

Keen to hedge its bets, Fox decide to pull the already once postponed release forward, from summer 1977 to 25 May, the Wednesday before Memorial Day, traditionally the start of summer. Despite that, the film was only able to book fewer than forty cinemas to screen the movie, with pre-orders coming in at around $1.5 million, far less than the $10 million that might be expected for an average movie of the period. 'People ask why *Star Wars* only opened in forty theatres,' said Fox executive Gareth Wigan (the film opened in just thirty-two cinemas, in fact). '*Star Wars* only opened in forty cinemas because we could only get forty theatres to book it.' It seemed few people, other than those who had made it, had faith in *Star Wars* prior to release. As a result, only ten 70 mm prints of the film were made at a cost of $7,000 each for screening in prestige cinemas in major cities like Los Angeles, San Francisco and New York. The usual promotional marketing campaign to push awareness of a new movie to audiences was virtually non-existent for *Star Wars*, as Fox cut back all spending on the movie, believing it had an expensive flop on its hands. There were only two basic posters and one, rather poorly conceived, trailer.

In the event, Lucas was proved to be right and the studio shown to be wrong. The astonishingly successful opening of *Star Wars* in May 1977 took everyone by surprise, even those – like Steven Spielberg and Fox's Alan Ladd Jr – who had expressed their belief that the movie would be a hit. The first screenings on opening day were at 10 a.m., but lines had started forming outside some cinemas from 8 a.m. Business would be booming at cinemas screening the movie until they closed their doors, with managers turning people away after the final screening by putting up 'house full' signs. The usual practice at cinemas at the time was to allow free access into movies at any time, and people could stay as long as they liked – many did on the first day, watching the movie up to four times in a row. However, for the following days cinemas had to implement a policy of clearing the auditorium after each screening to fit in another entire full house desperate to see the film.

One cinema manager, Al Levine, who ran the Coronet on San Francisco's Geary Boulevard, was widely quoted in the press, conveying his sense of what was happening with *Star Wars* in the days following the film's opening. 'I've never seen anything like it,' said Levine, before going on to describe the kinds of people *Star Wars* was attracting to his cinema. 'We're getting all kinds. Old people, young people, children, Hare Krishna groups . . . They bring cards to play in line. We have checkers-players, we have chess-players. People with paint and sequins on their faces. Fruit-eaters like I've never seen before. People loaded on grass and LSD.' In a sign of things to come, Levine even noticed that 'at least one guy's been here every day. It's an audience participation film. They hiss the villain; they scream and holler and everything else. When school's out [for the summer vacation], they'll go crazy!'

Lippincott clearly recalled the arrival of the film he worked so hard to promote. 'Oh boy, do I? Opening day I went to the main theatre on Broadway in New York. The people coming out of the first screening were acting out lightsaber battles on the street! It was overwhelming, watching that. They were just buzzing.'

House box-office records for a single day of screenings fell across the country, with those lucky thirty-two cinemas nation-wide bringing in just under $255,000, beating the previous opening day records of *The Sound of Music* (1965) and *The Towering Inferno* (1974). A sneak preview of the movie had taken place earlier in May at the Northpoint cinema in San Francisco. The hugely positive audience reaction to that screening had suggested that Fox executives might be wrong in thinking the film was not going to do much business, but in no way did anyone expect it to be an instant record-breaker. Press screenings packed with young audiences were arranged just a week before the film opened to the public to catch the major newspaper and magazine critics before they left for the Cannes Film Festival.

The reviews were incredibly positive. *Variety* – the Hollywood film industry trade paper – gushed: '*Star Wars* is a magnificent film. George Lucas set out to make the biggest possible adventure-fantasy out of his memories of serials and older action epics, and he has succeeded brilliantly.' Believing that the new movie had captured a more positive, upbeat public mood following the years of Watergate and Vietnam, the *Variety* reviewer continued: 'Like a breath of fresh air, *Star Wars* sweeps away the cynicism that has in recent years obscured the concepts of valour, dedication and honour. Make no mistake, this is by no means a children's film, with all the derogatory overtones that go with that description. This is instead a superior example of what only the screen can achieve, and closer to home, it is an affirmation of what only Hollywood can put on a screen. This is the kind of film in which an audience, first entertained, can later walk out feeling good.'

Variety wasn't alone in its effusive praise. Charles Champlin, of the *Los Angeles Times* – a long-term supporter of the work of Lucas – noted the director 'had been conducting a life-long double love affair, embracing comic strips on one hand and movies on the other. Now he has united his loves with *Star Wars*, the year's most razzle-dazzling family movie, an exuberant and technically astonishing space adventure . . . *Star Wars* is *Buck Rogers* with a doctoral degree, but not a trace of cynicism, a slam-bang, rip-roaring gallop through a distantly future world.'

Even the normally staid and proper *Time* magazine joined in the celebration of this new type of movie. With a cover-promoted feature headed '*Star Wars*: The Year's Best Movie', *Time* called the film 'a combination of *Flash Gordon*, *The Wizard of Oz*, the Errol Flynn swashbucklers of the '30s and '40s and almost every Western ever screened – not to mention *The Hardy Boys*,

Sir Gawain and the Green Knight and *The Faerie Queene*. The result is a remarkable confection: a sublimation of the history of movies, wrapped in a riveting tale of suspense and adventure, ornamented with some of the most ingenious special effects ever contrived for film.'

The reaction of critics wasn't the important factor, though: it was the reaction – and repeated re-viewings – by the audience that made *Star Wars* a genuine phenomenon. By the end of the week – three days after the film opened – *Variety*'s front page headline told the story: 'Fox's *Star Wars* Heads for Hyperspace: House Records Tumble.' The report opened with 'There was only one topic of conversation in the film industry yesterday – the smash opening of George Lucas's *Star Wars*.' An additional nine cinemas had taken the film on, but that did little to ease the queues as word of mouth about the movie spread and it rapidly became the 'must see' film of the summer. Fox were taken totally by surprise, as few had previously had any faith in the film. As the studio had abdicated its usual role as promoter, part of its success could only be laid at the door of Charles Lippincott and his tireless efforts in the months leading to May in selling the film to the dedicated, niche science-fiction fans and largely ignored teen audience. '*Star Wars* was a tough campaign,' admitted Lippincott. 'A lot of the other films I worked on were a lot simpler.' That the movie's appeal had rapidly spread beyond that heartland was due to the filmmaking skills of George Lucas.

For his part, Lucas had his first inkling of the success of his movie when he and Marcia had dinner in Hamburger Hamlet – their favourite Hollywood fast-food joint – opposite Grauman's Chinese Theatre. The lines around the block waiting to see his movie tipped the director off that something special was happening. He didn't hang around to find out more, however. He had a tradition of heading off to Hawaii on holiday whenever he had a movie opening, as he found it a stressful occasion. While the executives at Fox were coming to terms with their good luck towards the end of that week, Lucas and Marcia were staying at the Mauna Kea Hotel in Hawaii.

The question the people at Fox were asking themselves was whether *Star Wars* was a sustainable success – would it continue playing to full houses or was the opening day a weird aberration? Would the movie's box office (remarkable though it had been) tail off rapidly?

By the following week they had an idea of the phenomenon that *Star Wars* had become: *Variety* reported that the six-day box office take for the film was the highest since Steven Spielberg's *Jaws* the previous summer. Domestic US ticket sales had reached $2.55 million over the Memorial Day holiday weekend. *Jaws*, however, had played at over 100 cinemas from its opening, while *Star Wars* was now screening on just over forty, nationwide.

The press rapidly picked up on the *Star Wars* effect, rushing into print with news items and 'think pieces' about the success of the movie, thereby reinforcing that success. The core science-fiction fan audience quickly gave way to the mainstream and youth audiences who wanted to see what all the fuss was about, continuing the film's record-breaking run at the box office. Soon, more and more cinemas across the United States were screening *Star Wars*, as quickly as Fox could produce (or redistribute) more prints. By August, the film Fox predicted would fail was playing in over 800 cinemas across the United States.

Steven Spielberg called Lucas in Hawaii to congratulate him on his success. He was putting the finishing touches to *Close Encounters of the Third Kind* and was exhausted, so jumped at the invitation from Lucas that he and Amy Irving should fly out and join them. On a beach in Hawaii, Lucas and Spielberg discussed what they might do next. After *American Graffiti*, Lucas had done some work with writer and director Philip Kaufman (who had been involved in a failed attempt to get a *Star Trek* feature film made) on a movie modelled after MGM's 1950 film version of H. Rider Haggard's *King Solomon's Mine*. The pair had made notes on a Clark Gable or Spencer Tracy-style 1930s treasure hunter who enjoyed globetrotting adventures. Kaufman had come up with the gimmick of having their hero track down the mythical biblical Ark of the Covenant.

Now Lucas and Spielberg discussed the concept of another series-style film, featuring this rough-hewn adventuring hero. In the immediate wake of *Star Wars* the seeds sown were sown for the blockbusting adventures of Indiana Jones.

When Lucas had first visited the old Hollywood studios, he had found them virtually empty of production and in decline. Now, his *Star Wars* movie almost single-handedly saved Fox. The studio went from being a near-bankrupt takeover target to being talked of by the financial press as a potential future entertainment powerhouse, as its share price doubled in the days following the film's release. Before the movie, the most the studio had earned in a single year had been $37 million. By the time the 1977–8 financial year was over, the studio had taken in $79 million in pure profit. This was after paying out the amount on the 60/40 split on gross profits due to Lucas. The unassuming, often shy filmmaker now found himself a multi-millionaire and his company Lucasfilm awash in cash.

This was before any money from Lippincott's merchandising deals – including the popular soundtrack LP – even kicked in. Lucasfilm's marketing director had signed up Kenner to produce a range of *Star Wars* toys, but the company was as taken by surprise by the success of the film as everyone else. It had nothing ready when the movie opened (leaving the way clear for a lot of unofficial, knock-off, cheaply made merchandise to feed the worldwide *Star Wars* frenzy).

Kenner came up with a brilliant response: it would sell an empty box to *Star Wars* fans and kids who wanted to own a piece of the film! The 'Star Wars Early Bird Certificate Package', on sale before Christmas 1977, offered a presentation box of vouchers in exchange for cash that could be redeemed for toys once they became available (promised sometime between February and June 1978), when the Far Eastern manufacturing plants had made enough plastic action figures to catch-up with the unprecedented demand. The promised first four action figures were to be of Luke Skywalker,

Princess Leia, R2-D2 and Chewbacca, and they launched a lucrative and hugely successful merchandising empire (as well as a serious collecting hobby) that is still going strong today.

Having made a success of wistful nostalgia with *American Graffiti*, George Lucas had captured and shaped a more optimistic American zeitgeist for the second half of the 1970s. His feel-good space adventure movie appealed widely – as the seemingly endless box-office success proved – bringing in teenagers who had never seen such a flashy science-fiction adventure before, and their parents who vaguely recalled the otherworldly fun of *Forbidden Planet* or the intellectual thrills of *2001: A Space Odyssey*. Now, an entire generation had a movie phenomenon to call their own, and George Lucas was well on his way from being a rebel to becoming the commander of an all-encompassing empire.

Chapter 6

Summer of '77

It's just a movie. It's no big deal. I don't think it's altogether that well-made a movie, because I was working under extremely diffi-cult conditions.

George Lucas

America couldn't get enough of *Star Wars* in 1977. People (especially younger people) returned again and again to the cinema to see the film over and over, often in large groups of friends. Screenings of *Star Wars* were collective, almost interac-tive, events with audiences cheering on the heroes and booing the villains. For the first time since 1963, weekly cinema attend-ances in the United States exceeded twenty million. While children patiently waited for 1978 and the arrival of their long-promised *Star Wars* action figures, George Lucas found his life had changed – and he had changed cinema.

Wherever he went, Lucas found it hard to escape the impact of *Star Wars*. Darth Vader had become an instant cinematic icon, the villain audiences loved to hate. Vader (or rather more accurately, an anonymous actor dressed as the character), alongside droids C-3PO and R2-D2, joined the ranks of cinema greats of the past when – on 3 August 1977 – they added their unique foot- and hand-prints to the cement in the foyer of Grauman's Chinese Theatre in Hollywood, following in the hooves of fellow non-human star Trigger, Roy Rogers's famous movie horse.

Lucasfilm was inundated with requests to license *Star Wars* merchandise items, everything from creature masks to 'Force-filled' instant meals and 'Wookiee cookies'. Although Lucas had always believed that there were strong merchandising possibilities in *Star Wars*, he never expected anything like this, and certainly not so quickly. He tried his best to impose a quality standard upon any items to be produced, although this brought him into conflict with Twentieth Century Fox, which was keen to make the most of its surprise success, just in case the *Star Wars* boom went bust very quickly. Speaking to the *Los Angeles Times*, Lucas admitted: 'In a way, this film was designed around toys. I'm not making much for directing this movie. If I make any money, it will be from the toys.'

Star Wars characters dominated the T-shirts worn by American kids and teenagers during the summer of 1977, pushing aside previous favourites like *Wonder Woman*, *Charlie's Angels*, the Osmonds and tennis star Bjorn Borg. Both Marvel and Del Rey were astonished as the *Star Wars* comic book and novel entered reprint after reprint in order to keep up with soaring demand. To his horror, Stan Lee discovered that Marvel would be paying royalties to Lucasfilm almost immediately as sales rapidly soared past the once seemingly impossible 100,000 hurdle he had set. He also knew he faced a new negotiation for any future *Star Wars*-related comic books, and the power this time lay with Lucas.

Lucasfilm began hiring new staff simply to deal with the volume of calls and letters coming in requesting rights to produce *Star Wars* tie-ins. Kenner and its suppliers went into overdrive in an attempt to meet the promised delivery date of *Star Wars* action figures. The company's early interest in taking on the main *Star Wars* toy licence proved to be prescient: it would go on to sell $1 billion worth of toys each year over the next seven years.

The unexpected success of *Star Wars* had seen some of those involved come into equally unexpected, but very welcome, wealth. Alec Guinness's decision to take percentage 'points' in the movie's profits now also looked like far-sighted wisdom, rather than the gamble it had been. He would make around $6 million overall from his participation in the three *Star Wars* movies, by far the biggest payday the veteran actor had ever seen. Lucas had a habit of rewarding key collaborators by issuing profit share points or fractions of points – although he also kept upfront fees and payments on the low side. Hamill, Ford and Fisher each gained two-thirds of a point, worth around $650,000 each.

Overall, Lucas dished out a full 25 per cent of his *Star Wars* profits in profit-point participation given to friends and co-workers. Producer Gary Kurtz scored five points, while most of the crew got one-twentieth of a point each, and back-office staff were given one two-hundredth each. Writers Huyck and Katz – who had helped polish the screenplay – got two points, while Lucas's lawyer – who had helped to negotiate his unprecedented, immensely rewarding merchandise deal – was awarded a profit point. Soundtrack composer John Williams also got a point, while sound supervisor Ben Burtt was recognized for his contribution with a quarter-point. Others received cash bonuses, including $50,000 to Alan Dean Foster, who had written the *Star Wars* novel published under the Lucas byline, and James Earl Jones, the voice of Darth Vader, received an additional $10,000. Lucas even gave John Milius and Steven Spielberg a profit point each in an exchange that saw him take points in *Big Wednesday* and *Close Encounters of the Third Kind*.

The key cast also had to deal with their new fame, but – aside from Harrison Ford – none at first was really adequately able to capitalize professionally on their *Star Wars* notoriety, although Carrie Fisher found a rewarding sideline appearing on weekly TV satire show *Saturday Night Live*.

By the end of August 1977, *Star Wars* had taken $100 million at the box office, passing Spielberg's *Jaws*. The big question everyone was asking was 'When will there be more *Star Wars*?' Although he had always planned on there being sequels if the film was a success (and he had enough material and concepts to provide various storylines, cut from the original overlong script outlines), Lucas knew he had to decide soon: if he didn't act within two years, the sequel rights to *Star Wars* would revert to Twentieth Century Fox. Lucas was also aware that it could take another two-to-three years before he could get a second *Star Wars* film in cinemas, and the mania surrounding the first movie might have cooled dramatically by then.

There was another option to keep *Star Wars* alive in the minds of audiences: television. Almost a year after the success of *Star Wars*, Lucas was approached by a TV company to create a *Star Wars* TV special. Smith-Hemion had a track record of producing effective television specials, such as *My Name is Barbra* (1965), starring Barbra Streisand, *Frank Sinatra: A Man and His Music* (1965) and a 1976 television special adapting *Peter Pan*, starring Mia Farrow. Dwight Hemion and producing partner Gary Smith saw the Thanksgiving holiday weekend in late November 1978 as a prime spot for a spectacular television special that would attract lucrative advertising spots: their subject would be *Star Wars*.

Lucas was deep in pre-production on *Raiders of the Lost Ark*, his archaeologist adventurer movie to be directed by Steven Spielberg and starring Harrison Ford, so he was unable to give the proposed TV special his full attention. Lucas did agree to cooperate with the venture, providing the storyline and the main cast (except for veteran British actors Peter Cushing and Alec Guinness – who only appears in deleted footage from *Star Wars*). The deal gave Smith-Hemion access to the *Star Wars* costumes and props from the movie, the unique sound effects library and any unused footage.

Lucas went to material from his first draft of *Star Wars* for the story, reviving an idea he once had for a wrap-around to the main action of the film. Kurtz recalled that the original opening for *Star Wars* featured a visit to the Wookiee homeworld where a mother prepared to tell her son a bedtime story – that story would be the film of *Star Wars*. Hamill remembered that it was 'an enchanted forest ... You see a Wookiee mother trying to breastfeed this squealing baby Wookiee. He keeps gesturing toward the bookshelf, and there's all this Wookiee dialogue going on. She goes and points to one particular book and the baby gets all excited. She takes the book off the shelf and we see it is titled "Star Wars". She opens the book, and that's when the ship comes overhead and the film as we know it starts.'

Kurtz recalled why this original opening concept had been rapidly discarded: 'As soon as we got to discussing it over dinner one night, we realized what a fatal mistake it would be. When we found out how difficult it was to get one Wookiee costume looking right, we never considered creating a whole planet of them.'

Lucas now revived the idea of visiting the planet of the Wookiees – Chewbacca's people – for the Smith-Hemion project. Scriptwriter Lenny Ripps was presented with a list of things to avoid and things to use in the story, and a rough outline (he was one of five writers who would work on the ninety-seven-minute special). The result was a story that saw Han Solo and sidekick Chewbacca escape Imperial entanglements in order to return to the Wookiee planet of Kashyyyk in time for the 'Life Day' holiday that Chewbacca hopes to spend with his family. According to director David Acomba, Lucas attended a couple of early production meetings, but was not involved in the show much beyond that.

The much-derided TV special opens with a lengthy sequence of Wookiee family life as Chewbacca's relatives – wife Malla, father Itchy and son Lumpy – entertain themselves while waiting for Han and Chewie to arrive. There's much incomprehensible Wookiee grunting dialogue, but no subtitles to make it clear what is being said. Imperial stormtroopers arrive searching for the rebels, including Chewbacca, and place a guard outside the Wookiees' home.

Originally intended to run just an hour, the special was extended due to overwhelming advertiser interest in being associated with new *Star Wars* material. Kenner was a major sponsor, seeing the special as an opportunity to promote sales of its line of *Star Wars* action figures in the pre-Christmas holiday period. As a result, the already thin drama was stretched out, with the addition of comedy, musical and animated sequences. En route to Kashyyyk, Han and Chewie stop off at places viewers would recognized from the *Star Wars* movie, including a cantina run by *Maude* star Bea Arthur. Comedian Harvey Korman appears in a variety of guises as a four-armed cookery instructor, an incompetent robot and an amorous barfly. Art Carney plays a human purveyor of Life Day gifts. A Jefferson Starship perform-ance and a song sung by Bea Arthur provided musical interludes. There are brief appearances for Mark Hamill as Luke Skywalker, Kenny Baker as R2-D2, Anthony Daniels as C-3PO and Carrie Fisher as Princess Leia, who sings a terrible song to the tune (almost) of the 'Star Wars Main Theme' at the climax.

The best part of this very poor production turned out to be an animated adventure Smith-Hemion commissioned from Canadian animation company Nelvana. Presented in the form of an entertainment watched by Chewie's son, Lumpy, the cartoon introduces bounty-hunter Boba Fett (who would feature briefly in the *Star Wars* sequel, *The Empire Strikes Back*, and become an instant fan favourite). The cartoon – originally commissioned to pad the special out to length – chronicles a battle over a talisman and sees Han, Leia and Luke encounter Fett for the first time. Don Francks voiced Boba Fett, a part later played by British actor Jeremy Bulloch. It's the most *Star Wars*-like segment of the special and the first ever animated *Star Wars* adventure (several more would follow over the years). The most notorious sequence involved an erotic dance number performed by Diahann Carroll, viewed by a seemingly aroused Itchy (Chewbacca's father).

Having abdicated his involvement in *The Star Wars Holiday Special*, Lucas was shocked when the finished item turned out to be nothing like the semi-sequel to his movie that he had origi-nally envisaged. By the stage he saw the production, it was far too late to prevent the broadcast without incurring huge legal problems. All Lucas could do was ensure his name did not appear on the production as a scriptwriter or credited for the storyline, implying a lack of approval. The special aired on CBS on 17 November 1978 between 7 p.m. and 9 p.m. but – unusually – the Nielsen ratings recording how many viewers watched the show have never been officially released.

To the horror of Lucas, *The Star Wars Holiday Special* rapidly became one of the most notorious television broadcasts of all time. In his book *What Were They Thinking? The 100 Dumbest Events in Television History*, author David Hofstede places the special at number one, calling it 'the worst two hours of television ever'. Fox News Channel anchor Shepard Smith called the show a '[19]70s train wreck, combining the worst of *Star Wars* with the utter worst of variety television'. Kenner quickly axed its plans for a range of action figures based around Chewbacca's extended family in the wake of the poor reaction to the special.

Never rebroadcast, *The Star Wars Holiday Special* built up a legendary reputation. A bootleg VHS recording of the original transmission (complete with commercials) became a 'must have' item of bad taste merchandise for committed *Star Wars* fans. Lucasfilm attempted to erase the special from its official history of *Star Wars*, but to no avail. Elements from the *Holiday Special* have turned up in various official Lucasfilm *Star Wars* products, ranging from comic strips and storybooks to videogames and novels.

Lucas told *Maxim* magazine in 2002 that the *Holiday Special* was just 'one of those things that happened, and I just have to live with it'. In an online discussion with fans he admitted that the special 'does not represent my vision for *Star Wars*', and he reportedly told an Australian fan at a convention that, 'If I had the time and a sledgehammer, I would track down every copy of that show and smash it.' For her part, Carrie Fisher – whose notorious contribution was the out-of-tune singing at the end – claimed she asked Lucas for a copy of the special as payment for recording her DVD commentaries for the *Star Wars* films. She said she screens it at parties, 'mainly at the end of the night when I want people to leave'.

The legacy of *The Star Wars Holiday Special* is the animated sequence, commonly referred to as 'The Faithful Wookiee'. The special was the first full-length sequel to *Star Wars*, and the cartoon in particular offered fans a glimpse of the wider universe in which these adventures took place, two years before the release of the official movie sequel, *The Empire Strikes Back*, in 1980. Nelvana's animation was basic and some of the characters barely resembled their movie counterparts, but the cartoon was an exciting, brand new *Star Wars* story that wasn't ruined by terrible variety acts and songs. It was played straight – certainly compared to the rest of the TV special – and it has endured as a genuinely interesting early *Star Wars* spin-off. The Boba Fett cartoon was eventually released officially as part of the *Star Wars* saga Blu-ray set in 2011.

Lucas eventually told StaticMultimedia.com in 2005 that he had learned from the experience of *The Star Wars Holiday Special*. 'We let them use the characters and that probably wasn't the smartest thing to do, but you learn from those experiences.'

After falling out with George Lucas over the early days of ILM, John Dykstra had set up on his own as Apogee Inc., using many of the same staff and the same Van Nuys warehouse that had given birth to ILM. One of the first projects that Apogee worked on was the Glen A. Larson TV series *Battlestar Galactica* (initially called 'Star Worlds'). Larson had a track record of producing short-lived TV series riding on the back of successful movies (such as the *Butch Cassidy and the Sundance Kid*-inspired *Alias Smith and Jones*) and, to Lucas, *Battlestar Galactica* looked no different. It also rankled him that the new show was being made for Universal, against whom he still carried a grudge after *American Graffiti*.

As a result, Lucasfilm encouraged Twentieth Century Fox to sue Universal, claiming the series was simply a television copy of *Star Wars*. Writing to *Variety*, Lucas outlined his case: 'I feel strongly that Glen Larson and Universal Pictures have attempted to copy what I created for *Star Wars* and are continuing to attempt to pass their series off as some sort of *Star Wars* for television. This will be very harmful to what I have created and I strongly hope that Fox will be successful in attempts to protect us.'

Battlestar Galactica depicted a ragtag fleet of humans on the run from deadly robot Cylons, with whom they were at war, in search of a fabled planet called Earth. It was quite different in plot terms from *Star Wars*, but the look of the series and the special effects techniques used to achieve the space dogfights were very familiar, additionally helped by the fact that conceptual artist Ralph McQuarrie and designer Joe Johnston had contributed to the show's early development.

Universal counter-sued, claiming that *Star Wars*' droid R2-D2 had been copied from the diminutive robots Huey, Dewey and Louie in their *Silent Running* from 1973. Years of acrimony and additional lawsuits followed before a judge found against Fox and *Star Wars* and in favour of Universal and *Battlestar Galactica* in 1980. The judge claimed that so strong was the cultural impact of *Star Wars* that there were, in fact, 'hundreds of films guilty of infringing on *Star Wars*'. *Battlestar Galactica*'s initial run was short-lived (it was revived far more successfully with a TV mini-series in 2003, ironically in anticipation of the final *Star Wars* film, *Revenge of the Sith*), and the show was soon forgotten along with the lawsuit: so much so that Fox eventually hired Larson to run its television division.

Another casualty of the post-*Star Wars* Lucasfilm clearout had been marketing head Charles Lippincott. As the company grew, he had felt increasingly marginalized within the new structure and had gone by 1978.

One undoubted winner from the success of *Star Wars* was Kenner toys, which had taken an early risk by signing up for the action figure rights before the movie was released (thanks to Lippincott's enthusiastic encouragement). The company issued ninety-two figures from the movie, selling over forty-two million units in 1978 alone, reaching sales of over 250 million units over the next eight years covering the first three *Star Wars* movies. It was reported in *Newsweek* in 1981 that Kenner had created $1 billion in retail sales, with between 6 and 15 per cent going straight to Lucasfilm. The toys were making more money than the movie ever had.

The summer of 1977 was an extraordinary time in movie culture, and the release of *Star Wars* had a major impact. The movie business would never quite be the same again, with merchandising and spin-offs becoming a much more accepted part of filmmaking. Other directors and studios tried to cash in on the '*Star Wars* effect', producing the likes of Disney's turgid *The Black Hole* (1979), the Italian Luigi Cozzi's *Starcrash* (*Scontri Stellari Oltre la Terza Dimensione*, 1979) and the Roger Corman-produced *Battle Beyond the Stars* (1980). None of these, nor any of the many other *Star Wars* knock-offs, attracted the same phenomenal attention, box office success or dedicated fan following. Only George Lucas could produce an authentic follow-up to *Star Wars*, and he would take his space fantasy saga in a darker, more serious direction in *The Empire Strikes Back*.

Chapter 7

Striking Back

I hate directing. It's like fighting a fifteen-round heavyweight bout with a new opponent every day. By the end of the day, you're usually depressed because you didn't do a good enough job. It was easy to let go of directing.

George Lucas

It was a much more confident George Lucas who embarked upon making the *Star Wars* sequel, *The Empire Strikes Back*, but that didn't stop the production from becoming a troubled one.

The first production meeting on the second movie took place the day after the 50th Academy Awards ceremony, held on 3 April 1978. *Star Wars* had received ten Oscar nominations, winning six in mainly technical categories. Lucas was up for Best Director and Best Screenplay, with *Star Wars* in line for Best Film, none of which he won. Instead, he watched as Oscars went to his film for its look more than anything else, with wins for the teams involved in production design, costume design and visual effects. John Williams won for Best Score, while Ben Burtt was awarded a separate Oscar for Special Achievement in Sound Effects Editing. Perhaps the highlight of the night for Lucas was when Marcia Lucas was one of the team honoured for Best Editing. Alec Guinness had been rewarded for his participation with a nod for Best Supporting Actor, but lost out to Jason Robards for the movie *Julia* (Guinness had already won Best Actor in 1957 for *The Bridge on the River Kwai*).

Lucas was not a fan of awards anyway, so he was able to brush off Woody Allen's multiple wins with *Annie Hall* as Best Picture, Best Screenplay and Best Director. While Lucas reluctantly attended the event, as was his usual habit Allen was instead playing jazz clarinet in New York.

Star Wars was quickly re-released to take advantage of the Oscar wins, and grossed an additional $46 million over five weeks. By the time the movie completed its run in US cinemas in November 1978, just as the ill-fated *Star Wars Holiday Special* was airing on CBS, it had grossed an all-time high of $273 million, with overseas box office bringing in an additional $68 million. With an additional re-release in 1979 – in advance of *The Empire Strikes Back* – the box office totalled $430 million worldwide before the second film hit cinemas.

The inevitable *Star Wars* sequel had been confirmed to Hollywood at large in a front-page headline in *Variety* on 24 February 1978: 'It's Definite Now: 20th Century Fox Gets the *Star Wars* Sequel.' It was only then that wider Hollywood became aware of the unusual deal that George Lucas had been able to strike with the studio over *Star Wars*, given Fox's initial lack of faith in the project. Fox would continue to distribute the *Star Wars* films, but as Lucas now owned the sequels, he would fund the next movie himself, meaning the majority of the profits from the film would also come back to his company. Although this looked like a licence to print money from the outside, the truth was that in order to fully control the first *Star Wars* sequel (and, hopefully, everything that might flow from it in the future), Lucas had to put everything he had already earned on the line.

Officially, the budget for the second movie would be $10 million, just slightly higher than the first. Lucas, though, knew different. His plans for the film would mean an initial expenditure of at least $18 million, if he were to realize his storytelling ambitions on screen. As a result, Lucas reinvested almost all of the $20 million he had made from *Star Wars* into Lucasfilm to fund the production of the sequel. If the film worked, then he would get his money back – and even more – but if it flopped (and he believed that was perfectly possible), then he stood to lose everything.

The Empire Strikes Back wasn't the only financial drain on Lucas at that time. He had long harboured the notion of creating an independent filmmaking 'utopia' in Northern California, ever since his involvement with Francis Ford Coppola's American Zoetrope back in the late 1960s. Now he had the funds to begin to make it happen. He started by buying up land with the first money he earned from *Star Wars*, purchasing the 1,800 acre Bulltail Ranch in a valley near San Rafael (coincidentally, the property was accessed by the already named Lucas Valley Road). It cost him $2.7 million, but he was already negotiating to buy-up adjoining plots in order to secure the isolation and privacy of his planned facility (and to prevent the building of housing nearby). This was the seed for Skywalker Ranch, Lucas's filmmaking base, which would fully blossom only after he had finished with the first trilogy of *Star Wars* movies in 1983. For this project to continue, though, Lucas needed the second *Star Wars* movie to succeed. 'We are taking the profits from *The Empire Strikes Back* and the next film and investing them in companies, then using those profits to build the ranch. If it doesn't happen with this [movie] and the next, then that's the end,' admitted Lucas.

The Oscars had not been good for Lucas personally, but the work went on. 'The next morning,' recalled Oscar-winning costume designer John Mollo, 'we had a production meeting on the second movie.' The idea of a follow-up had long been considered, with Fox executive Alan Ladd Jr suggesting in the closing weeks of filming on the first film that Lucas should consider shooting some additional footage for a future sequel. The director, however, was far too busy struggling to complete *Star Wars* adequately to worry about filming extra scenes for a sequel he had not yet fully conceived.

Ladd knew how much additional material and ideas Lucas had from his development work for the first *Star Wars*, so he was confident (especially in the wake of the film's astonishing opening) that a sequel would not only be possible, but also highly anticipated by audiences, so it was as near to a sure thing as Hollywood ever saw. Lucas was reluctant: making *Star Wars* had shown him beyond all doubt that writing did not come easy and the rigours of directing were not good for his health. There was huge pressure for him to make another *Star Wars* movie quickly and he was interested, but he wondered whether he could survive the process intact. It was then he came up with the idea of delegating as much of the future of *Star Wars* to other people, while still retaining strict control.

In preparation for the new movie, Lucas had relocated his special effects facility, Industrial Light and Magic, to San Rafael in Marin County, divesting the company of those he felt had let him down. Many of the original pioneers stuck with the company, happy to be involved in the creation of what would essentially be a brand new (and now well-funded) movie-making venture.

The story for the sequel was the first problem to be confronted. The first movie had been designed to be self-contained (in case there were no sequels), but it was also clearly a small part of a larger story. Now, it was Lucas's task to develop that larger story, while still retaining all the elements that had made *Star Wars* such an unexpected success. When the movie was reissued in 1981 the film would have a new subtitle at the top of the yellow text 'crawl' that set-up the film: *Episode IV – A New Hope*. In keeping with his love of 1930s serials, Lucas had now decided that *Star Wars* came in the middle of an ongoing story, although he was really only committing to the relatively short-term goal of getting the next instalments – Episodes V and VI – made, so completing a trilogy, despite statements in early interviews that he had once envisaged a nine- or even twelve-film sequence, according to early press interviews.

Lucas knew he would need help in writing his second instalment of *Star Wars*. He had a ring-binder folder packed with notes outlining the basic story in which the rebels escape an opening attack by Vader, only to be scattered. A wise old Jedi Master named Yoda trains Luke in the ways of the Jedi, while Han and Leia fall into a trap on Cloud City, a floating palace in the sky straight out of *Flash Gordon*. Attempting to rescue his friends, Luke confronts Vader in a lightsaber battle and learns a troubling secret.

Lucas decided he needed someone better versed in writing pulp science fiction than he was to flesh out his story notes into a shootable screenplay. He was pointed in the direction of Leigh Brackett, a pulp writer from the magazine golden age of science fiction in the 1940s, who still lived in Los Angeles. The legend goes that Brackett was invited to an interview with Lucas, who was keen to capture the pulp touch seen in her novels *Queen of the Martian Catacombs* and *Black Amazon of Mars*. Unaware of her wider Hollywood background, Lucas innocently asked the sixty-two year-old whether she had ever written for the screen. Patiently, Brackett outlined her impressive screenplay résumé, including scripts for classic films like *The Big Sleep* (1945), *Rio Bravo* (1959) and the more recent *The Long Goodbye* (1973). Suddenly the penny dropped with Lucas: 'Are you that Leigh Brackett?' he asked, surprised. Despite that confusion, Lucas felt he had found the screenwriter he needed for *The Empire Strikes Back*.

Brackett accepted the role, declining to share with Lucas the fact that she had been diagnosed with terminal cancer. She completed a draft of the film before succumbing to her illness, dying on 18 March 1978. This development left Lucas with a first draft *Star Wars* sequel screenplay, but no writer to revise the material. He now had to look elsewhere – although he didn't have to look too far. Lucas worked on the script himself, then drafted in a new writer, Lawrence Kasdan, who he and Steven Spielberg had hired to write *Raiders of the Lost Ark*.

Although the majority of the material in *The Empire Strikes Back* screenplay came from Lucas and Kasdan, the wider sense of the space-opera universe and some of the dialogue displayed Brackett's touch. A credit was given on the final film to Brackett in recognition of her input and her role in kick-starting the always difficult scripting process for Lucas.

With the script in place, attention turned to casting the sequel. While it was expected that the central trio of Hamill, Ford and Fisher would all return, only Hamill and Fisher had been signed up from the beginning to appear in any sequels (hence the focus on them in Alan Dean Foster's 'cheap sequel' novel, *Splinter of the Mind's Eye*). Neither actor had prospered despite the success of *Star Wars*. Hamill had spent time recovering from a road accident during the closing stages of making *Star Wars* that had resulted in cosmetic reconstruction on his face. He had appeared in a couple of movies (*Corvette Summer*, 1978; *The Big Red One*, 1980), but was basically floundering (he would later find a lucrative niche as a cartoon voiceover actor). Fisher had become more of a personality than an actress, with her frequent appearances on *Saturday Night Live* alongside her friends John Belushi and Dan Aykroyd (she briefly appeared with them in *The Blues Brothers*, 1980). Although they had little choice, as they were contractually obliged to appear in the second and third movies, it is likely that Hamill and Fisher welcomed the work.

The same could not be said of Ford. His career was faring little better than those of Hamill and Fisher, although he had made more movies. Unfortunately they were all flops, and included *Force 10 from Navarone* (1978), *The Frisco Kid* (1979) and *Hanover Street* (1979). A cameo in Francis Ford Coppola's *Apocalypse Now* had been severely reduced during editing. Ford was, however, very concerned about being typecast as Han Solo and was looking to his leading role as Indiana Jones in *Raiders of the Lost Ark* to save him. For the *Star Wars* sequel, he wanted the character of Han, whom he saw as two-dimensional and comic book, to be developed further. Lucas and Kasdan had taken this on board during their script revisions, and Ford was lured on to the production by a screenplay he saw as a significant improvement over that of *Star Wars*. As he had not been signed up for sequels, he was also in a stronger bargaining position when it came to increasing his remuneration for the role, winning the profit points and a share of merchandising revenue that had eluded him on the first movie.

A key criticism of the first *Star Wars* film had been the almost all-white nature of the cast. This was something Lucas set out to address in casting actor and singer Billy Dee Williams in the key role of Lando Calrissian, the original owner of the *Millennium Falcon*, who unwittingly lures Han and Leia into Vader's trap on Cloud City. The only other sticking point proved to be Anthony Daniels, the man in the golden armour of droid C-3PO. He, like David Prowse (Vader) and Kenny Baker (R2-D2), had been annoyed by the lack of public recognition they had received for their roles in *Star Wars*. It had been especially galling when they discovered that others had filled their suits to place their footprints at Grauman's Chinese Theater. Prowse had done much to advance his own cause, especially in the UK, doing his best to put himself forward publicly as the man who had played Darth Vader. For his part, Kenny Baker was the least troubled of the trio, being not particularly interested in fame. Daniels was annoyed by PR attempts by Lucasfilm to claim that C-3PO wasn't an actor at all, but a real-life robot. 'They denied I existed,' whined Daniels. His complaints were noted by Lucasfilm and for the second film he was offered profit participation (just like Ford) and higher billing. He quickly signed on to play 'goldenrod' once more.

Knowing Lucas did not want to direct the second *Star Wars* film, producer Gary Kurtz faced the task of finding a suitable replacement. It was a tricky job, as he needed someone who could work closely with Lucas, could deliver a great movie, but would also be happy to be subservient to the *Star Wars* creator. In many ways, experienced Hollywood movie directors looked upon the *Star Wars* sequel gig as a poisoned chalice. Any director, no matter how experienced, would not be able to be his own man, only a puppet of Lucas. Others worried that if they messed up the sequel to the biggest grossing film of all time, they would never work in Hollywood again. It was a risk not worth taking. If the film succeeded, it was unlikely the director would get the kudos. It would be Lucas who would soak up the acclaim – and the profits.

As so many of Lucas's old film-school friends and acquaintances had found roles on *Star Wars*, Kurtz returned to this source in his search of a director willing to take on *The Empire Strikes Back*. Irvin Kershner had been a tutor at USC and Lucas had been in his class – the *Star Wars* creator looked upon Kershner (known as 'Kersh' to all his friends) as something of a mentor. Kershner was an all-round renaissance man, with interests in music and art as well as movies. His most recent work included a sequel, *The Return of a Man Called Horse* (1976), a war movie in *Raid on Entebbe* (1977) and a supernatural mystery, *The Eyes of Laura Mars* (1978). This combination made him an attractive option for Lucas and Kurtz. For his part, Kershner had come to the original *Star Wars* through his son, but had appreciated the mythic depth obvious in the story and the archetypes with which Lucas was working. A deal was soon done and Kershner was quickly named as the director of the *Star Wars* sequel. Later he would go on to direct an unofficial Sean Connery James Bond movie, *Never Say Never Again* (1983), and another science-fiction sequel in *RoboCop 2* (1990).

Kurtz had settled on the UK once more as the best location to shoot the studio work for *The Empire Strikes Back*, booking Elstree from February to September 1979. It also gave easy access to other areas the film would use, especially Finse in Norway, which would double for the snowbound planet of Hoth featured in the film's opening battle. March 1979 saw an ill-prepared film crew arrive in the remote location hoping to capture the area's natural grandeur. Just as unprecedented rain had greeted their arrival in Tunisia three years earlier, the *Star Wars* crew arrived in Norway during some of the coldest weather the region had seen in many years. Based in the Finse Ski Lodge, on the Oslo–Bergen rail line, the crew discovered they were to shoot in the same area where Captain Scott had taken his men to acclimatize for their doomed expedition to the South Pole in 1911 – not a great omen.

Even without the persistent weather problems, the unit had terrible difficulty working in the snow and capturing even the most basic shots in the sub-zero temperatures. Much of the shooting took place 7,000 feet above Finse, on the Hardanger-jøkulen glacier. Hamill and Ford (who had not been originally scheduled to work in Norway, but was flown in at the last minute) in particular were to suffer as they struggled to capture the opening scenes of the film in which their characters spend an awful night out in the open on the planet Hoth. For them both, little acting was required: they really were frozen and scared to death.

Kurtz had planned the shoot like a military operation, importing snow vehicles and hiring helicopters to move the cast and crew on and off the glacier. Relations were strained between Kurtz and Kershner as the production fell behind schedule. All involved were only too aware they were spending Lucas's own money on the movie and his plans to build his ranch complex in Marin County depended on the second *Star Wars* movie being as big a smash hit as the first. 'We have to be careful with [the money], so be sure to do a good job,' Lucas had warned the pair during his fleeting visit to Norway. This responsibility weighed heavily on those in charge every minute the crew spent indoors, sheltering from the weather and not shooting.

Amongst the snow, wind and ice, the cast and crew struggled to capture what they could, although their efforts were frequently abandoned as they rushed back to the relative warmth of their base camp hotel pursued not by the deadly Wampa creature that featured in the scenes but by the equally deadly winds and whiteouts that were frequent in Finse in winter. Many were grateful when the unit wrapped and everyone returned to Elstree Studios in the UK to work on the more controllable studio-bound sequences. The estimated budget for the movie had grown to $22 million following the delays in Norway.

Major sequences of the film followed Luke in his quest to find and train with renowned Jedi Master Yoda on the swamp planet of Dagobah. Kurtz initially wanted to shoot this material on location either in the Florida Everglades or the Caribbean, but concerns about controlling such an environment and working with a puppet main character (as Yoda would be) meant that he reorganized the Dagobah scenes to be shot on a soundstage in London. Kurtz found that due to a fire on one soundstage and the fact that perfectionist director Stanley Kubrick (shooting *The Shining*, 1980, on the specially built 'George Lucas Stage' at Elstree) was over-running, he couldn't get his crews started on building the needed sets as quickly as he would have liked. Lucas, following his brief visit to Norway, left Kurtz and Kershner to deal with the problems, returning to the United States to supervise the start of the special effects and model work for the film at ILM.

Kershner took advantage of the creator's absence to craft the film he wanted. His vision was for a darker sequel, a film built more around the characters, their relationships and trials than on startling spectacle and special effects. The cast welcomed this new approach, finding Kershner much more communicative as a director of actors than Lucas had ever been. Kershner was collegiate, welcoming contributions from the actors regarding their characters and dialogue. For Ford, this fresh approach validated his decision to return, making playing Han Solo a much more enjoyable experience than during the first film. Ford constantly questioned Kershner's choices, which the director either adapted or defended, while being receptive to constructive debate. It all made for a better film in the end, certainly far better than if Lucas had elected to direct. The developing romance between Han and Leia in Kasdan's script had been welcomed by both Ford and Fisher, despite the fact that their own friendship had cooled considerably since the summer of 1976. She was now involved with singer-songwriter Paul Simon and that helped bring additional tension to their scenes and their on-set behaviour. Kershner did his best to bring their frustrated relationship across on screen. Some of the lingering traces of Leigh Brackett's acidic 1940s-style Bogart-and-Bacall type dialogue also helped.

Where Lucas had not allowed the cast to ad-lib during the

first film, Kershner's more relaxed approach resulted in one of the all-time great movie lines. As the captured Han Solo was being lowered into the carbon-freezing chamber, Leia finally admits her feelings for him with a simple 'I love you'. The scripted reply was the rather banal, 'Just remember that, 'cause I'll be back', but during a frustrating day of shooting an irritated Harrison Ford came up with a waspish 'I know' as his character's response. Kershner was delighted with the development, something Lucas would probably not have allowed, and determined to keep the revised response in the finished film.

Two more essential elements were necessary for the final success of *The Empire Strikes Back*: the wizened Jedi Master Yoda and the secret of Luke Skywalker's parentage. In devising Yoda, Lucas had reacted against the expectation that such a great warrior would be a superhero figure. He was to be a tiny, ancient alien with a face that character-sculptor and make-up wizard Stuart Freeborn would model on a combination of Albert Einstein and his own visage. The big worry was how to bring this character to life on screen, and Lucas had to rely on some very old tried and tested methods. He brought in *The Muppets*' puppeteer Frank Oz both to manipulate the Yoda puppet and to provide the character's voice (which gave the Jedi Master an occasional vocal resemblance to *The Muppets*' Fozzie Bear, also operated and voiced by Oz). The secret to making the Yoda puppet work on screen – as became clear during the uncomfortable shooting in the studio set of the Dagobah swamp – was in Mark Hamill's truthful and convincing rapport with the Muppet-like creature (which didn't come easily to the actor under the conditions he had to work in). If Hamill had been unable to buy in to the reality of Yoda, it was unlikely that audiences in cinemas would.

In order to maintain the core secret of the film – that Darth Vader was in fact Anakin Skywalker, Luke's father, as mentioned by Obi-Wan Kenobi in the first film – fake dialogue was shot during the confrontation between the two characters. Darth Vader actor David Prowse had no idea of his character's relationship to Luke as he delivered different lines to those that Vader voice-actor James Earl Jones would dub on to the soundtrack later in post-production. Those who were in the know on the crew (and there were very few) were sworn to secrecy. The gamble worked, as the first most viewers discovered about this aspect of the movie was when it happened on screen in front of them. That kind of narrative development is so much harder to keep under wraps today. Alec Guinness also returned, without an additional fee as a favour to Lucas, playing the ghostly form of Obi-Wan Kenobi and recording a handful of disembodied lines of dialogue that motivate Luke's search for Jedi Master Yoda.

As filming drew to a close on *The Empire Strikes Back*, tragedy struck the unit as Oscar-winning production designer John Barry died suddenly on 1 June 1979 of infectious meningitis. When the production had fallen behind schedule, Lucas and Kershner had turned to Barry (who had directed the science-fiction movie *Saturn 3*, eventually released in 1980) to also take on the role of second unit director. The production had to be shut down, giving Kurtz a chance to look again at the film's ballooning budget that he feared was about to soar past the new estimate of $22 million. He and Lucas were concerned, but a report in *Variety* that their sequel had secured over $26 million in pre-release guarantees from US cinema chains eased their concerns. It meant, barring some calamity, that *The Empire Strikes Back* would almost certainly be in profit from the day it opened in May 1980. Nonetheless, Lucas returned to London to supervise the final shooting days, attempting to speed up the slow Kershner and get the film completed.

Weeks later Lucas viewed a rough cut of his sequel in London, compiled by *Star Wars*' Oscar-winning editor Paul Hirsch, who had been editing as shooting had progressed. As with the first disappointing cut of *Star Wars*, Lucas did not like what he saw. He felt the slow pace of the character scenes that Kershner had built up damaged the movie overall, and he was uncomfortable with the romance between Han and Leia. Lucas locked himself in an editing suite for two whole days in an attempt to salvage his movie, emerging with a cut that Kurtz felt was worse than the first one. 'It was awful,' the producer maintained. 'It was chopped into tiny pieces and everything was fast.' Feeling overwhelmed by the fact that it was his money on the line, Lucas had panicked and over-reacted to what was essentially a work in progress. Hirsch had another go at reshaping the original material, resulting in a new cut that Lucas described as 'coming together beautifully'.

The next disaster to hit the film was beyond anyone's control. The movie had been financed through a loan arranged with Bank of America, with Lucas's own substantial cash reserves put up as collateral. In July 1979, the bank suddenly called in the loan, jeopardizing the production entirely. The spiralling budget had finally got beyond what the bank could tolerate: they would advance no more money to the production and demanded repayment of the $22 million already loaned out. It was a catastrophe, not only for Lucas but for all those working on the film who faced not being paid at the end of the week (a wage bill that itself reached almost $1 million).

Kurtz swung into action, working out that a further $3 million would be needed to complete the movie. A new loan from First National Bank was quickly arranged for $25 million, which paid off Bank of America and saw the production receive the additional funds needed. The move rescued the film from oblivion, but it came at a cost, with National First Bank demanding extremely high rates of interest to cover the risk it perceived in loaning so much money to make a movie.

However, Kurtz had miscalculated, and an additional $3 million was needed by the production. This time, First National also said 'No'. Lucas had no option but to swallow his pride and go to his distributor, Twentieth Century Fox, in an attempt to secure the vital final tranche of production funding. Unfortunately, Alan Ladd Jr, his long-term ally at Fox, had long gone, moving into independent movie production. Lucas had to deal with the new regime at the studio, including executive

Sherry Lansing. Knowing the director was in a difficult position, the studio demanded a 15 per cent share in the profits of *The Empire Strikes Back* in return for the last $3 million the film needed for completion. Having been at the mercy of studios before on *THX 1138* and *American Graffiti*, Lucas had hoped never to be put in that position again. He had felt that the amazing success of *Star Wars* would guarantee this would never happen to him once more, yet here he was, cap in hand to the studio that he had enriched through *Star Wars*, a film most at Fox had little faith in originally. The final negotiation gave Fox a greater share of the gross from distribution but also guaranteed them distribution rights to the promised third *Star Wars* film. Lucas complained for years after that he was still 'suffering' from losing out to the studio.

The fall-out of the affair landed on Kurtz, and the producer would not be back in charge of that third *Star Wars* film. 'The problem with *Empire*, as George saw it, was that it went over budget,' said Kurtz. 'It was his money and it was my fault because I was in charge. I have to accept that responsibility. Also, he felt a bit grated by the style, and I had picked the director. [Kershner] wasn't controllable enough.'

Three days before the opening of *The Empire Strikes Back* on 21 May 1980, lines began forming outside Hollywood Boulevard's Egyptian Theater where the movie was set to run non-stop for a full twenty-four hours from opening night. The small band of dedicated *Star Wars* fans – including one who had seen the first movie 178 times (in cinemas between 1977 and 1979) – soon attracted the attention of the media. So began the phenomenon of the advance fan line that would reach epidemic proportions with the release of the first *Star Wars* prequel in 1999. Inspired by the crowd outside the Egyptian, fans across the United States dug out their sleeping bags in preparation for a night or two on the sidewalk in order to ensure they would be first to see the new *Star Wars* movie.

The first film had been an unknown quantity and had the

element of surprise on its side. The same could not be said of *The Empire Strikes Back*: there were very few people across the modern world who didn't know who Luke Skywalker, Han Solo and Darth Vader were. This time out, Vader featured on the cover of *Time* magazine (much to the annoyance of Lucas, who hoped he might feature himself). Premieres were held for the film worldwide, including in London and Washington, DC. As before, house records tumbled across the United States as fans flocked to see the latest adventures in the galaxy far, far away.

Equally, critics now knew what to expect from *Star Wars*. Some, like Pauline Kael, who had been negative about the first film, found much to like in the second. 'There is no sense that this ebullient, youthful saga is running thin in imagination', she wrote, 'or that it has begun to depend excessively on its marvellous special effects – that it is in any danger, in short, of stiffening into mannerism or mere billion-dollar style.' She did offer one caveat, though: 'I'm not sure I'm up [for] seven more *Star Wars* adventures [as some sources had promised at the time], but I can hardly wait for the next one.'

Some critics were thrown by the fact that the film was the middle part of a larger story, beginning mid-action and ending on a cliffhanger, relying on audiences to return for the third instalment to see how the story ended. The surprise ending, which saw Han Solo trapped in carbonite and taken off to gangster Jabba the Hutt by bounty hunter Boba Fett, while the rebels were defeated by Darth Vader and the Empire, was something of a downer but necessary to George Lucas's storytelling. It played up to his inspiration from the old-style 1930s serials that ended every week with a seemingly impossible situation.

Much of the credit for the success of *The Empire Strikes Back* went to director Irvin Kershner, despite what Lucas felt. The *Los Angeles Herald Examiner* noted that 'after a long, honourable, unjustly neglected career, Kershner fully comes into his own at last. He's produced a contemporary marvel.' Other were equally positive, calling the film 'classic in style, design and narrative' (*Houston Chronicle*), praising it's 'sense of wonder' (*Detroit News*) or it's 'charm, spectacle [and] child-like glee. It's a near flawless movie of its kind' (Gene Siskel, *Chicago Tribune*). Veteran critic Roger Ebert of the *Chicago Sun-Times* hailed the movie as 'one of the most visionary and inventive films of all time'.

Not all the reviews were as gushing, though, with Judith Watson of the *Washington Post* denigrating *The Empire Strikes Back* because it had 'no plot structure, no character studies, no emotional or philosophical point to make', oddly all elements that the film has been widely praised for by fans since 1980. Watson went on to say of the film that it had 'no original vision of the future, which is depicted as a pastiche of other junk-culture formulae, such as the Western, the costume epic and the World War Two movie. Its specialty is "special effects" or visual tricks, some of which are playful, imaginative and impressive, but others of which have become space-movie clichés.'

Watson was not alone, as the *Village Voice* called the film 'minor entertainment', while the UK's *New Statesman* labelled the sequel 'far less entertaining than the first'. Critic Robert Asahina, writing in the *New Leader*, claimed: 'no amount of lightness can lift this movie out of the swamps of Dagobah'.

Audiences clearly did not agree with these negative critics. Although Fox had been concerned that the underperformance (compared to its excessive cost) of Paramount's *Star Trek: The Motion Picture* (1979) and Disney's misguided *The Black Hole* (1979) signalled that the science-fiction movie boom launched by *Star Wars* was over, the film opened to a $9 million first week. *The Empire Strikes Back* was rolled out to as many cinemas nationwide as the studio could book as quickly as possible. Within a month, domestic box office take stood in excess of $31 million, out-grossing every one of that summer's rival big screen entertainments, including the big-budget *The Blues Brothers* (featuring Carrie Fisher in a cameo). Within three months, the movie had made a profit, and by 1987 the domestic box office stood at $141 million, with an additional $363.5 million world-wide. Including later re-releases, *The Empire Strikes Back* claimed a final total of $290 million at the US box office and almost $540 million worldwide.

Despite the success of the finished film (financially and creatively), Lucas was determined not to lose control to the same degree next time. 'I never got on Kersh about the fact that he was over schedule and putting a great burden on me and my life,' admitted Lucas. 'Everything I owned was wrapped up in that damned movie. If he blew it, I lost everything. He would go on and do another movie, but I was really under the gun at that point.' Things would be very different on the third film, then titled 'Revenge of the Jedi'.

Between the second and third *Star Wars* movies, George Lucas focused on the building work at the old Bulltail Ranch. In October 1980 work had begun in earnest in shaping the ground for the sympathetic, traditional buildings he planned to use as the headquarters for his idealistic filmmaking 'community'. The past three years had seen Lucas accumulate a personal fortune in the region of $100 million, his strategy of risking all his proceeds from *Star Wars* (film and merchandise) on the making of *The Empire Strikes Back* having paid dividends. Lucasfilm had grown, too, from a handful of people way back at the start of The Star Wars Corporation to around 200 employees in 1980, overseeing all aspects of the growing Lucas empire, from merchandising to public relations.

Lucas saw Skywalker Ranch as 'a kind of creative-filmmakers retreat. The idea came out of film school. It was a great environment: a lot of people all very interested in film, exchanging ideas, watching movies, helping each other out. I wondered why we couldn't have a professional environment like that . . . an environment that gets people excited.' It was, however, also to be an emblem of his rebel credentials. 'They don't do that in Hollywood.'

Although running such a facility would inevitably have overtones of running a business like any other (if it was to succeed, anyway), Lucas was clear that he didn't see himself that way at all. 'I don't want to be a businessman,' he said in 1980. 'My ambition is to make movies.' At all costs, he didn't want to be the small-town businessman his father had been.

At that time, though, besides the planned third *Star Wars* film, Lucasfilm only had two other projects underway: fellow Northern Californian filmmaker John Korty's animated fantasy *Twice Upon a Time* (1983) and the Spielberg-directed *Raiders of the Lost Ark*. Lucas would function as executive producer on both projects (and help provide the storyline for *Raiders*), but Lucasfilm didn't fund either film, with the hated studios (Warner Bros. and Paramount respectively) footing the bills. While the *Star Wars* creator continued to hold his grudge against the American film-making establishment (especially Universal), he was equally happy to use them on his own terms when it suited him.

He did make a final break with much of Hollywood, however, when he quit the Directors Guild of America (DGA). Both *Star Wars* movies to date had a 'cold open', meaning that they went straight into the action without running any significant credits. This was against union rules, and the DGA issued a $250,000 fine against Lucasfilm as *The Empire Strikes Back* had not displayed Irvin Kershner's directorial credit up front. The DGA was joined by the Writers Guild (the screenwriting union), which similarly claimed that the film had failed to properly credit screenwriter Lawrence Kasdan in the same upfront manner. This was the last straw for Lucas: he angrily paid the fines and quit both unions, declaring that his fully independent future productions would be made outside the union agreements. The argument, from the point of view of Lucas, was about creative artistic decisions rather than the working conditions or compensation agreements that the unions would normally arbitrate on (the kind of thing he normally supported).

In April 1981 *Variety* reported the events under the headline: 'George Lucas Cuts H'Wood Ties.' The industry trade paper announced Lucas had not only quit the DGA and the Writers Guild, but had also withdrawn from the Academy who awarded the annual Oscars. At the same time, the long-term Lucasfilm offices in Hollywood (ironically opposite Universal Studios on Lankershim Boulevard, where they had been established at the time of *American Graffiti*) were closed and all staff moved to Northern California. Step-by-step, George Lucas was almost inevitably becoming the businessman with a loathing for the sin city of Los Angeles that his father had been. 'For every honest, true filmmaker [in Los Angeles] trying to get his films off the ground, there are a hundred sleazy used-car dealers trying to con you out of your money. I've never made a film in Hollywood. Now, I'll never have to.' The maverick movie-making rebel was now fully out on his own, finally in charge of his own destiny.

Chapter 8

Creature Feature

With [Return of the] Jedi I have finished what I began more than ten years ago. When Jedi is launched, I'll take a couple of years off. The company [Lucasfilm] was created to serve me, but it has turned out the opposite: I serve it.

George Lucas

By 1980, Hollywood rebel George Lucas was well on his way to building a new empire. The third *Star Wars* film was clear in his mind. It would be called 'Revenge of the Jedi'. It would be directed by Steven Spielberg. It would develop the conflict between the Emperor, Vader and Luke Skywalker (rather than seeing Leia becoming leader of her people and the central trio separating in a bitter-sweet way, as had originally been discussed with Gary Kurtz). Howard Kazanjian, who had handled *More American Graffiti* (the 1979 TV movie sequel to Lucas's original) and *Raiders of the Lost Ark* for Lucas, had replaced Kurtz as line producer on the third film following the budget over-runs on the second movie.

Kazanjian's first task was to deal with the fallout from Lucas quitting the Hollywood guilds, meaning that any director on the third movie would have to be non-union: that ruled out Spielberg. Although Irvin Kershner had delivered a critically acclaimed movie that had succeeded in extending and deepening the unfolding *Star Wars* saga, it was not entirely to Lucas's liking. He found it too dark and less child-friendly than the original, something he set out to rectify with the third film. Lucas also wanted a director who would be more amenable to being supervised by the *Star Wars* creator.

Weirdly, his next choice was David Lynch, the maverick director of *Eraserhead* (1977) and *The Elephant Man* (1980). Lynch was as baffled as everyone else at the suggestion that he should take on a family-friendly blockbuster science-fiction movie (although he would go on to tackle science fiction – not entirely successfully – with Frank Herbert's *Dune*). Lynch claimed he had 'next door to zero interest' in taking on the film, but he met with Lucas anyway claiming to suffer an increasingly severe headache as the meeting progressed. 'I've never even really liked science fiction. I like elements of it, but it needs to be combined with other genres. And, obviously, *Star Wars* was totally George's thing,' he said in the interview book *Lynch on Lynch*. He later told MTV that *Star Wars* 'was his thing. I said, "You should direct this. It's your thing! It's not my thing."'

Despite Lynch's encouragement, Lucas was not ready to return to directing even though he had regretted giving up so much control to Kershner on *The Empire Strikes Back*. Undeterred, Lucas then approached Canadian filmmaker David Cronenberg, who turned the film down in favour of making *Videodrome* (1983) and *The Dead Zone* (1983) instead.

Finally, filling the director position on the third *Star Wars* movie was Richard Marquand, a minor British director who had most recently helmed the Second World War thriller *Eye of the Needle* (1981). He had started out making television documentaries for the BBC before graduating to directing drama (similar to Kershner's career progression in the United States). Lucas felt that Marquand 'had done some great suspense films and was really good with actors. *Eye of the Needle* was the film I'd seen that he had done that impressed me the most; it was really nicely done and had a lot of energy and suspense.' Marquand's relative inexperience would make him more controllable by Lucas.

Once again the screenplay was to be written by Lawrence Kasdan. He based his work heavily on the lengthy outline supplied by Lucas. Marquand contributed what he could during rewrites, while screenwriter David Peoples (*Blade Runner*, 1982) also made uncredited contributions. Between July and December 1981, Kasdan wrestled with his first draft of what was then still called 'Revenge of the Jedi'. Four drafts were accumulated, while Marquand sketched storyboards fulfilling Lucas's demand for more action than in the previous film. The story threads from *The Empire Strikes Back* had to be concluded, but that story had departed from the direction Lucas originally intended. The result was a compromised conclusion to the saga in which the proposed deaths of both Han Solo and Lando Calrissian were dropped in favour of a happy ending for all. Ford was keen to see the back of Solo, telling Lucas, 'He's got no mama, no papa, and he's got no story. Let's kill him and get some weight to this thing.' Ford was contractually committed to the film as a result of his deal on the second movie, but the eventual resulting performance betrayed his boredom during filming.

The film was planned around three major sequences. The opening would see the rescue of the frozen Han Solo from the Tatooine palace of Jabba the Hutt, with the reunited team of Han, Leia (now revealed as Luke's sister) and Luke preparing a new assault on the Empire. As Han and Leia attempt to switch off a shield generator on the moon of Endor, Lando Calrissian flies the *Millennium Falcon* in an attack on a second Death Star, now under construction. Luke attempts to rescue his father from the clutches of the dark side of the Force, while confronting the Emperor. The whole movie was designed to wrap up the *Star Wars* trilogy, providing a happy ending for all the main characters. The only significant characters to die would be bad guys: Jabba the Hutt, Boba Fett and Darth Vader.

For the first time, the bulk of the location work for the film would be shot in the United States, rather than in the UK, Tunisia or Norway. After scouting possible locations near Denver and Las Vegas, it was decided that Tatooine's desert scenes would be captured in Buttercup Valley, near Yuma,

Arizona, an area rich in barren sand dunes. Nearer Lucasfilm's home territory, the green landscape of Endor would be brought to life in the giant redwood forests of Northern California, specifically near Crescent City. Although studio work would still be carried out in the UK, Lucas wanted the rest of the locations to be as close to his home base at Skywalker Ranch as much as practically possible.

The budget for the third *Star Wars* film was significantly increased over the previous two at $30 million, with at least a third of that allocated to ILM for special effects work. Never one to waste an idea, Lucas had revived Jabba the Hutt (played by an actor in a fur coat in scenes cut from the first film) for *Jedi*, using Yoda-style puppetry to bring the galactic crime kingpin to life. Surrounding Jabba would be a whole host of unlikely creatures (including a house band) as Lucas set out this time to redo the cantina scene from *Star Wars* properly, with more money and better resources. Believing that *The Empire Strikes Back* had been 'too grown up', Lucas set out to redirect 'Revenge of the Jedi' to appeal to what he saw as the core *Star Wars* audience: eight to twelve year-olds. A monster mash of Muppet creatures was his answer to the more human emotional depth of the second film.

Shooting on 'Revenge of the Jedi' was faster than on the previous movie under Kershner, taking six weeks less to complete. Between January and May 1982 work progressed on the live action components, while Industrial Light and Magic got to work on the special effects sequences. Principal photography in London would begin on 11 January and run until the beginning of April, when cast and crew would relocate to the United States for major location shooting during May. By the end of the year, it was expected that ILM would have completed much of its work, with the final pieces being delivered by March 1983, just two months before the film opened in cinemas that May.

The first scenes shot in London at Elstree Studios saw Han, Luke, Leia, Chewbacca, Lando and the droids caught up in a sandstorm on Tatooine. It was a scene that would not be seen by filmgoers as it was ultimately cut from the movie (although patient fans finally got to see the by then legendary deleted scene when the *Star Wars* saga hit Blu-ray in 2011). The lateness of the script (a habit Lucas had formed by now and would almost fatally maintain through the creation of the prequels) had caused line producer Robert Watts some serious concern: 'The screenplay is the blueprint for everything, and without it you do tend to flounder a bit. We'd had drafts, but the final script did come very, very late . . .' He had planned for a seventy-eight-day shoot across both UK and US locations, but without a final screenplay this was essentially guess work.

In featuring a second Death Star, the third film was largely a retelling of elements of the first, just done on a grander scale. Another old idea revived for 'Revenge of the Jedi' (soon retitled *Return of the Jedi*, as Lucas decided Jedi Knights would not be so base as to seek mere revenge) was that of a Wookiee army. Still fearing they might be difficult to pull off, Lucas essentially cut the Wookiees in half, and partially inverted the name to call his new teddy-bear-like creatures Ewoks. As played by a group of little actors in furry costumes, the Ewoks would be Lucas finally telling the Vietnam-inspired story he didn't get to make with *Apocalypse Now*. These 'primitive' and 'simple' characters would use their low technology to defeat the high technology Empire, just as the low-tech Vietcong had defeated modern America. It also proved convenient that the Ewoks were ready-made for spin-off merchandising possibilities.

The Ewoks had originally been teamed up with the 'Yuzzums', twenty-foot tall, spindly creatures that would have been operated by stilt-walking puppeteers. It was only after Kazanjian had discovered a Venezuelan troupe of professional stilt-walkers who could manipulate the puppets that Lucas scrapped the creatures, sticking with his pint-sized Ewoks instead.

Stuart Freeborn and Phil Tippett established two 'creature shops' for *Return of the Jedi*, one in California, the other in London. 'This is the monster movie,' said Robert Watts of the creature laden Jedi. 'They are terribly difficult because you are breaking new ground each time on each new creature.' As well as Ewoks and Wookiees, the biggest problem for the production was realizing the much-discussed but not yet seen intergalactic crime lord, Jabba the Hutt.

Originally intended to appear in the first *Star Wars* movie, Jabba had been described in the script as a 'fat, slug-like creature with eyes on extended feelers and a huge ugly mouth'. Technical limitations at the time meant that the creature could not be adequately brought to life, despite various concept designs being worked out for him (one was used for the humanoid, dog-faced version of Jabba that appeared in the Marvel comic book adaptation of *Star Wars*). The decision was taken to film the scene with an actor playing Jabba. Wearing a scruffy fur coat, actor Declan Mulholland played opposite Harrison Ford, but Lucas finally decided to drop the scene, both because he was unhappy with the portrayal of Jabba and with the phoney-looking background aliens. His wife, Marcia, had fought to keep the scene in the movie as she felt it reflected well on the character of Han Solo, but she was overruled.

For the final film in the trilogy, Lucas felt he now had the technology to make Jabba a key figure in the drama. The entire opening sequence revolves around Jabba and his court on Tatooine, and was necessary to pay off the Han Solo storyline that had been built up across the previous two movies and provided the cliffhanger at the end of *The Empire Strikes Back*. Using several Ralph McQuarrie sketches as inspiration and input from Phil Tippett, the building of the eighteen-foot long Jabba the Hutt puppet became the responsibility of Stuart Freeborn and his team. It took three months to build, weighed one ton and cost a total of $500,000. Several puppeteers were required to operate the Hutt's head, tiny arms and remote control eyes. Mike Edmonds, who played Ewok Lograv elsewhere in *Return of the Jedi*, was deemed small enough to operate Jabba's tail from inside the puppet. Lucas reportedly felt let down by the finished product, believing it not to be lifelike or flexible enough for what he needed, but he was forced to make the best of it in filming. 'Jabba was my biggest headache,' admitted Freeborn. 'I think we just about made him work.' Lucas later admitted that if CGI technology had been developed enough in 1982, that's how he would have realized Jabba the Hutt. The technology was eventually used to bring the character to life, with a CGI Jabba the Hutt replacing Mulholland in the *A New Hope Special Edition* in 1997 as well as in the first prequel movie, *The Phantom Menace*.

Roaming the background of Jabba's Tatooine Throne Room was a variety of creatures, some reused from *Star Wars* while others were fresh creations. Among those present were Jabba's tiny, wily sidekick Salacious Crumb, a court jester-like character; Bib Fortuna, a Twilek (with distinctive, thick head tentacles) who functions as Jabba's major domo; Ephant Mon, Jabba's unwieldy, long-faced head of security; and Hermi Odle, Jabba's saggy-faced weapons-maker.

Each of these distinctive creatures had to be designed and then constructed, before being operated in front of the cameras by a combination of actors in costumes and puppeteers. Phil Tippett led the design team that created many of these creatures and he admitted drawing on his childhood viewing for inspiration: 'A lot of us watched horror movies when we were children, and we therefore had a pretty good foundation on what had been done already and what we didn't want to do. Our first designs were models for George to accept or turn down.' Out of between fifty and sixty creature concepts presented to him, the director selected around twenty-five to be further developed.

One line in the script – 'And then the band strike up . . .' – resulted in a huge amount of work for Tippett and his team in creating the band members and their instruments, as the characters had to not only appear in the background of many shots but also provide accompaniment for a central musical sequence (one repeatedly revised in various released versions of the film over the years). Three main characters made up the Max Rebo Band: the blue-hued Max Rebo himself on keyboards; Droopy

McCool, a pudgy pipe player; and Sy Snootles, the group's long-lipped singer. Rebo and McCool were played by actors under latex costumes, while Snootles was a mix of a rod puppet operated from below and a marionette manipulated from above, depending on what she was required to be doing in any given individual shot. Cable controls operated separately were used to simulate her lip movements for singing scenes.

One of the Throne Room creatures that took on a life of his own was Salacious Crumb. Intended as little more than a tiny pet or sidekick for Jabba to torment, the Muppet-style, beak-faced, long-eared puppet won the hearts of all who saw it in action. Puppeteer Tim Rose (who would also play rebel leader Admiral Ackbar) gave the little Kowakian monkey-lizard such personality that the film crew began to build up his role beyond what was specified in the script. 'We enlarged his role when we saw him,' admitted Kazanjian of Crumb. 'He was added way late. [The puppeteer] would have him do something unexpected, such as peck at somebody's ear or some other impromptu action. We couldn't help but fall in love with him, so gradually we enlarged his part.' On 29 January, Tippett and Freeborn featured in a photo shoot for publicity purposes in which they posed on the Throne Room set surrounded by their menagerie of creatures.

By mid-February, the creature-heavy scenes in Jabba's palace had been completed, but the movie was not yet finished with Jabba. The scenes set inside his giant sail barge followed, during which the slug-like crime lord met his end thanks to a feisty Princess Leia. Director Richard Marquand would regard the Jabba scenes as the most difficult in the entire film. 'The hardest scene in every way was the one in Jabba's Palace Throne Room,' he said. 'It's a very, very crowded set. It's full of characters. It was incredibly hot and we had all these people wearing rubber suits, and they couldn't move very easily. Nobody could escape. Telling the story was very, very difficult. I wanted great performances from the actors, and from these ridiculous, manic creatures. That scene was by far the hardest.'

The following weeks of production were less creature-intensive, focusing on scenes in the rebel briefing room, Yoda's home on Dagobah and the Emperor's Throne Room on the second Death Star. While Yoda was a known quantity (after his appearance in *The Empire Strikes Back*), the character of rebel leader Admiral Ackbar was something else. A fish-headed alien, Ackbar was a combination of a slip-on head mask worn by *The Muppets* veteran Tim Rose or a half-body puppet with radio-controlled articulation. Ackbar was to feature as a major character, commanding and directing the rebel alliance attack on the incomplete Death Star. Audiences had to believe in him, but as always, Lucas was full of doubts as to whether the puppet would be convincing enough (especially following his experiences with Jabba). So concerned was Lucas that he shot all of Ackbar's scenes twice. In the second set, the human General Madine (Dermot Crowley) replaced Ackbar's character and delivered his lines charting the progress of the space battle. It was a sensible back-up in case the Ackbar material did not work as well as Lucas hoped it might (these kind of production worries would be significantly lessened by the digital and CGI technology of the prequel trilogy). In the event, Ackbar passed muster and the character went on to become something of a fan favourite, especially given his inadvertent catchphrase of 'It's a trap!' (A young Captain Ackbar was featured in the first three episodes of *Star Wars: The Clone Wars* fourth season on TV in 2011, further developing the once almost abandoned character). The creature-laden London shoot drew to a close in March 1982, but when the film crew relocated to the United States the movie would have another new title . . .

Having wrapped filming the studio portion of the movie at Elstree, the production moved to the Unites States under the banner of a movie called 'Blue Harvest', complete with the slogan 'Horror Beyond Imagination'. The ruse was intended to disguise the making of the new *Star Wars* movie from an ever-curious fan base and to ensure that external contractors did not artificially increase their fees as they believed the *Star Wars* producers were rolling in cash.

Two weeks in Arizona's Yuma Desert saw the production capture all the Tatooine scenes from the opening sequences. The 'Blue Harvest' plan failed, however, when the production's cover was blown by a report in the *Los Angeles Times*, resulting in hordes of keen *Star Wars* fans turning up to watch the production's progress in the Northern Californian woods where they filmed for another two weeks. If nothing else, the code-name gambit resulted in the creation of a host of 'Blue Harvest' tagged material that has since become collector's items for fans.

Preparation work had begun in the dense woods over a year before, with tracks being cleared and special ferns being planted that were now several feet high, just in time for shooting. Overall, the movie was now expected to cost around $32.5 million, again financed by Lucas himself – an easy enough task now that *Star Wars* had grossed $524 million and *The Empire Strikes Back* had reached $365 million.

The *Star Wars* B-team of Peter Mayhew as Chewbacca, Anthony Daniels as C-3PO, Kenny Baker as R2-D2 and Dave Prowse as Darth Vader (who had been suspected by Lucasfilm of leaking the revelation of Luke's parentage prior to the release of *Empire*, even though the actor had claimed to be unaware of the secret plot development) had been joined by the 3 foot 11 inch eleven-year-old Warwick Davis as the Ewok Wicket (he would later go on to star in Lucasfilm's *Willow* and feature in the *Harry Potter* movies). All of them would face a post-movie future that largely consisted of repeated appearances at *Star Wars* fan conventions.

Lucas had met his 'need for speed' that had been with him since his teenager years in almost every movie he had made, and *Return of the Jedi* would be no different. From the futuristic car chase that climaxed *THX 1138* through the hot-rodding antics of *American Graffiti*, his earliest commercial work had been built around fast-moving vehicles. The *Star Wars* films had their fair share of 'fast cars', albeit disguised as vehicles from a galaxy far,

far away. Luke had his landspeeder in the first movie, while the fast-paced assault on the Death Star had brought aerial dogfights into space (Lucas would later tackle their inspiration, Second World War dogfights, in *Red Tails*, 2012). *The Empire Strikes Back* had seen the *Millennium Falcon* outmanoeuvre Imperial TIE Fighters and giant Cruisers alike as it sped through a dangerous asteroid field. Now, in *Return of the Jedi*, a central portion of the film would feature a speeder bike chase through the redwoods that stood in for Endor. Mixing location work, models and special effects trickery, the sequence astonished audiences, who felt they were riding along with the rebels and stormtroopers on their rocket-powered bikes, just narrowly dodging the massive redwood tree trunks as they flew past the camera.

The sequence was achieved by the use of relatively new Steadicam technology. A film camera mounted on a rig attached to an operator was walked through the redwoods at a steady pace, shooting on high-speed film. The resulting images, combined with live action footage of the actors atop the speeder bikes, and models, made for a convincing action sequence that livened up the rebels encounter with the Ewoks on Endor.

The long-term investment that Lucas had made in Industrial Light and Magic paid off on *Return of the Jedi*. The climatic space battle had to be bigger and better, faster and more intense than those seen in either of the two previous films. Now he had the technology, the technicians and the resources to bring amazing images to the screen. Instead of two or three ships on screen at once, Lucas could now show dozens, all interacting with each other in spectacular style.

Despite the presence of the annoying Ewoks, *Return of the Jedi* concluded the *Star Wars* trilogy in some style. Even as a replay of the highlights of the first *Star Wars* with a bigger budget and better technology, it worked well. Where the film really scored, though, was in paying off the emotional promise of the shocking revelation in *The Empire Strikes Back* about Luke Skywalker's parentage. The crackling confrontation between Luke, Darth Vader and the Emperor aboard the under-attack Death Star II saw the major character arcs resolved, the villain get his comeuppance and the trilogy's central tragic character (and who could have foreseen that on the basis of *Star Wars*?) redeemed by the love of his son. It was a satisfying conclusion to the story, even if some major characters (like Han Solo and Princess Leia) were essentially sidelined by this concentration on the 'dark father' arc. The movie even repeated the celebratory climax of *Star Wars* by having a victory party among the Ewoks (a sequence hugely expanded in 1997's *Special Edition* to show celebrations of the defeat of the Empire elsewhere in the galaxy with a whistle-stop tour of the major planets of the trilogy). This is where *Star Wars* on the cinema screen would rest for over a decade-and-a-half as Lucas expressed a wish to concentrate on the creation of experimental and personal movies instead.

Lucas had decided after *Star Wars* that he would not direct again, hence hiring Kershner and Marquand to handle the sequel movies. However, on *Return of the Jedi* he was to all intents and purposes directing by proxy. This meant he didn't escape having to deal with the problems that came up on the film. As well as Harrison Ford wanting to see Han Solo killed off, Carrie Fisher wanted to see Princess Leia become a stronger character, essentially a role model for young women – although Lucas recast her as a sex symbol in a metal slave bikini. Billy Dee Williams seemed to be the only one happy with his more heroic and action-oriented role, especially as he wasn't to be killed off after all. Mark Hamill simply wanted the *Star Wars* series to end so he could be free of Luke Skywalker and get on with playing new and more challenging parts – a development that was never to really happen for him or many members of the *Star Wars* cast. Ian McDiarmid, an acclaimed British stage actor, was signed up to play the Emperor (a role he would reprise through all three of the *Star Wars* prequels), but he still enjoyed a burgeoning stage career in the UK.

The lines began earlier than ever before for the newest *Star Wars* movie. Eight days before the official opening night of *Return of the Jedi*, enterprising fans were camping outside cinemas across the United States. The film opened on 25 May 1983, six years to the day since *Star Wars* had made its unprepossessing debut in 1977. The film quickly claimed the biggest opening day in the history of American movies, grossing $6.2 million. Within a week, *Return of the Jedi* had garnered over $45 million at the US box office and would go on to take over ten times that amount (around $475 million) worldwide.

In what would later become something of a habit, Lucas used the release of a new *Star Wars* film to force new technology upon some movie theatres. Four cinemas, including the Avco in Westwood, paid $15,000 to be equipped with Lucasfilm's new THX Sound system. The new technology had been named after developer Tomlinson Holman (TH) with the X standing for 'crossover' as well as paying convenient homage to Lucas's first movie, *THX 1138*. THX Sound rapidly became a widely accepted, industry standard, quality-assurance system for theatrical movie soundtracks, alongside Dolby Stereo.

Despite the huge popular success of the *Star Wars* saga, the critics were not as kind to the third *Star Wars* film as they had been to the first two. The original *Star Wars* had come as a surprise, a return to a 1930s swashbuckling adventure that had beguiled many. In *The Empire Strikes Back*, many critics had seen a maturing of the themes and characters of *Star Wars* under the steady hand of Irvin Kershner. With *Return of the Jedi*, however, there could be detected something of a soulless retread with a nonentity director failing to put his own stamp on Lucas's universe. The proliferation of weird creatures and the dominance of the climax of the movie by merchandisable 'teddy bears' made some critics suspicious.

'The innocence that made *Star Wars* the movie phenomenon of the 1970s has long since vanished,' wrote David Ansen in *Newsweek*. He went on to identify the rise of Lucas's new empire as the root of the problem. *Star Wars* 'has become its own relentless Empire, grinding out "fun" with soulless efficiency'. Others were happier to accept the film for what it was: superior entertainment. Under a headline declaring the *Star Wars* finale a 'triumph', *Washington Post* critic Gary Arnold described *Return of the Jedi* as 'a feat of mass enchantment'. The film was 'robustly diverting . . . a crowd pleaser, a breathtaking, exhilarating special effects achievement'. *Variety* dubbed the movie 'a visual treat throughout' with 'enough menacing monsters to populate a dozen horror pictures [yet] it suffers in comparison to [*Star Wars*] when all was fresh'. The *New York Times* concluded the film would be a success, but that *Star Wars* had lost something along the way: 'The Force is with them, but the magic is gone.'

Darth Vader actor David Prowse was more vocal in his dislike for the concluding film of the six-year saga: 'They killed me off. They killed Yoda off. They killed Boba Fett off, and they had all these silly little Ewoks. It was designed to clear up the [story] odds and ends. [It was] by far the worst of the three. I hated it.'

Prowse's opinion, or those of the critics, didn't trouble Lucas for long. *Star Wars* merchandising was as lucrative as ever, but claims that he had created characters simply so they could be toys did get to him. 'A lot of people say the films are just an excuse for merchandising,' Lucas said. '"Lucas just decided to cash in on the teddy bear?" Well, it's not a great thing to cash in on. People tend to look at merchandising as an evil thing, but ultimately a lot of fun things come out of it, and at the same time it pays for the overhead of the company and everybody's salary.'

The *Star Wars* trilogy had made George Lucas a fortune, bought him filmmaking independence and paid for the building of Skywalker Ranch. However, the eight-year commitment to making the movies had taken a huge toll on his private life. It came as a shock to many friends and those working at Lucasfilm when – just a week after the triumphant release of *Return of the Jedi* – it was announced that Lucas and his wife Marcia were to be divorced.

They had married in February 1969, long before *Star Wars* had come to dominate their lives. Their homes had been their workplaces, whether it was Lucas struggling to write *Star Wars* during the early 1970s or Marcia editing movies for other film-makers throughout that decade. His transformation from a low-budget moviemaker to the biggest film director in the world was something Marcia never expected to happen.

She had always wanted a family, but Lucas's burgeoning career meant putting that moment off, seemingly indefinitely. Discovering they couldn't have children together, Marcia had put her foot down following completion of *The Empire Strikes Back*. As a result, the pair adopted two-year old Amanda in 1981, but the gambit didn't work and they continued to drift apart both as people and professionally.

Where Marcia was outgoing and had a love of travel and culture, Lucas had often been caricatured as a cold, stay-at-home type, slow to engage with people and not comfortable with displaying emotion, either in real life or in his movies. Initially, it was their opposite natures that had brought them together. The period of the making of *Return of the Jedi* and the first phase of designing and building Skywalker Ranch saw Marcia disconnect further from her husband. Although she was the obvious choice to edit the movie, Lucas was never clear about her role when asked (she did work briefly on the film). 'It's been very hard on Marcia,' Lucas said of his work–life balance (or lack of). She had been 'living with somebody who is constantly in agony; uptight and worried, off in never-never land'.

Finally, tired of waiting for Lucas to come around to her way of living, Marcia looked elsewhere. She found solace with Tom Rodriguez, a contractor supervising the installation of stained-glass panels at the ranch. She soon began an affair with Rodriguez, who was a decade younger than her husband. When he found out, Lucas was taken aback, having never imagined such a scenario was possible. Rejecting Marcia's suggestion of marriage counselling or a trial separation, he moved straight to the option of divorce (something that would prove to be expensive, given his *Star Wars* earnings). Marcia went on to have the child she had long wanted with Rodriguez, while Lucas later adopted two more children: a daughter, Katie, and a son, Jett. While he went on to have a series of relationships (including one with singer Linda Ronstadt), it seemed another marriage would not be on the cards.

By 1983, George Lucas was the lonely Emperor of all that he surveyed. He had completed the trilogy of *Star Wars* films he had been hopeful of making back in 1976. The astonishing success of the films had brought him huge wealth, worldwide fame and the ability to make any movie he wanted, independent of the Hollywood machine he distained so much. However, having started out as a rebel filmmaker who wanted to do things differently from 'the system', in building his own moviemaking empire, George Lucas was well on the way to becoming the embodiment of the system himself.

Chapter 9

Empire Building

I haven't read any of the novels. That's a different world than my world, but I do try to keep it consistent. We have two universes: my universe and then this other one. They try to make their universe as consistent with mine as possible, but obviously they get enthusiastic and want to go off in other directions.

George Lucas

The sixteen years between the two *Star Wars* movie trilogies were often referred to by fans as the 'dark times', a period devoid of new *Star Wars*. While there were no new movies, there was plenty of creative activity at Lucasfilm (and beyond) that prepared the way for the prequel trilogy released from 1999. A huge amount of technological progress took place that changed modern filmmaking, while the development of the 'Expanded Universe' proved there were many more *Star Wars* stories to be told in all sorts of media. There was also a very receptive audience patiently waiting to hear them . . .

The Expanded Universe of *Star Wars* adventures began in the world of comic books. First to tell an all-new *Star Wars* story was Marvel's *Pizzazz Magazine*. Running across nine issues (October 1977 to June 1978), 'The Keeper's World' by Roy Thomas and Archie Goodwin saw Luke and Leia involved with a quartet of android children and their computerized 'Keeper', a plot more reminiscent of *Star Trek*. A second adventure – 'War on Ice' – followed, but remained incomplete when the magazine was cancelled in January 1979. The story was only finished when collected in 1981.

Following the six-issue adaptation of the original movie, the Marvel *Star Wars* comic book (released in September 1977) embarked upon all new stories beginning with 'New Planets, New Perils'. Writer Roy Thomas and artists Howard Chaykin, who had adapted the movie, developed the new stories along with others at Marvel, including Don Glut, Archie Goodwin and Chris Claremont. The initial story sees Han and Chewie fall foul of space pirates – led by the notorious Crimson Jack – when on their way to settle their debt with Jabba the Hutt.

Star Wars had come along at just the right time for Marvel. According to Marvel editor Jim Shooter, the company was in turmoil in the mid-1970s, admitting that 'sales were falling. It seemed like the company as a whole was in a death spiral. Then Roy Thomas proposed we licence some upcoming science fiction movie called *Star Wars*. The prevailing wisdom at the time was "science fiction doesn't sell". Adapting a movie with a hokey title like *Star Wars* seemed like folly to most.'

According to Shooter, the strong opposition to taking on *Star Wars* (despite the approaches from Lucasfilm's Charles Lippincott) included company head Stan Lee. Despite that, Thomas prevailed. 'Driven by the advance marketing for the movie, sales were very good,' said Shooter. 'Then about the time the third issue shipped, the movie was released. Sales made the jump to hyperspace. Not since The Beatles had I seen a cultural phenomenon of such power. The comics sold and sold and sold. It is inarguable that the success of the *Star Wars* comics was a significant factor in Marvel's survival through a couple of very difficult years.'

Despite being instrumental in bringing the comic book to Marvel, Thomas wouldn't stick with *Star Wars* as he found working with Lucasfilm's then-developing continuity 'rules' to be limiting (he'd had the same experience with the Edgar Rice Burroughs estate when working on *Tarzan*). Thomas told *Alter*

Ego magazine that Lucas and Lippincott 'thought *Star Wars* might appeal to the same people who read Marvel comics'. According to Thomas, Lippincott outlined the *Star Wars* plot and showed him the pre-production concept artwork. 'My head was spinning,' he admitted, but it was only when he saw the artwork featuring Han Solo that he said, 'I'll do it!' That character gave Thomas a handle on the as yet unmade movie. The presence of Alec Guinness among the cast list caused Stan Lee to change his mind, especially as the terms of the deal were now more favourable to Marvel.

Between 1977 and 1986, the Marvel run of *Star Wars* comics would comprise 107 issues and three special editions. Each of the subsequent movies would be adapted (*The Empire Strikes Back* in issues 39–44, while *Return of the Jedi* was published as a 'Super Special' which was then reprinted with new splash pages as a separate four issue mini-series). Although the Marvel comics were aimed at younger readers, the creators of the stories had a relative freedom that those who followed would be denied. The accumulation of stories across the years (in all media) resulted in a tangled web of continuity of which Lucasfilm attempted to keep track (it now has a full-time member of staff who fills this role). In later years potential stories and time periods in the saga would be off limits, as they were reserved for Lucas himself to explore.

The light-hearted Marvel tales usually ran for two or three issues, with Luke, Han and Leia meeting new adversaries. Occasionally Darth Vader would turn up, sometimes with a part-cyborg female Sith sidekick named Lumiya. More often, the film's heroes would encounter members of crime lord Baron Orman Tagge's family. Perhaps the most notorious character Marvel introduced was the smuggler Jaxxon, a six-foot tall green carnivorous rabbit – an influence on the prequel trilogy's Jar Jar Binks?

The Marvel stories resulted in some continuity glitches that would be superseded by later films and novels. An early Marvel story established Anakin Skywalker and Darth Vader as two separate people (was this approved by Lucasfilm to mislead fans, or had Lucas not fully developed their relationship at that stage?). Similarly, Jabba the Hutt appeared in the comics as a yellow-skinned humanoid character before *Return of the Jedi* established him as a giant slug-like creature.

The Marvel *Star Wars* comics, along with the *Star Wars* newspaper strips, would form the cornerstone of the Expanded Universe – a term that came to encompass almost all the non-movie *Star Wars* material created, including comic books, novels, videogames, TV series and film spin-offs, even toys. From this small acorn, a mighty empire called Lucas Licensing would grow.

The Alan Dean Foster *Star Wars* novelization was only published due to the tenacity of Charles Lippincott. The deal with Del Rey was initially seen (like the comic book) as a marketing opportunity, a chance to pre-sell the movie to science-fiction fandom. However, after the success of the film Lucasfilm investigated producing a second novel that would fall between the first two movies. This time Alan Dean Foster would get his name on the cover. *Splinter of the Mind's Eye* was the first original *Star Wars* novel, and it would eventually lead to a thriving industry in spin-off fiction.

The possibility of a second book had been built into Foster's contract, with any story developed intended to double up as the basis of a low-cost sequel should the first film be a less-than-stellar success. Given the unprecedented impact of *Star Wars*, such considerations were now unnecessary. Foster was allowed simply to develop the outline (drawn from concepts in Lucas's source material) as he saw fit. However, the novel remained something of a hangover from the original concept of a low-budget sequel, with locations and props from the movie reused and the setting of a jungle-covered, mist-shrouded planet intended to make the film easy to shoot. Han Solo and Chewbacca were absent from the novel, suggesting that Lucas was prepared to make a sequel without them. The focus was on

Luke and Leia and their quest for the mysterious Kaiburr crystal, a Force-amplifying artefact (included in early drafts of 'The Star Wars' as the 'Kiber' crystal).

In the swamplands of the planet Minban (an opening space battle was cut at an early stage to make any resulting film cheaper), Luke and Leia – accompanied by faithful droids C-3PO and R2-D2 – hunt for the Force-enhancing gem while battling Imperial stormtroopers, the elements and, eventually, Darth Vader. The novel climaxes in a lightsaber duel between Luke and Vader in which Luke severs Vader's arm (an inconsistency with both the second movie and all the following Expanded Universe material). Additionally, the novel plays upon the sexual tension between Luke and Leia, suggesting that their familial connection had not yet been devised (further reinforced by Lucas teasing their will-they, won't-they status at the end of *The Making of Star Wars* TV special). Lucas later claimed he left that element of the story intact in order to indicate the pair had feelings for each other, but that they did not yet understand the true nature of their connection.

The second novel's sales proved there was an audience for non-movie related *Star Wars* paperbacks, making viable a new series of novels. Between April 1979 and August 1980 (following the release of *The Empire Strikes Back*) a trilogy of adventures featuring Han Solo and written by Brian Daley were released. Set two years before the events in *Star Wars*, the novels told of the previous adventures of Solo and Chewbacca in their smuggling days. *Han Solo at Stars' End* launched the trilogy and saw the *Millennium Falcon*'s pilot pals trying to track down 'Doc', a missing outlaw technician, in the company of two droids (with the unusual names of 'Bollux' – changed to 'Zollux' in the UK for obvious reasons – and 'Blue Max'). Two more novels followed – *Han Solo's Revenge* and *Han Solo and the Lost Legacy* – that saw Solo and Chewbacca caught up in a slavery ring and embarking on a treasure hunt for the lost loot of the Xim. The third book saw the pair preparing to borrow money from Jabba the Hutt in order to embark on the Kessel

Run, a smugglers' route, making a direct connection with the beginning of *Star Wars*.

A growing awareness of the need for continuity within the burgeoning *Star Wars* universe saw Daley constricted on the elements he could use in his novels. 'I was told that it had to take place before, not after [*Star Wars*],' said Daley. 'I could not use the Force or any other powers. I could not use Vader, the Empire, TIE fighters, the rebellion, or any of the other major characters from the movie, save Han and Chewie. [I was allowed] nothing about gambling or a resort planet because comic strip [writers] were developing [those] ideas. I was very much hemmed in, but I understood why. If some of the tie-in folks had gotten the bit in their teeth, they'd have been all over the galactic landscape.' It would be a sign of things to come as Lucasfilm began to exert more direct control over the creation of Expanded Universe material.

Following the second and third movies – and the publication of novelizations by Donald F. Glut, Lucas's old film-school friend, and James Kahn respectively – Lando Calrissian was the next character to get the trilogy novel treatment. Collectively known as *The Adventures of Lando Calrissian*, the three novels were titled *The Mindharp of Sharu*, *The Flamewind of Oseon* and *The Starcave of ThonBoka*, and were released between July and December 1983. Written by fantasy author and political activist L. Neil Smith, best known for his alternate American history series set in the Gallatin universe, that trilogy turned out to be the last adult *Star Wars* novels for eight years. Despite the success of the books, in the mid-1980s Lucas wanted to move his company away from *Star Wars* and concentrate on other projects. 'My heart is in other areas now,' he said. 'I can make more *Star Wars* and make zillions of dollars, but I don't really have the interest right now.'

Having started at Lucasfilm as Lucas's assistant, Lucy Autrey Wilson had been put in charge of the company's publishing programme. In the early 1990s, in consultation with Bantam Books, she felt the time was right for a return to publishing original *Star Wars* novels. However, no one at Lucasfilm or the publisher could be confident that the books would sell beyond the hardcore *Star Wars* fans that had stayed loyal to the franchise during the 'quiet' period. Fantasy novelist Timothy Zahn was contracted to write a new trilogy, to be set in the aftermath of *Return of the Jedi* and to be released in hardback over a three-year period from 1991. He would be asked to draw on an unusual, non-movie source as his core reference for *Star Wars* continuity.

Starting in 1987, West End Games began publishing a *Star Wars Roleplaying Game* system. This consisted of a handbook, a series of guidebooks and several scenarios that allowed groups of players to run their own *Dungeons and Dragons*-style role-playing games. Despite its limited appeal to a gaming subset of *Star Wars* fandom, the material created for this game would – through Zahn's work – feed further into the foundations of the Expanded Universe.

Zahn's resulting novel – *Heir to the Empire* – was effectively sold as an official sequel to the *Star Wars* trilogy. It was a strategy that worked, propelling the novel on to the *New York Times* bestseller list, and kick-starting a whole new era of *Star Wars* publishing. Set five years after the defeat of the Empire, the novel has Han and Leia married while Luke is training a new generation of Jedi. However, the remnants of the Imperial fleet regroup under the leadership of Grand Admiral Thrawn and attack the Republic once more. Alongside other movie characters, like the droids and Lando Calrissian, Zahn introduced several new characters that became fan favourites. These included smuggler Talon Karrde and Mara Jade, who sets out to kill Luke Skywalker in revenge for the death of the Emperor (only to later marry him in a spin-off comic book). The planet of the Wookiees – Kashyyyk – is depicted for the first time in depth (beyond *The Star Wars Holiday Special*) and Zahn named the homeworld of the Republic as Coruscant (taken up by Lucas in the prequel trilogy). Two further books – *Dark Force Rising* and *The Last Command* – appeared in 1992 and 1993, respectively. Combined sales of Zahn's *Thrawn Trilogy* would eventually hit fifteen million copies, and 2011 would see a twentieth anniversary edition of *Heir to the Empire* published with copious notes from the author.

The twenty years between those two editions saw an unstoppable boom in *Star Wars* novels. Kathy Tyers picked up the *Star Wars* baton post-Zahn with *The Truce at Bakura* in 1994, with a host of authors following including Dave Wolverton, Kevin J. Anderson, Roger MacBride Allen and Barbara Hambly. By 1996, Michael A. Stackpole was chronicling the adventures of Wedge Antilles's 'rogue squadron' in a series of X-Wing novels, while other post-*Return of the Jedi* adventures continued throughout the later 1990s. *Shadows of the Empire* gave the novel series a sales and promotional boost in 1996 (see Chapter 10), with the entire novel series relaunched in the wake of *Star Wars: Episode I – The Phantom Menace*. *Vector Prime* by R. A. Salvatore was the first in the new series (under the umbrella title 'The New Jedi Order'). That novel took the radical step of killing off the much-loved character of Chewbacca, the first time someone significant from the movies had been killed off in the Expanded Universe. The publishing arm of Lucasfilm sought the approval of Lucas, and it certainly brought the *Star Wars* book series a welcome wave of new publicity. Between 1999 and 2003 the nineteen-book 'New Jedi Order' series would chronicle the adventures of a more mature Han, Leia and Luke (and their children), with the stories set up to two decades after *Return of the Jedi*. The series introduced a villainous new species, the fierce alien Yuuzhan Vong, who invade the galaxy.

Hundreds of *Star Wars* novels across over two decades have hugely expanded the universe of characters, creatures and locations that now make up the saga beyond the films. Many dedicated *Star Wars* fans follow the adventures of their heroes in print as they did at the movies, with the depth of the Expanded Universe growing month on month with every new novel published.

From the 1920s until the popular advent of television in the 1950s, there was a golden age of radio drama in the United

States. Although variety entertainment and soap-operas (domestic dramas, so called due to their sponsorship by soap powder manufacturers) were family favourites, it was the pulp dramas of the 1930s and post-war years that caught listeners' imaginations. Hollywood movies were often adapted, while thrilling fantasy series like *Lights Out* and *Suspense* entertained a young George Lucas.

By the 1970s, though, radio drama in the United States had gone into a dramatic decline (although it continued to thrive in the UK and elsewhere in Europe). One last outpost was the part-publicly funded National Public Radio (NPR), where Richard Toscan – associate dean of the University of Southern California School of the Performing Arts – was trying to keep the artform alive. He had been encouraged by John Houseman, then USC's artistic director. He had once been Orson Welles's Mercury Theatre on the Air producer, responsible for the controversial 1938 radio adaptation of H. G. Wells's *The War of the Worlds*. Starting with the NPR-affiliated campus station, KUSC, Toscan adapted the short stories of Raymond Carver to audio.

In the early 1980s, NPR Playhouse was looking to expand its radio drama productions, but wanted a property that would benefit fully from advances in audio technology and the full range of dynamic audio and music effects now available. While Houseman and Toscan began a search for suitable material, it fell to Joel Rosenzweig – one of Toscan's students – to suggest 'Why don't you do *Star Wars*?' Toscan, Houseman and NPR producer Frank Mankiewicz immediately recognized the challenge – movies had been adapted before for radio, especially during the golden age, but *Star Wars* was one of the most visually impressive and successful movies of all time. How could they capture the sheer excitement and drama of *Star Wars* on radio? The serial nature of any adaptation would draw on those old movie serials, like *Flash Gordon* and *Buck Rogers*, which had inspired Lucas in the first place. The movie also had the kind of broad appeal that NPR was looking for, as it saw its dramas as a way of attracting new, perhaps younger audiences to its long established service.

The USC connection offered by Toscan and Houseman would pay off when the plan was put to Lucasfilm. The fact that Lucas's old school had originated the idea went a long way to it getting a favourable hearing, as well as the feeling that adapting *Star Wars* to radio would both be breaking new boundaries and going some way to restoring radio drama to its long-lost place as a prime American art. The rights to the radio version of *Star Wars* were quickly offered to KUSC, the university station, for the token amount of just $1, including the rights to the use of all *Star Wars* music and sound effects.

That deal saved the station a lot of money, but nonetheless the cost of adapting the hit movie to audio (involving writing a script, hiring actors, renting studio space and hiring technicians) was budgeted at around $200,000. While NPR had an annual $21 million budget, there was no funding available for this particular project. Looking for international partners, NPR's Mankiewicz persuaded Britain's BBC to become involved as a co-production partner, giving it the right to air the serial in the UK. The quid pro quo on the deal was that the BBC would supply key members of the production team, due to its long-standing experience in audio drama. This brought twenty-nine-year-old director John Madden on to the production (later the director of such award-winning films as *Mrs Brown*, 1997, and *Shakespeare in Love*, 1998). Madden was teamed with US sound engineer Tom Voegeli, with Toscan and Lucasfilm's Carol Titelman acting as executive producers.

After a failed attempt at adapting the movie by an unnamed BBC-nominated writer, the task fell to Brian Daley, writer of the Han Solo trilogy of Expanded Universe novels. Over three months, Daley devised scripts for a thirteen-episode version of the story that would run for almost six hours, about four hours longer than the movie. Daley's scripts were witty and fast-moving, finding solutions to many of the daunting problems of adapting droid dialogue and Wookiee wails to radio. He had access to early drafts of the *Star Wars* script and as a result the 1981 radio version included several scenes cut from the movie and many others expanded or invented for audio. The entire first episode is built around cut scenes exploring Luke Skywalker's pre-rebellion life on Tatooine, while the method by which Princess Leia acquires the plans for the Death Star is expanded. Han Solo has an encounter with another of Jabba the Hutt's agents (not just Greedo) named 'Heater', while Vader's interrogation of Leia is longer and Admiral Motti's attempts to use the Death Star as a political tool are deepened. Some of the ideas came from Alan Dean Foster's novel, itself based on early movie material that was cut. Daley's innate understanding of myth and fantasy in storytelling helped him reorder Lucas's original material to the best advantage of audio drama.

Recording took place in Los Angeles in June 1980. Casting the radio drama should have been an easy matter, with the film actors reprising their roles, but that was not to be in several key cases. While Mark Hamill and Anthony Daniels were available to play Luke and C-3P0 respectively, Harrison Ford was busy making the first Indiana Jones movie, *Raiders of the Lost Ark* (1981). Given those circumstances, Solo was played by American voice actor Perry King (who had auditioned for the film role), while Ann Sachs performed Leia, due to Carrie Fisher's unavailability. Brock Peters (*Star Trek II: The Wrath of Khan*, 1982) gave new voice to Darth Vader, while Bernard Behrens played Luke's Jedi mentor, Obi-Wan Kenobi. A variety of lesser-known voice actors filled out the other parts, although some – like David Paymer, Jerry Hardin and Adam Arkin – would rise to later prominence. With union minimum performance fees of $200 per day for the actors, Madden recorded the drama's thirteen instalments in a swift thirteen days, with Daley on hand to edit or rewrite scenes as necessary.

The resulting serial was given a big push by NPR, including a star-driven launch at Los Angeles' Griffith Observatory, where an episode was played in concert with a starry light show. Broadcast from March 1981 on NPR (and on the youth-oriented BBC Radio 1 in the UK), the unusual series brought a 40 per cent rise in NPR's audience, with 750,000 listeners. More than mere quantity, however, NPR was delighted with the demographic results that saw the network's all-important twelve to seventeen age group soar fourfold. Promoted with the slogan 'You may think you've seen the movie; wait 'til you hear it!', the *Star Wars* radio drama brought very positive critical reaction endorsing the cliché that the pictures are always better on radio.

Madden knew why the radio version succeeded so well: 'Anyone who's ever listened to radio drama will testify to the fact that a play you hear will remain in your mind; twelve years later you'll remember it vividly. And the reason you'll remember it vividly is because you've done the work . . . it lives in your imagination.'

Demand for a sequel was high, and with *The Empire Strikes Back* the material was ready and waiting. Just as the third *Star Wars* movie, *Return of the Jedi*, went before the cameras, the second was being adapted to audio, again for NPR. The same $1 deal was struck for the rights, and the core cast was already established, making the set-up simpler. Some new key roles had to be filled, including wise Jedi Master Yoda (with John Lithgow replacing the movie's Frank Oz), while *Star Wars* screen newcomer Billy Dee Williams reprised his role of Lando Calrissian. As before, Daley's scripts (this time forming a four-hour, ten-episode version of the film) expanded upon some key scenes, notably those involving a rebel attack on an Imperial convoy that comes before the movie starts, and additional conversations between Han and Luke when they are trapped in Hoth's snowy wastes.

Recorded in just ten days at the start of June 1982, much effort went into the post-recording sound mixing, adding music and effects, a role that again fell to Tom Voegeli. He regarded his work on *The Empire Strikes Back* as a step up from his efforts on *Star Wars* as he now felt more comfortable in the audio version of Lucas's universe. New digital production methods only just available to KUSC sped things up and allowed for much more dynamism in the sound production. Promoted like a movie (complete with a new poster), *The Empire Strikes Back* was premiered at the Hayden Planetarium in New York during a blizzard on 14 February 1983. Success with listening audiences followed, suggesting that the third movie, *Return of the Jedi*, would be rushed into audio production.

Except it didn't happen, at least not then. US Republican President Ronald Regan's public funding cutbacks hit NPR hard in early 1983, causing the planned audio version of *Return of the Jedi* to be scrapped. The $400,000 cost for ten episodes (or even the estimated $250,000 for just six) was now beyond the organization. The first two dramas were repeated to continuing acclaim, but nothing could be done to salvage plans for the third.

NPR eventually returned to the project in the mid-1990s. Writer Brian Daley was contacted by Lucasfilm directly in 1995 and asked if he wanted to finish the job he had started over ten years before. There was one big problem: the forty-seven-year-old had been diagnosed with terminal pancreatic cancer.

Daley had moved on to other things since *Star Wars*, including his epic *GammaLAW* novel series. His writing partner and later *Star Wars* novelist Jim Luceno took over that series, while Daley committed to the welcome task of finishing the *Star Wars* trilogy. It was clear there was a new audience for audio *Star Wars*. With the post-Timothy Zahn growth of the Expanded Universe and the advance of CDs and sales of audio books, Lucasfilm and NPR were sure they could recoup the costs of production by selling the complete trilogy to fans.

Audio sales company Highbridge Audio bought the rights to the first two audio dramas, and cassette and CD sales were so high it decided to complete the trilogy itself, selling the finished drama directly to NPR for broadcast and to fans on cassette and CD. Highbridge, however, did not normally produce full-cast audio dramas, focusing instead on single-actor readings of novel manuscripts. The challenges involved and the high cost seemed too much for the company. The only way to achieve the production to the standards of the previous entries was to limit the running time to around three hours, meaning a six-episode version of the movie rather than the expansive audio versions of the previous films. Daley completed his scripts by the end of 1995, but was unable to commit to revisions due to his failing health. Others, including John Whitman, who had scripted the audio books of the *Star Wars Dark Empire* graphic novel series for Time Warner Audio, worked on preparing the final scripts for production.

Daley was able to include some significant expanded scenes within the three hours he had available for *Return of the Jedi*. His scripts opened with additional Tatooine scenes that saw Luke back in the company of his old pals Fixer and Camie. The nascent Jedi Knight saves his friends from a 'Gunmetal' warbot battle droid, before preventing them from joining Jabba's gangster gang. Lucasfilm nixed these scenes, replacing them with Luke constructing his own lightsaber in Ben Kenobi's old Tatooine hovel. This scene had been shot but cut from the movie (and was finally seen, complete with effects, in the deleted scenes on the 2011 Blu-ray release).

Recording on the final *Star Wars* audio drama took place in February 1996, although neither Mark Hamill nor Billy Dee Williams returned. Instead, Luke was voiced by Joshua Fardon and Arye Gross (from then-popular TV sitcom *Ellen*) played Lando. Ed Begley Jr provided the vocals for the taciturn character of Boba Fett, while acclaimed actor Ed Asner (*The Mary Tyler Moore Show*, *Lou Grant*) vocalized Jabba the Hutt. BBC radio stalwart Martin Jarvis appeared, as did *The Simpsons* voice-actor Yeardley Smith (the voice of Lisa Simpson), with David Birney giving voice to the small but important role of Anakin Skywalker (as distinct from Brock Peters' Vader). C-3PO's Anthony Daniels was the only actor to appear in all three *Star Wars* films and all three radio dramas. The actor was particularly taken with Daley's interpretation of his character on audio as he had to function properly as a protocol droid, translating many of the sounds made by other characters into English (or 'basic' as it is known in *Star Wars*).

On 11 February 1996, mere hours after the cast completed recording on *Return to the Jedi*, Daley succumbed to his illness and died at home in Maryland. His handwritten final lines in the drama's script saw Luke Skywalker speak of the Jedi's return: 'Our fire is back in the universe . . . Let it burn high and bright, to be seen by friend and foe alike. The Jedi have returned.'

Since 1982, LucasArts has been a top computer games company behind a variety of games, from traditional adventure games to first-person shooters and puzzle-based amusements. Many of its games were based around movies, such as Jim Henson's *Labyrinth* (1986) and *Indiana Jones and the Last Crusade* (1989). The Monkey Island series, starting with *The Secret of Monkey Island* (1990), helped build the company's reputation as a groundbreaking videogame developer.

The first *Star Wars* videogames were licensed to Atari, with *The Empire Strikes Back* debuting on the Atari 2600 console in 1982. Further games, including *Death Star Battle* and *Jedi Arena*, followed the release of *Return of the Jedi* in 1983. In the 1990s, LucasArts took over control of the *Star Wars* videogames directly, launching the X-Wing series of flight simulator and combat games from 1992. A host of games followed, including the popular *Rebel Assault* (1993) and first-person shooter *Dark Forces* (1995).

The launch of the prequel trilogy of *Star Wars* movies from 1999 would see a flood of computer games released across a variety of platforms. The business continues to be hugely successful in the post-prequel world, launching games based around *The Clone Wars* animated TV series and the LEGO *Star Wars* range of construction kits.

The second publisher of *Star Wars* comics was established in 1986, around the time that Marvel concluded its nine year run of tie-in titles. Dark Horse Comics was founded by comic storeowner Mike Richardson with the declared aim of creating 'sequels to the movies we love'. The company started with licensed tie-ins to 1980s movie franchises *Aliens* and *Predator*. In 1991 Dark Horse secured the licence for *Star Wars* comic books, starting with *Dark Empire*. Originally in development at Marvel Comics, and written by Tom Veitch and illustrated by Cam Kennedy, *Dark Empire* was published between December 1991 and October 1992. Set six years after *Return of the Jedi*, the series explored several story threads, including a bounty offered on Leia for the death of Jabba the Hutt and the creation of a clone of Emperor Palpatine. Sticking to the *Star Wars* trilogy formula, that successful six-issue series was followed by two sequels, entitled *Dark Empire II* (1994–5) and *Empire's End* (1995).

Dark Horse launched several other *Star Wars* series in the 1990s, including *Tales of the Jedi* (1993–8) set during the height of the Old Republic 4,000 years before the *Star Wars* movies; *Jabba the Hutt* (1995–6); and *Droids* (1994–7), aimed at younger readers like the original Marvel strips. Other series would be based around the character of Boba Fett or drawn from *Star Wars* novel series such as *X-Wing* or *Jedi Academy*. The end of the decade saw the *Crimson Empire* series chronicle the exploits of the formidable red clad Imperial Guards seen briefly in *Return of the Jedi*.

Mike Richardson wanted to take the *Star Wars* comics in a more grown-up direction, given that the original *Star Wars* fans from 1977 had grown older themselves. According to Richardson, Dark Horse banned 'giant rabbits with ray guns', preferring to 'make [the comics] very cinematic and as close to the films as possible'. The company would also publish comic book adaptations of Timothy Zahn's *Thrawn Trilogy* of novels, to huge sales.

The 1999 release of *The Phantom Menace* (and the following films) gave Dark Horse a whole new set of characters and environments to explore. However, the company found the sheer amount of available material at the start of the twenty-first century across all media (plus a revitalized toy line from Hasbro, taking over from Kenner) hit it hard, and sales actually fell. According to Dark Horse editor Randy Stradley, 'Sales stayed at that lower level pretty much across the board until after the release of *Revenge of the Sith*. There was so much *Star Wars* available that fans were forced to make choices. After the third film, as the product wave subsided, our sales went back up . . .'

Dark Horse produced a plethora of new titles exploring the previously off-limits prequel era, while continuing to create new adventures for the cast of characters from the original trilogy. A series of titles, under the *Infinities* banner, explored a few 'what ifs?' of the *Star Wars* universe. Alternative retellings of the original movies explored the consequences of slight changes in circumstances, allowing these alternative histories to unfold free of Lucasfilm's usual continuity restrictions. The period after the final movie, *Revenge of the Sith*, saw Dark Horse continue to develop new and old stories, including a third entry in their *Crimson Empire* series, more explorations of the Old Republic era and various mini-series and ongoing comic books.

All George Lucas had hoped for in 1977 was a successful movie that might cover its cost of production and maybe even make a little profit. Instead, *Star Wars* became a phenomenon and launched a fan movement that endures to this day. The first *Star Wars* fans were kids in 1977, most aged between eight and twelve years old, Lucas's self-declared target audience. Alongside them were the older science-fiction fans, from their teens into their forties, for whom the last great science-fiction film had been *2001: A Space Odyssey* almost a decade earlier (although many held a secret affection for the *Planet of the Apes* series). *Star Wars* was a science-fiction film that was both serious in its intention and fun in its execution, using cutting-edge special effects to show what many science-fiction fans could only previously have imagined. The acceptance of *Star Wars* by the already established, well-connected science-fiction fan community allowed the new 'franchise' to rise quickly.

However, it was those fans that were kids in the late 1970s that would go on to form the basis of *Star Wars'* enduring fandom. They had been too young to see *Star Trek* on first transmission in the United States in the late 1960s, but could well have caught it in the endless reruns of the 1970s. Certainly in Britain, *Star Wars* caught up many fans of the BBC's mid-1970s screenings of *Star Trek* and those who had followed the various incarnations of *Doctor Who* on Saturday nights since 1963. *Star Wars* fans moved through their teen years with the original trilogy. Those who were ten-years-old in 1977 were hitting sixteen in 1983 when *Return of the Jedi* was released. They had stuck with the trilogy through the dark middle chapter of *The Empire Strikes Back*, but many now older fans were dismayed by what they saw as the 'kiddie' element of the Ewoks in the third – and at the time final – movie. However, ten-year-olds coming to *Return of the Jedi* for the first time didn't react the same way, enjoying the antics of the Ewoks that their older brothers disparaged.

Lucasfilm made an early attempt to organize *Star Wars* fandom with the establishment of The Star Wars Fan Club and its newsletter, *Bantha Tracks*, in 1978. The newsletter, edited by Lucasfilm's first Director of Fan Relations Craig Miller, ran until 1987, by which time the *Star Wars* juggernaut had virtually come to a halt in the wake of the last movie. *Bantha Tracks* was replaced by the *Lucasfilm Fan Club Magazine* in 1987 (covering other Lucasfilm projects such as the Indiana Jones movies and *Willow*, as well as *Star Wars*), which ran for twenty-two issues before being replaced by the widely available newsstand magazine *Star Wars Insider* in 1994 (which continues today having endured the prequel era).

Many *Star Wars* fans would prove to be very creative and rapidly filled the gap left by the absence of new *Star Wars* movies or any new *Star Wars* adventures in the 1980s beyond the child-focused *Ewoks* TV movies and *Ewoks* and *Droids* TV cartoons (see Chapter 10). Fan fiction boomed, published by aspiring writers in fanzines distributed through the mail to local fan groups or traded for other fanzines. The first fan-written *Star*

Wars story (a tradition established in the late 1960s by *Star Trek* fans) appeared in the fanzine *Warped Space #28* in 1977, primarily a *Star Trek* fanzine. By 1978, Sharon Emily had written the first novel-length piece of fan fiction, entitled *Dark Interlude*, while the first dedicated *Star Wars* fanzine, *Empire Star*, appeared from Australia. That same year saw a boom in *Star Wars* dedicated fanzines, including *Falcon's Flight*, *Falcon's Lair*, *Moonbeam* and the *Mos Eisley Tribune*, many of which featured fan fiction. *Skywalker* was the first *Star Wars* only fan fiction fanzine, launched in 1978 and lasting for six issues.

The arrival of *The Empire Strikes Back* was a catalyst for the growth of *Star Wars* fandom. Science-fiction movie and TV magazine *Starlog* had pre-empted one of the big revelations of the movie by publishing a rumour that Darth Vader was, in fact, Luke Skywalker's father in a February 1980 issue. The release of the film did little to dampen fan speculation on the subject, with many arguing that Vader may have been lying, while others speculated that the 'other' Force-sensitive figure spoken about by Yoda must be Han Solo (*Return of the Jedi* revealed Vader's relationship to Luke to be true and Luke's sister, Leia, to be the 'other' that Yoda mentioned). This early tendency by fandom to appropriate the story for themselves and reshape it according to their own imaginations would store up trouble for the future when Lucas returned to *Star Wars* with the prequel trilogy, disappointing many long-term fans who had their own version of Vader's iconic genesis in their imaginations.

The second movie also saw Lucasfilm become more concerned about fan appropriation of their 'intellectual property'. In August 1980 Maureen Garrett, director of the Official Star Wars Fan Club, sent several fanzine editors an official letter asserting Lucasfilm Ltd's ownership of the *Star Wars* characters and settings, and warning of possible litigation, especially if fan publications contained 'pornography'. This was a reference to the increasing tendency of fan writers to put the *Star Wars* characters into sexual scenes, often homosexual in nature (known as 'slash fiction', a term developed to cover homosexual *Star Trek* stories concerning a Kirk/Spock relationship and drawn from the 'slash' between their names). Irate fans responded by publishing an 'adult' fanzine called *Organia* in 1982. Described as an 'adult fanzine of ideas', *Organia* featured heterosexual stories and art, but was criticized by some fans for going against Lucasfilm's warnings. The creation of 'original' *Star Wars* material by fans was taken one step further in 1983 when John Flynn submitted 'Fall of the Republic' as a 'fan script' for the third *Star Wars* movie. Many fans who came across the script, prior to the release of *Return of the Jedi*, were convinced it was the real thing.

Participation in fandom and the creation of material became much easier in the mid-1980s with the arrival of affordable home computers and the implementation of early computer bulletin board systems (a precursor of internet newsgroup and web pages or blogs). A new age of fan communication dawned, in which isolated individuals or small local groups could communicate with a much larger fandom worldwide. By the 1990s, the newsgroup rec.arts.sf.starwars was a popular host for fan fiction, while 'A Certain Point of View' (between 1996 and 1998) became established as a dedicated fan-fiction review site. By 1997 and the arrival of the *Star Wars Special Editions* in cinemas, Lucasfilm had become much more reconciled to the existence of fan fiction (six years after establishing its own line of official tie-in fiction). In *Wired* in October 1997, Lucasfilm's then director of internet development, Marc Hedlund, confirmed that the company would 'tolerate' the publishing of fan fiction as long as it was a not-for-profit activity or commercial gain and that it 'did not sully' the family image of the *Star Wars* characters. It was a welcome – if late – development, although Lucasfilm would face a much more challenging time with the internet during the *Star Wars* prequel era of the late 1990s and early 2000s.

Others would pursue their fandom through their love of drawing and painting, creating *Star Wars*-inspired artwork (some would later go on to become officially recognized Lucasfilm artists). Others used the newly available video equipment (most often used in the 1980s to capture family vacations) to make backyard movies with their friends, some more professionally put together than others. The 'fan film' phenomenon, driven by cheap video equipment and the development of digital special effects and editing packages, was officially recognized by Lucasfilm with their Fan Film Awards. From 2002 onwards, Lucasfilm allowed the use of their intellectual property in non-profit, fan-created short films, as long as the 'family friendly' stricture was observed. From spoofs and comedy skits, to serious, earnest dramas and animated versions of the saga, fan films flourished with this official recognition, making 'stars' of some of their creators within *Star Wars* fandom.

Other fans would go beyond simply collecting Kenner/ Hasbro's *Star Wars* action figures and would build life-size stormtrooper armour or character costumes for them and their friends to wear (sowing the seeds of the later 501st Legion, a worldwide Cosplay fan group that raises money for charity). All this activity proved one thing to Lucasfilm: there was still an audience for new *Star Wars* material even through the 1980s when they were not producing anything of any significance. *Star Wars* fandom was now well-established and here to stay.

While the ongoing series of novels and comic books of the 1980s and 1990s had fed fans appetites for new *Star Wars* stories, their biggest desire was always for a new trilogy of films. From the first rumours in 1993 that George Lucas would be returning to *Star Wars*, it looked like fans' hopes were finally to be fulfilled and a sense of excited anticipation swept *Star Wars* fandom.

Chapter 10

The Road to the Prequels

When I did [Star Wars], we were really bumping up against the ceiling of technology. I was able to push the limits of the medium and the cinematic form just a tiny bit. What I really wanted to do was much grander, but I could only do so much with the technology I had. I've always been pushing that technology.

George Lucas

The first film project to get George Lucas's attention following the completion of the second Indiana Jones movie, *Indiana Jones and the Temple of Doom* (1984), was an unexpected return to the *Star Wars* universe, though not perhaps in the way that fans wanted. In 1984 Lucas had stepped back from detailed involvement in Lucasfilm, beginning a divorce from all things *Star Wars* that would last over a decade. 'I've put up with *Star Wars* taking over,' said the frustrated filmmaker, 'pushing itself into first position, for too long.' Now he had a family to which he wanted to devote time, with two adopted daughters – Amanda and Katie – and an adopted son, Jett (named after James Dean's character, Jett Rink, from *Giant*, 1956).

It was to please his young children that Lucas gave the go-ahead to two made-for-TV movies featuring the Ewoks, the Empire-thwarting 'teddy bears' of *Return of the Jedi*. His original plan was for a simple one-hour special, but this rapidly grew into a more elaborate project. As with CBS in 1978 and the ill-fated *Star Wars Holiday Special*, ABC commissioned *Caravan of*

Courage: An Ewok Adventure for their Sunday Night Movie spot for the Thanksgiving holiday season in 1984. Lucas developed the storyline, inspired by the fairy-tale Hansel and Gretel and a dash of Edgar Rice Burroughs's *Tarzan of the Apes*, but left it to Bob Carrau to write the teleplay (he later made a career of writing for various animated TV series including *Tiny Toon Adventures*, *Manic Mansion* and *Dragon Tales*, as well as various *Star Wars* tie-in books for kids).

Lucas wanted to avoid the mistakes that had been made with the *Holiday Special*, so Lucasfilm itself retained full control of the project and brought in Bay Area filmmaker John Korty (who had made the Lucas-produced animation *Twice Upon a Time*) to direct. Aimed at children, the simple story sees a young brother and sister (Eric Walker and Aubree Miller) stranded on Endor (home of the Ewoks) when the family spaceship crashes and their parents head off in search of help. The pair – Mace (a name from Lucas's earliest *Star Wars* drafts later used for Samuel L. Jackson's Jedi character in the prequels) and Cindel Towani – fall in with the Ewoks, led by Wicket (Warwick Davis reprising his role). Lacking the scope or epic feel of the big-screen films, this low-budget production (filmed simply as 'The Ewok Adventure') was released in cinemas across Europe. Simply told, with the help of folksy narrator Burl Ives, the film was shot in the Northern California redwoods. Industrial Light and Magic art director and concept artist Joe Johnston helped keep the *Star Wars* feeling through his production design, while ILM contributed stop-motion animation for various creatures.

Premiered on 25 November 1984, *Caravan of Courage* was successful enough for ABC immediately to request a follow-up for the following year. *Ewoks: The Battle for Endor* (shot under the title 'Ewoks II') was again based on a story developed by Lucas. This instalment featured an injection of traditional fantasy elements into the *Star Wars* universe, partly due to Lucas working on the screenplay for *Willow* at the same time. Although many of the cast from *Caravan of Courage* returned, all but Aubree Miller's Cindel were (in a bizarre storytelling decision, given the young target audience) killed off near the beginning when King Terak (Carel Struycken, Lurch in the 1991 film *The Addams Family*) stages a raid on the Ewok village. Escaping with Wicket, Cindel encounters friendly hermit Noa (Wilfred Brimley) and is captured by wicked witch Charal (Siân Phillips), before finally leaving Endor.

The second Ewoks TV movie was scripted and directed by brothers Jim and Ken Wheat and was shot in Marin County during the summer of 1985. As before, according to Ken Wheat, Lucas regarded the project as a gift for his own children. 'Lucas guided the creation of the story over the course of two four-hour sessions we had with him,' Wheat told *EON* magazine. 'He'd just watched *Heidi* with his daughter the weekend before, and the story idea he pushed was having the little girl from the first Ewok TV movie become an orphan who ends up living with a grumpy old hermit in the woods. We'd been thinking about the adventure films we'd liked as kids, like *Swiss Family Robinson* and *The Seventh Voyage of Sinbad*, so we suggested having space marauders, which was fine with George – as long as they were seven feet tall'. Screened on ABC TV on 24 November 1985, audience figures were 30 per cent less than the first TV movie, but nonetheless there were discussions about another – dubbed 'Ewoks III' – but the third TV movie was never made.

The two Ewok movies, and the concept of producing *Star Wars* TV material aimed at children, led to two short-lived animated TV series on ABC. *Star Wars: Ewoks* and *Star Wars: Droids* (often screened together as *The Ewoks and Droids Adventure Hour*) ran between 1985 and 1986. For these series, Lucas turned to Nelvana Studios, the Canadian animation house that had produced the Boba Fett cartoon sequence for the *Holiday Special*. The only characters from the movies available to the animators were Wicket and the Ewoks and the two droids, C-3PO and R2-D2. While the former were restricted to adventures on Endor, the nomadic droids were free to wander the *Star Wars* universe, moving from master to master.

With a bizarre theme tune performed by Stewart Copeland of the Police, the *Droids* series was probably the most interesting to fans. Set prior to the first movie, the thirteen episodes filled in much of the back-story of the droids. Episodes saw C-3PO and R2-D2 encounter space pirates, gangsters, agents of the Empire and even *The Empire Strikes Back*'s Boba Fett and droid bounty hunter IG-88. Anthony Daniels returned to voice C-3PO, with several episodes written by sound specialist Ben Burtt. Aspects of the series would turn up in the later prequel movies, such as Tatooine's Boonta race, the planet of Bogden (where Jango Fett was recruited by Darth Tyranus, according to Episode II), and in Episode III Droid General Grievous is seen to ride a 'wheel bike' similar to one seen in the series.

Acclaimed *Batman: The Animated Series* writer Paul Dini got his start working on the *Ewoks* and *Droids* shows. 'It was better animated than most of the stuff on air at the time,' recalled Dini in *Star Wars Insider*. Each episode cost around $500,000 and featured between 8,000 and 10,000 animation cells, a high number for 1980s Saturday morning cartoons that then employed so called 'limited animation' to cut costs. A one-off forty-eight-minute *Droids* special, called *The Great Heep* and aired in June 1986, saw C-3PO and R2-D2 confront a creature constructed from the remains of destroyed droids (voiced by blues singer Long John Baldry). However, this wasn't enough to save the show. Only the *Ewoks* made it through to a second season of half-hour adventures in a simplified format that increased the cuteness factor in an attempt to attract more young girls. By December 1986, the party was over for both the *Ewoks* and the *Droids*.

Following the conclusion of *Return of the Jedi*, George Lucas wanted to get away from *Star Wars* altogether and move Lucasfilm in new directions. Things got off to a disastrous start with 1986's *Howard the Duck* (or *Howard: A New Breed of Hero* as it was optimistically retitled outside the United States). Based on the Steve Gerber satirical Marvel comic that began in 1976 (much admired by Lucas), the movie – written by Lucas's old USC classmates Willard Huyck and Gloria Katz and directed by Huyck – was intended as a rival to Columbia's *Ghostbusters* (1985). Produced through Universal, the studio required Lucas to act as a financial guarantor, securing him a producer credit (although he actually had little direct involvement). Released in 1986, the film was a magnet for criticism, mainly surrounding the use of actor Ed Gale (among others) in a duck suit to play Howard, rather than producing an animated movie. Despite the presence of Tim Robbins, Lea Thompson and Jeffrey Jones and sterling work by ILM attempting to make a talking duck believable, *Howard the Duck* was a flop, taking just $16 million at the US box office against a production budget of $36 million.

For his part, Lucas was more invested in *Willow* (1988), providing the story for this family-focused fantasy adventure directed by Ron Howard (who had featured in *American Graffiti* before going on to develop a career as a director following Disney mermaid movie *Splash*, 1984). Ewok actor Warwick Davis, by then eighteen years old, starred as Willow, a would-be sorcerer who embarks on a series of adventures while trying to protect a human baby from the evil witch Bavmorda (Davis would go on to star in the *Leprechaun* and *Harry Potter* movies). The storyline for *Willow* had been long in development by Lucas and he had mentioned the project to the then eleven-year-old Davis during *Return of the Jedi* in 1981, believing him ideal to play the title character. Released in May 1988, the $34 million movie also underperformed at the US box office, only bringing in $27 million and attracting a series of negative reviews (although none as bad as those for *Howard the Duck*). *Willow* would later find more appreciative audiences on home video.

After these two relative failures, Lucasfilm needed a post-*Star Wars* hit. That came in the form of the third Indiana Jones movie, *Indiana Jones and the Last Crusade* (1989), directed by Steven Spielberg. As with the previous two movies, Lucas generated the storyline but was a much more hands-on producer, and is widely regarded as the co-author of the Indiana Jones films alongside Spielberg. 'George is in charge of breaking the stories. He's done it on [the Indy] movies. Whether I like the stories or not, George has broken all the stories. I'm going to shoot the movie the way George envisaged it,' Spielberg told *Empire* magazine. 'I'll add my own touches, I'll bring my own cast in, I'll shoot the way I want to shoot it, but I will always defer to George as the storyteller of the Indy series. I will never fight him on that.'

From the opening sequence of River Phoenix as young Indiana Jones through the comic double act of father and son adventurers (Sean Connery, Harrison Ford), *Indiana Jones and the Last Crusade* was a fitting conclusion to this trilogy centring on a hunt for the holy grail of biblical legend. The film's opening week US box office take of almost $47 million eclipsed the total takes of the previous two most recent Lucasfilm productions. The movie would go on to take a total of $474 million worldwide, putting it more on a par with the *Star Wars* movies. A belated fourth Indiana Jones adventure, *Indiana Jones and the Kingdom of the Crystal Skull*, followed in 2008, to a mixed reception.

The opening sequence of *The Last Crusade* inspired the spin-off TV series *The Young Indiana Jones Chronicles* that would serve multiple functions. Not only was the show intended as an educational history series, putting young Indy in the middle of historic events or in contact with historical figures, but it was also to be a test-bed for the technologies and production processes that would make the *Star Wars* prequel films possible and affordable for Lucasfilm. The series also served to gather many of the individuals who would work on the prequel films, including producer Rick McCallum, production designer Gavin Bocquet and cinematographer David Tattersall.

Four actors played Indiana Jones across the various iterations of the series. Sean Patrick Flanery featured in the bulk of the episodes as Indy in his late teen years, while Corey Carrier played him as a younger child. George Hall played the ninety-three-year-old Indy featured in the bookends to many episodes, while Harrison Ford returned to the role for a single episode's bookends (in 'Young Indiana Jones and the Mystery of the Blues'). The series ran between 1992 and 1996, with twenty-four regular episodes and four TV movies rounding out the run.

Lucas was heavily involved in the project, creating an exhaustive timeline for Indy's life (which spanned almost the entire twentieth century) from 1905 up to the already produced movie trilogy, with enough material for up to seventy episodes. Over thirty of these story ideas were produced by the end of the show (one not made evolved into *Indiana Jones and the Kingdom of the Crystal Skulls*, 2008).

'Young Indy was a testing bed to learn new ways of making films,' said McCallum. 'It had to do with the way we structured it. We would do seventeen episodes, but we treated it as one film – a film made all over the world, as inexpensively as possible, but with the highest quality. [We blurred] the line between production and post-production, so we could go back into production after the initial shoot, after we'd had a chance to see how the story was evolving. It meant shooting with a crew of thirty people, rather than the standard crew of sixty to one hundred. It meant building sets months beforehand and letting them stand so we could return to them as necessary – which meant shooting in places other than traditional studios. Finally, it meant using a great deal of digital technology to provide sets and landscapes, which saved a fortune in construction and production travel costs. We started to set the boundaries of non-linear filmmaking. We were learning and figuring out how we could apply this new way of making films to Episode I.'

Across the run, *The Young Indiana Jones Chronicles* won 10 Emmy Awards, including for actor Corey Carrier and cinematographer David Tattersall. In 1994, the series scored a Golden Globe for Best TV Series: Drama. More importantly, the innovative techniques developed for that show would be pivotal in making the new *Star Wars* movies possible.

There was a five year gap between *Indiana Jones and the Last Crusade* and Lucas's return to filmmaking with his long-in-gestation project, *Radioland Murders*, in 1994 (an obligation Lucas owed Universal from the *American Graffiti* contract). Once again, Lucas had developed the story and produced the movie, leaving the direction to British comic actor and director Mel Smith (*The Tall Guy*, 1989). Set behind the scenes of radio production in the 1930s, this project – like *The Young Indiana Jones Chronicles* TV series before it – was a testing ground for the technology Lucas would require to produce a new trilogy of *Star Wars* movies. The lively film was a critical and commercial failure, costing $15 million to produce but taking only a paltry $1.3 million at the US box office. However, the experiment in digital filmmaking, involving the use of computers as a basic movie-making tool, more than paid off for Lucas. Speaking to *American Cinematographer* Lucas presciently declared: 'Soon, *Radioland Murders*' fix-it shots and digital set extensions and enhancements will be so commonplace we will not regard them as special effects.'

With the digital tools needed for his future movies in development, Lucas also wanted to be sure his company was still capable of all the ancillary activity that the next *Star Wars* movies would require.

Lucasfilm's 1996 *Shadows of the Empire* started life as a novel filling in the events between *The Empire Strikes Back* and *Return of the Jedi*. However, the ambitious multi-media project grew to encompass not only a novel, but also comic books, a videogame, trading cards, action figures and even a soundtrack album. In preparation for the *Special Editions* of the original *Star Wars* trilogy and the prequel trilogy, Lucasfilm essentially used *Shadows of the Empire* to explore all the commercial possibilities of a movie event without actually producing the film itself.

Central to the project was the novel by Steve Perry, bridging the narrative gap between the second and third films. This was an area that no tie-in novel had been allowed to tackle before.

The storyline was developed further in a comic book from Dark Horse (written by John Wagner and illustrated by Kilian Plunkett) and was playable as a videogame on the Nintendo 64 games console or on a PC. Around twenty-five licensees would produce tie-in material.

'There was some nervousness,' admitted Perry of the project. 'You want to be sure to get it right. I also knew going in, I wasn't going to please everybody. I knew I was going to get flak [from fans] no matter what I wrote, so I just did the best I could and hoped most of the fans would approve.'

The novel introduced a major new villain to the *Star Wars* universe. Prince Xizor, a humanoid criminal gang lord, plans to replace Darth Vader at the side of Emperor Palpatine. Featuring Luke's growth as a Jedi, Leia's search for Boba Fett and Han Solo (frozen in carbonite at the end of *The Empire Strikes Back*) and Vader's hunt for his lost son, the novel also introduced a Han Solo-replacement character in the form of space pirate Dash Rendar.

While the novel told the main story (complete in itself), it was supplemented with the comic book's account of Boba Fett's attempts to hang on to the frozen form of Solo (and also featuring some of the other bounty-hunters seen in the second movie), while the videogame allowed players to control Dash Rendar in events that weaved in and out of the main storyline. The videogame started during the battle of Hoth and moved on through encounters with the bounty-hunters, Luke Skywalker and Lando Calrissian. The criminal underworld explored in this 'movie campaign without a movie' (as Lucasfilm termed it) was also proposed as the potential setting of the long-in-development live action *Star Wars* TV series. The event was even launched with a trailer using footage from *The Empire Strikes Back*, *Return of the Jedi* and a voice-over pitching the story of *Shadows of the Empire*. Shortly after releasing the trailer, however, Lucasfilm withdrew it, fearing that mainstream audiences might mistakenly believe it was for a brand new *Star Wars* movie.

Perhaps the most unusual element of the *Shadows of the*

Empire project was the soundtrack CD. It's rare for books to come with soundtracks (although later *Star Wars* author Joe Schreiber accompanied his books *Death Troopers* and *Red Harvest* with suggested playlists). Performed by the Royal Scottish National Orchestra, the fifty-one-minute soundtrack included a few distinctive cues from the movies (such as the main theme, the Imperial March and others), but composer Joel McNeely was allowed to come up with his own thematic accompaniment to the novel, while under instruction to stay true to the work of John Williams. Freed from composing to images, McNeely – who had been recommended by Williams – was able to produce a different kind of soundtrack. 'Unlike with film music,' he noted, 'I have been allowed to let my imagination run free with the images, characters and events from this story. I have also had the luxury to loiter as long as I like with a character or scene. Every passage represents some person, place or event in this story.'

At one stage Lucas said he could have seen himself making a film of *Shadows of the Empire* back in the 1980s if he'd had the available time. All the aspects of the ambitious project were chronicled in Mark Cotta Vaz's book *The Secrets of Star Wars: Shadows of the Empire.* The film that never was certainly generated a whole lot of buzz in *Star Wars* fandom and beyond, but it was only a warm up for the real thing: *The Phantom Menace.*

From the very beginning, the filmmaking of George Lucas had involved pushing the available technology to its limits. Eventually, by inventing entirely new technologies, he changed the way movies were made altogether.

Finding special effects technology was not adequate to his needs in the mid-1970s, Lucas established Industrial Light and Magic to develop the cameras, computer-control systems and techniques he needed to put his vision on screen. From then, ILM continued to grow, developing new technologies and new filmmaking techniques through the next two films of the growing *Star Wars* saga.

After the conclusion of that trilogy in 1983, the company continued to be at the forefront of the digital revolution in special effects and filmmaking. Lucas had already opened up his facility to provide special effects for other filmmakers. Several significant milestones in modern filmmaking were achieved by ILM, including the first completely computer-generated sequence (the Genesis planet scene in *Star Trek II: The Wrath of Khan*, 1982), the first fully computer-generated character (the 'stained glass' man in *Young Sherlock Holmes*, 1985), the first 'morphing' sequence in which one object or person seamlessly transformed into another without any cuts or cross fades (in *Willow*, 1988), the first computer-generated 3D character (the 'pseudopod' tentacle in James Cameron's *The Abyss*, 1989) and the first partially computer-generated main character (the T-1000 in *Terminator 2*, 1991).

The company continued to innovate, pioneering digital filmmaking technology with the creation of photorealistic dinosaurs in Steven Spielberg's *Jurassic Park* (1993), and providing photorealistic hair and fur for *Jumanji* (1995). It was these last two developments, especially the dinosaurs, that convinced Lucas that technology had now developed enough for him seriously to consider returning to making *Star Wars* movies in an affordable way and on his own terms.

ILM was not the only company within Lucasfilm that was driving forward filmmaking technology from the 1980s. A major development in digital filmmaking was Lucasfilm's EditDroid, a computerized non-linear editing system that pioneered the concept of digital editing for movies. Although not a commercial success, the concept provided the impetus for the development of the AVID system and the consumer level Final Cut Pro software.

The Lucasfilm in-house computer graphics department was sold off in 1986 to Apple Computer's Steve Jobs, who reshaped it into Pixar, which drove the computer-generated animated movie field with 1995's *Toy Story*. Skywalker Sound, based at Skywalker Ranch, began life as Sprocket Systems in 1975 but developed into a cutting-edge facility for sound design (always important to Lucas), editing, mixing and creating sound effects, servicing virtually all of Hollywood's top moviemakers.

As the twentieth anniversary of 1977's *Star Wars* approached, George Lucas saw the perfect opportunity to test much of the digital technology he had developed over the past twenty years in a proper filmmaking situation. Steven Spielberg had pioneered the vogue for 'special editions' of movies with his revised *Close Encounters of the Third Kind*. Re-cut and with added footage (both originally deleted scenes and newly shot), the movie was re-released in 1980. Lucas reckoned he could do the same with his most famous films.

The release of the *Star Wars Special Editions* to cinemas in 1997 was a huge event. As originally planned, the movies would be returned to cinemas one each month between January and March. However, *Return of the Jedi* was delayed by a further week due to continued box office demand for the second movie. The re-release had several purposes: it allowed Lucas to test the digital technology he would use on the prequel films, it raised additional revenue for Lucasfilm to help fund the prequels, and it renewed awareness of *Star Wars* for older audiences and prepared younger audiences for the 1999 release of *Star Wars: Episode I – The Phantom Menace*.

Speaking at the press conference for the release of Episode I on DVD, producer Rick McCallum explained Lucas's thinking behind the creation of the *Special Editions*. 'One of the great things about doing the *Special Editions* was we were able to go back and do the original *Star Wars: A New Hope* exactly the way George wanted it. The way he had written it. Whether people liked it, it didn't matter; it was his movie and he couldn't make it [the way he wanted] when he first made it because there were so many compromises he had to go through.'

Fans blasted Lucas for making changes to the *Special Editions*, but these versions were far from the first alterations made to the films. Lucas had constantly tampered with his own movies across the years, seeing each re-release (in whatever medium) as a chance to 'fix' things he saw wrong with them. The first *Star*

Wars film was a constant source of frustration due to the compromises forced upon Lucas thanks to a lack of funds, a lack of time and the inadequacies of the then available technology to match his vision. Fans, however, had become used to the films as they had been through twenty years of repeated viewings in cinemas, on television and on videotape.

The first alterations Lucas made came within hours of the release of the film in 1977. That evening, after dinner with his wife Marcia in Hamburger Hamlet, Lucas had returned to the editing suite and dragged Mark Hamill in to re-loop a line of dialogue for the movie's mono sound mix. Hamill had driven past the Avco cinema in Westwood and witnessed the massive lines as audiences waited to see the movie. Lucas greeted him with 'Hi kid, you famous yet?'

The subtitle to the first film was only added for the 1981 re-release. Until then it had just been *Star Wars*, as indicated at the head of the opening text crawl. With Lucas now making the further instalments that had not been guaranteed until the success of the first movie, he wanted to emphasize the serial nature of his saga by giving each movie an individual episode number and title. The first film became *Star Wars: Episode IV – A New Hope*, with each subsequent instalment following a similar pattern. Other changes would be made, mostly minor, to each of the movies through the years but usually so subtly that few fans even noticed.

Early home video releases, such as on VHS and Laserdisc, saw each of the movies' soundtracks regularly overhauled, supervised by Ben Burtt, among others. The years 1985 and 1993 saw alterations to the soundtrack of *Star Wars*, but it was the advent of the 1997 *Special Edition* theatrical re-releases that really put the issue of Lucas changing his movies into the public discourse. Lucas had a long-held dislike of movies being changed by others, and had spoken out in a Congressional hearing regarding the issue of colourizing black-and-white movies in the 1980s. 'People who alter or destroy works of art for profit or as an exercise of power are barbarians, and if the laws of the

United States continue to condone this behaviour, history will surely classify us as a barbaric society,' he said in 1988. 'These current defacements are just the beginning. Today, engineers with their computers can add colour to black-and-white movies, change the soundtrack, speed up the pace, and add or subtract material to the philosophical tastes of the copyright holder. Tomorrow, more advanced technology will be able to replace actors with "fresher faces," or alter dialogue and change the movement of the actor's lips to match.'

Ironically, Lucas himself would go on to do all of that, and so much more, to the *Star Wars* movies across various re-releases. The DVD versions of the original trilogy and of the prequel trilogy are not the same movies as seen in cinemas: they have all been changed in ways large and small (Lucas later grudgingly released the raw, unrestored theatrical versions of the original trilogy as extras on the re-released DVDs). The difference between this activity and the complaint Lucas made in 1988 is that the *Star Wars* movies are his saga – no matter what the fans might believe.

Lucas invested in renewing the movies that had made his fortune, knowing that future DVD releases as well as cinema box office would be profitable. Almost $10 million was spent sprucing up *Star Wars: Episode IV – A New Hope* (more than the film had originally cost to make in 1977). Around $3 million of that went on once again refreshing the movie's soundtrack. The other two movies were considerably cheaper to revamp at around $2.5 million each. Despite spending $15 million on reworking the movies and preparing them for presentation in modern cinema environments, the box office appeal of the *Special Editions* was hard to predict – Lucasfilm had no idea whether any audience beyond the core fans would turn out to see the films, hence the decision to have them only on release for one month each (that 'event' programming also helped to draw in large audiences in a concentrated period).

The company needn't have worried. The *Star Wars Special Edition* enjoyed a $35.9 million opening weekend (the biggest

January opening for any movie, until the release of *Cloverfield* in 2008), going on to gross $138.2 million across the United States. The next two films brought in less revenue, but still reached amazing numbers for releases of movies between fifteen and twenty years old. The *Empire Strikes Back Special Edition* had an opening weekend of $21.9 million, culminating in a US total of $67.6 million, while the *Return of the Jedi Special Edition* took $16.3 million on its opening weekend, with a final US total of $45.5 million. That $15 million expenditure on reconstructing the movies (plus print, distribution and promotions costs, of course) brought in a total of $251.3 million in US domestic box office, with a further $219.6 million earned in international markets (outside the US *Star Wars* took $118.6 million, *The Empire Strikes Back*, $57.2 million and *Return of the Jedi*, $43.8 million). The entire project brought Lucasfilm a $470.9 million return on its investment (although Fox retained a percentage of the gross for redistributing the movies). Given that the combined production budget for all three *Star Wars* prequel movies was $348 million, the *Special Edition* releases more than paid for the creation of the entire second trilogy of movies. The scene was set for the return of *Star Wars*.

Chapter 11

Digital Menace

I didn't want to write one of these movies unless I had the technology available to really tell the kind of story I was interested in telling. I wanted to be able to explore the world I'd created to its fullest potential, so I waited until I had the technological means to do that.

George Lucas

For George Lucas and fans worldwide, *Star Wars* had never really gone away. For the wider public, however, the release of *Return of the Jedi* had ended the *Star Wars* story: it had been impressively epic, huge fun and widely influential, but it was over. Dale Pollock's semi-authorized biography of Lucas was republished in 1990 with a new introduction that concluded that the *Star Wars* creator's 'biggest success [was] now behind him'.

The release of Steven Spielberg's *Jurassic Park* in June 1993 finally convinced Lucas the time was right to revive *Star Wars*. The success of the Timothy Zahn novels and the *Star Wars* Expanded Universe had proven to him that an audience for new *Star Wars* still existed. A new generation was discovering the original films through television and on video. The theatrical re-release of the *Special Editions* confirmed it: there was still a hunger for *Star Wars*.

Lucas had a story to tell: the material had been there since 1976, albeit in a rough form. The big question was whether filmmaking technology had developed enough to allow him to tell those stories in an economical way, as he would be funding them himself. Each of the original trilogy movies had been a struggle, but *The Empire Strikes Back* had been a huge personal financial risk. Now he was thinking of doing it all again, but he had to know he could both achieve his vision on screen and afford to do so.

Spielberg's *Jurassic Park* showed that digital filmmaking tools (many developed by ILM) had progressed to the extent that photoreal visions could be shown on screen, interacting with humans. The implications were immediately obvious. Additionally, through working on *The Young Indiana Jones Chronicles* with Rick McCallum, Lucas felt he had found his new Gary Kurtz or Howard Kazanjian – a man who could marshal the resources and command the troops to get such a complicated production underway.

Lucas first sat down seriously to begin work on crafting the first *Star Wars* prequel in November 1994. 'The story for the three new films was the back story of the other films,' said Lucas. '[It] was sketched out in rudimentary fashion when I wrote the first trilogy. There were certain things I knew even then, [such as] Anakin Skywalker grew up on a small planet, had special skills, and was found by the Jedi. A lot of the story points were there. The actual scenes and many of the characters were not.'

Lucas still saw writing as a chore and found it intensely difficult. He was determined, however, not to hand over the creation of his worlds to someone else. That might come later for the sequels, but he felt he needed to lay down the ground rules for these new *Star Wars* films himself. Despite having the original outlines to work from, a lot of new material was needed. Lucas wasn't the same man who had originally drafted this material. He would be filtering his original vision through the more experienced eye of a mature filmmaker who had built an empire of his own.

Technology had changed here, too. Writing was now largely done using computers. Lucas, however, stuck with his tried and tested method of writing his screenplays longhand in pencil on yellow, lined notepads, with a secretary to type them up. Much of what he had put down on those sheets of paper would dictate how the story would unfold across a brand new trilogy. It was important to take the time to get it right at this stage when all that was involved was a man and his imagination, before committing to spending millions of dollars and co-opting the labour of thousands.

The *Star Wars* prequels were a complicated storytelling puzzle. Not only had Lucas to tell the back-story of major characters from the original films – mainly Darth Vader, the Emperor and Obi-Wan Kenobi – he had to ensure that everything tied up too. He also had an ambition to work in pre-echoes of events in the existing *Star Wars* movies. Lucas was a huge history buff, and he had noticed how events were often repeated or replayed in slightly different ways by different generations. He wanted to bring this to *Star Wars* by featuring characters, situations and events that viewers might recognize from the first trilogy. His overall ambition, though, was to transpose the fall of a Republic – as in Rome, or the United States in the 1970s (with the fall of Nixon's presidency) – to his galaxy far, far away. Behind the space combat and all-out action would be the rise of the evil Empire that had dominated the original trilogy.

Fans had long been teased with an origin story for Darth Vader that had involved a final conflict with Obi-Wan Kenobi. A battle between the pair had seen Anakin Skywalker fall into a lava pit, being burned horribly and then reborn as 'more machine than man'. The specifics of these events had never been revealed. Most diehard fans of *Star Wars* were expecting the prequel films to fill in those blanks. Instead, Lucas decided to start with the adventures of a nine-year-old boy.

Lucas knew that selling his planned depiction of the most evil man in the galaxy as a nine-year-old would be difficult. He considered making the character older, maybe nearer to twelve. That would simplify a lot of things that Lucas could see as problems for a nine-year-old, such as triumphing in the Podrace and flying an unfamiliar starfighter. However, clear in his mind was the need to depict the inciting trauma that would set the young Anakin Skywalker on the road to becoming Darth Vader. The forced separation of Anakin from his mother would be all the more traumatic for a younger boy, so Lucas stuck with his original ideas, even while aware of the problems he was creating for himself – and the fans.

The main through-line for the film was to be the rise of Palpatine from Senator to Chancellor of the Republic, his first step to becoming galactic Emperor. Drawing on history, Lucas was riffing on the rise of Hitler, the Nazi party and the Third Reich in 1930s Germany. Around this Lucas dropped in several other connected plots. The taxation of trade routes (another important element of American history, but something much mocked when introduced to *Star Wars*) sees the arrival of two Jedi to negotiate between the planet of Naboo and the blockading Trade Federation. These Jedi are the young padawan Obi-Wan Kenobi and his rebellious Master Qui-Gon Jinn. Their involvement in political matters brings them to Tatooine and an encounter with Anakin Skywalker, a young boy clearly powerful in the Force. The boy's blood is rich in a microscopic life form called midi-chlorians that enhance the Force (a controversial addition to *Star Wars* mythology – although drawn from Lucas's original source material – that annoyed fans and was not referred to in subsequent films). The older Jedi recognizes in this boy the fulfilment of a prophecy about a figure who will bring balance to the Force. The exact nature of this 'balance' is not initially clear, but the rebirth of the 1,000-year-old Sith order (through dark-side practitioner Darth Maul and Palpatine's alter-ego of Darth Sidious) cannot be coincidental.

This may not have been the tale fans were expecting, but it was the one Lucas needed to tell. He knew he had two other movies to further deepen and complicate the story of Anakin Skywalker, depicting his fall to the dark side of the Force and his re-emergence as Darth Vader (not to be seen until the closing stages of the third movie). It may have all seemed rather simplistic in the finished film, but that was part of the overall plan. The original *Star Wars* was a simple adventure story, extended and deepened by the two sequels. Lucas wanted something similar this time around, although it did take him around twenty drafts to get this 'simple' story into a shape that would allow production to begin on what was one of the most-anticipated movies in film history.

Rick McCallum began work on the first *Star Wars* prequel without a finished script. Much of what had been learned through the three years of making the Indiana Jones TV series would be instrumental in his approach to Episode I (as the new film was now tagged) and many of the department heads would transfer over from that show.

Lucasfilm's challenge to the traditional movie-making production process extended to pre-production. With only a story outline and a breakdown of key scenes, McCallum could begin the conceptual design work while Lucas continued to write. There were entire worlds, new characters and creatures, spaceships and vehicles to design. As with the script, the cheapest part of production would be when it was all still confined to pencil and paper. Digital tools came into play here, too, as they increasingly replaced traditional paint, pencil and ink.

The initial art department for Episode I was established in an upstairs room of the main house on Skywalker Ranch. McCallum spent six months looking for new artists, preferably new talent fresh out of art school who would be both affordable and adaptable. Months were spent sifting through over 25,000 portfolio submissions. Out of this process, McCallum found Doug Chiang, who was already working at Industrial Light and Magic. He won the role of heading up the art department on Episode I. He started drawing his ideas for how the new *Star Wars* movie might look the same November in 1994 that Lucas sat down to begin drafting the full screenplay.

The process of 'pre-visualization' was extensive, but helped hugely in communicating the look and feel of the film to those responsible for production, set and costume design. Chiang's meetings with Lucas were inspirational. 'George wanted to see a wide range of styles,' said Chiang. 'He wanted Episode I to be completely different from the previous films, stylistically richer and more like a period piece. At our weekly meetings [he] would choose the designs he liked best and ask us to expand on them. The list of design elements kept growing, and George would tell us just enough information to keep us working.'

Following in the footsteps of three of the biggest movies of all time would not be easy for those who came fresh to *Star Wars*. It was their task to capture the special essence of those films in their designs, the things that made them distinct from regular science-fiction movies. The universe they were set to depict would eventually evolve into the one seen in *Star Wars: Episode IV – A New Hope*. The clue came in their realization that *Star Wars* was really mythic fantasy dressed up in the iconography of science fiction. With that in mind, the designers were able to mine inspiration from not only great civilizations of the past, but also epic tales of heroes and villains from folklore.

The new film would feature Tatooine, a world already depicted on screen, although the town of Mos Espa would have to be distinct from the already seen Mos Eisley. The rest of the planets in Episode I would be new, although the Republic capital of Coruscant had been briefly glimpsed in the *Return of the Jedi Special Edition*.

Lucas's design team drew upon Italian architecture, especially that of Venice, to provide a look for Theed City on Naboo. The underwater city of Otho Gunga, home of Jar Jar Binks and his fellow Gungans, was harder to visualize, with no earthly template to draw upon. The city – depicted as a series of pressurized bubbles – was art nouveau in its look, featuring the curves and shapes of natural forms from flowers and plants. It fitted well with the watery world the Gungans inhabited. Unused concept art by original *Star Wars* artist Ralph McQuarrie inspired the look of Coruscant – a high-tech city covering an entire planetary surface. Chiang admitted, 'All I did was take his vision, and expand on it a little.'

These planets also had to feature their own unique inhabitants. Terryl Whitlatch, an illustrator specializing in zoology, was
hired by Lucasfilm to create authentic creatures that would fit
with the planets. She was able to bring her knowledge of how
animals on Earth exist within their distinctive habitats to figure
out what kind of creatures would live in the undersea world of
Otho Gunga or deep in the bowels of the super-metropolis of
Coruscant. Combining features from several real world creatures, Whitlatch came up with odd-looking characters such as
Tatooine junk-dealer Watto, which Lucas then tinkered with
before approving. It was Whitlatch who would give form to the
notorious Jar Jar Binks, the comic Gungan who becomes an ally
of Obi-Wan and Qui-Gon. Disowned by his people due to his
bungling, Jar Jar saves the Jedi from Trade Federation forces and
helps them get to Theed City. The result is an alliance between
Naboo's surface-dwellers and the Gungans to defeat the invad-
ing Trade Federation.

Lucas originally thought of Jar Jar as being the equivalent to
Chewbacca, the loyal sidekick, or filling the comic relief role
C-3PO had played in the originals. He wanted to use digital
technology to bring the character to life, rather than the more
traditional 'man-in-a-suit' approach. Whitlatch's first attempts
to design Jar Jar were more duck-like than Lucas wanted, while
others resulted in a dog-like amphibian in an attempt to make
him appealing. In the end, they settled on a gangly teenager for
Jar Jar's overall body shape, with extended eyestalks atop an
elongated face and long, droopy ears. Initially intended to be
green, it was decided to make Jar Jar a warmer orange colour
instead. The character would form the template for the other
Gungans featured in the movie, including the rather larger Boss
Nass and Captain Tarpals.

A returning character requiring a makeover was Yoda. With the
use of digital animation focused on Jar Jar Binks, Lucas decided
that other characters – such as the Trade Federation's Neimoidians
and Yoda – should be a mix of animatronics, costumes and
puppetry. Designer Iain McCaig had the task of making Yoda

slightly younger than his appearance in *The Empire Strikes Back* while still retaining the core of the character. The new puppet seemed somehow less convincing than the one used back in the 1980s, and Lucas took the opportunity of the release of the films on Blu-ray in 2011 to update the Episode I Yoda with a digital CGI version, as seen in the two subsequent prequels.

The hardware of the movie was as important as its creatures and planetary environments. Lucas took a decision to replace the white armoured Imperial stormtroopers with robotic battledroids (although the origin of the cloned stormtroopers would prove central to the second prequel). As well as these cannon-fodder droids, the film also introduced rolling destroyer droids that unfurled into ruthless killing machines and an assortment of background robots seen walking and flying around on Tatooine.

Lucas once more indulged his need for speed with the central Podrace sequence that he modelled after the classic chariot race in *Ben Hur* (1959). Instead of horses, these carriages would be pulled by jet engines, ensuring an exciting and visceral sequence that would test the mettle of young Anakin and enable Qui-Gon Jinn to win the credits to buy spare parts needed to repair the queen's starship and get them all off the planet. Each Pod (and, indeed, its pilot Podracer) was unique. Attention was paid to each vehicle in order to suggest that they came from individual cultures.

Storyboards and animatics (semi-animated storyboard sequences) were developed for much of the movie, allowing Lucas to essentially direct the film before he got on set or loca-tion. These tools proved very important given how much digital work would be required. These pre-visualizations allowed the film's creative departments to see exactly what would be needed of them and to plan their work, thus helping to keep the budget under control. They proved vital to ILM when adding its work to the live action footage: there is virtually no scene in Episode I that does not have some digital effects involved.

Lucas had tried to work this way before, back in the low-tech, analogue 1970s. 'On the first film I used old footage of dogfights as temporary footage to figure out the choreography of the end battle,' he said. 'On *The Empire Strikes Back* and *Return of the Jedi*, we did a rough animated film for certain scenes to get a sense of what the action would look like. With Episode I, it was the first time I was able to use computerised animatics to pre-visualize the entire film before I even started shooting.'

The first sequence to be given the animatic treatment was the Podrace, which was only a few pages in the script but twelve minutes in the movie. There were already around 500 story-boards for this sequence, so animatic creator David Dozoretz had a lot of material with which to work. Low-resolution computer animation was employed to bring those storyboards to life, giving a feel for the potential speed and dynamism of the Podrace. It was a process of trial and error in attempting to get to the heart of the scene and dispensing with any ideas that didn't work. The final arbiter on what was kept and what was discarded was Lucas. Working with a first-cut animatic of twenty-five minutes, Lucas, editor Ben Burtt and Dozoretz fine-tuned the Podrace sequence until the director was satisfied. So successful was the process that Lucas expanded it to the whole movie, creating an animated 'guide track' for those involved in the shooting.

McCallum and production designer Gavin Bocquet had begun looking for real-world locations several months before Lucas even sat down to write. The summer of 1994 had seen them visit Tunisia, Portugal and Morocco in search of Tatooine and Naboo. Bocquet – a British production designer who worked in the art department on *Return of the Jedi* – had come to Episode I through Spielberg's *Empire of the Sun* (1987) and *The Young Indiana Jones Chronicles*.

The cast of the original trilogy had gone on to become famous and – at least in the case of Harrison Ford – stars, but they had all been virtually unknown when cast. Lucas had a similar idea in mind when it came to Episode I. Key among them was the role of the younger Kenobi, a character who would feature in all three films, growing older and wiser as the movies progressed. The actor taking on the part also had to pass as a younger version of Alec Guinness, something of a tall order for any young up-and-coming film actor.

The movie had been in development for over a year when Lucas began seriously to look at actors. Casting director Robin Gurland was hired to kick-start the process: it would take her two years and visits to seven different countries to find the cast for Episode I. Working from character profiles, the script outline and concept art, Gurland became familiar with the key characters and was able to suggest some actors right away. In the interests of secrecy, however, none of the prospective cast was given the film script to work from. Their suitability was instead determined through a series of conversations with Lucas, McCallum and Gurland about a wide range of topics, often anything other than *Star Wars*. 'George was looking to find out who the person was and how he or she matched the vision he had of a particular character,' said Gurland.

The earliest role filled was that of Qui-Gon Jinn, the Jedi Master who is a mentor to Kenobi. Described in the script as a man appearing to be in his sixties, Gurland had focused her search on older American actors but could find no one she and Lucas felt filled the brief. One name kept coming up, though: Liam Neeson, an Irish actor in his early forties. He had been Oscar-nominated for Steven Spielberg's *Schindler's List* (1993) and had already been cast in *Rob Roy* (1995) and *Michael Collins* (1996). He had the right physicality (at six foot four inches tall) and conveyed the distinguished gravitas of the Jedi, with Alec Guinness's Kenobi the only readily available model. Having chatted with Lucas about their children, Neeson finished off by admitting, 'For what it's worth, George, I'd love to be a part of this movie'.

Lucas was convinced that Neeson was right to fill the role. 'The Master Jedi is the centre of the movie, just like Alec Guinness was in the first movie,' said Lucas. 'Where were we going to find another Alec Guinness? Someone with that kind of nobility, strength, centre? Liam was the guy who could do it: there wasn't anybody else . . .'

Casting Guinness's direct replacement as the young Kenobi wasn't quite as straight forward. Gurland started with a list of fifty actors and a sheaf of photos of a young Guinness. One name high on the list early on was British Shakespearean actor Kenneth Branagh, star and director of *Henry V* (1989). Lucas instigated a technological approach to casting the role, digitally matching half of Guinness's face with that of prospective young Kenobis. One who made a good match was Scottish actor Ewan McGregor. His credits included two acclaimed UK TV series (Dennis Potter's *Lipstick on Your Collar*, 1993, and *Scarlet and Black*, 1993, with Rachel Weisz) and two movies (*Being Human*, 1993, and *Shallow Grave*, 1994).

Before meeting with McGregor, Lucas had no idea that the actor's uncle, Denis Lawson, had featured as X-wing pilot Wedge Antilles in the original trilogy and that the potential new Kenobi had grown up as a *Star Wars* fan. The family connection and McGregor's love for the movies cemented the feeling that Lucas had that he was right for the young Jedi who would grow and change significantly. Before he could start work on Episode I, McGregor came to international fame in his starring role as a drug addict in Danny Boyle's *Trainspotting* (1996). One of McGregor's earliest tasks was to undergo voice coaching so he could sound like a youthful Guinness.

The biggest casting headache was trying to find an actor capable of playing the nine-year-old Darth Vader. The role of Anakin Skywalker was unusually complex. Gurland embarked upon a series of one-to-one meetings with over 3,000 child actors across the world, knowing that this performance could make or break the movie. One who stood out as wise beyond his years was Jake Lloyd. 'He was too young at the time,' noted Gurland, 'but even then there was something magical about him, a quality that was perfect for Anakin. I kept him in mind, thinking that by the time we started shooting, he might be the right age.' Between then and being cast as Anakin, Lloyd appeared alongside Arnold

Schwarzenegger in *Jingle All the Way* (1996), where he gave an assured performance. Lloyd finally tested alongside two other young actors, and convinced Gurland and Lucas he was right for the challenging role. Lucas saw echoes of Mark Hamill's Luke Skywalker in Lloyd's carefree approach and he felt that helped sell the idea that this was Luke's father-to-be.

Anakin's future wife, Queen Amidala of Naboo, was another tricky role to cast. Supposedly fourteen years old, the part was filled by sixteen-year-old Natalie Portman. A professional actress from an early age, she had starred opposite Jean Reno in *Léon* (1994) and in Tim Burton's comic alien invasion movie *Mars Attacks* (1996). Referring back to the original trilogy, Lucas was keen to find someone who resembled Carrie Fisher's Leia, and – like Ewan McGregor – Portman had to embark on a course of voice work for her dual role as queen-in-disguise handmaiden Padmé and the more formal queen.

Filling the last of the main roles for the film came extremely easy for Gurland after the challenges of finding actors for Kenobi, Skywalker and Amidala. The new trilogy would follow the rise of Senator Palpatine to evil Emperor. Ian McDiarmid had been heavily made up for his role back in 1983, as he had only been thirty years old. Now, fourteen years, later he was exactly the right age to portray Palpatine during his corrupting rise to galactic power. Several smaller roles were filled by prominent actors, such as Swedish star Pernilla August as Anakin's doomed mother, Shmi, and Samuel L. Jackson as Jedi Knight Mace Windu. He had secured the role after lobbying for a part during a live British TV chat show. British actor Terence Stamp was cast as Chancellor Finis Valorum, Palpatine's predecessor as head of the Republic. Finally, returning to familiar roles were Anthony Daniels (voicing the under construction skeletal C-3PO) and Kenny Baker (hired more for the good PR value than through any real necessity). Lucas even found a role for Warwick Davis, *Return of the Jedi*'s Wicket the Ewok, as Wald, a Rodian friend of Anakin.

Perhaps the most thankless role in the movie went to Ahmed

Best, who not only played the physical role of Jar Jar Binks as a
reference for ILM's digital animators, but also voiced the character. Best suffered the indignity of performing dressed as
Binks, with a helmet with a Jar Jar face to indicate the character's
height and give the other actors an eye-line. Also on set for
reference were others playing eventual digital creations they
later voiced, including Brian Blessed as Gungan leader Boss
Nass and Andy Secombe as junk-dealer Watto.

Making the biggest impact in Episode I, given his brief screen
time and lack of dialogue, was martial arts expert and stuntman
Ray Park as Sith assassin Darth Maul. The red-skinned, tattooed
Maul is Darth Sidious's sidekick and weapon of choice. It is
Maul who is sent to terminate the two Jedi. Facing them in a
climatic confrontation, Maul unleashes a double-bladed lightsaber (first seen in an Expanded Universe comic book). During
the dramatic battle, Maul kills Jinn, prompting Kenobi to strike
back, chopping Maul in half. Park would build a career on the
back of Maul, including physical roles in *X-Men* (2000) and
G.I. Joe: The Rise of Cobra (2009) and in TV superhero saga
Heroes (2009).

It was almost two years from the beginning of pre-production
on the new *Star Wars* film (then entitled 'The Beginning') until
the first day of principal photography. On 26 June 1997 George
Lucas returned to directing for the first time since 1977. 'The
reason I wanted to direct Episode I was that we were going to be
attempting new things: I didn't quite know how we were going
to do them – nobody did,' said Lucas. 'I figured I needed to be
there at all times.'

The first shots were relatively simple: a brief conversation
between Darth Maul and Darth Sidious on a Coruscant balcony.
Although both Ray Park and Ian McDiarmid were in full make-
up and costume, they were shooting on a minimal set against a
huge blue screen, so the cityscape could be added later by ILM.
McDiarmid was in action again later that day, as Sidious's alter-
ego of Palpatine in a scene opposite Natalie Portman's queen.

The studio base for the new movie was in England once more. However, the *Star Wars* team had bypassed the traditional studios of Elstree or Pinewood in favour of a converted aerodrome in Leavesden. It had been converted for use as a studio for the 1995 James Bond movie *GoldenEye*. After Episode I, the site became the home of the Harry Potter films.

McCallum had taken out a two-year lease, giving the production free run of the facilities, so significant sets could remain standing for long periods in case of reshoots. This allowed for an innovative 'digital backlot' approach where partially built sets would be augmented by digital extensions. Flexibility became the keynote, with production as an ongoing process, and constant revision of the story, concept creation and special effects development running alongside principal photography and into post-production.

Leavesden would be a long-term base for the production, with a break in the middle of studio shooting for location work and then a return to the studio to finish off. The guiding rule for the physical sets was only to build what was absolutely necessary, leaving the rest of Tatooine, Naboo and Coruscant to be filled in by ILM. Despite this, around sixty individual sets would still be constructed.

Episode I shot for a total of sixty-five days, including an initial four weeks in the studios at Leavesden, under a week at Caserta in Italy and another two weeks filming Tatooine scenes in Tunisia. Following the decision that Naboo should be an ornate Italianate city, the Palace of Caserta in Italy was used as the home of the queen of Naboo. McCallum negotiated exclusive access to the palace for four consecutive days between midday and midnight, leading to an intense period of shooting in Italy. Nothing could be done that might damage the historical site, so scenes requiring explosions from the climactic battle would have to be restaged on replica sets at Leavesden.

It was obvious that the Tatooine scenes should be shot on the original locations in Tunisia, but finding them proved to be difficult. When the crew moved on to Tunisia the search was helped immensely by *Star Wars* fan and archaeologist David West Reynolds, who had tracked the original locations down. However, several of the sites had been modernized, making filming difficult. Similar locations in Tozeur, Hadada and Medenine were used (primarily for Mos Espa and Anakin's home), while digital trickery and camera angles helped overcome the other problems.

These weeks were the most difficult for cast and crew, who had to deal with the summer desert heat in July, with temperatures often exceeding 130°F. Much to his own surprise, Lucas was glad to be back. 'Difficult as it was, Tunisia was the place that brought back the most memories for me,' he said. 'It looks like Tatooine – it must be *Star Wars!*'

As with original filming in Tunisia and Norway, the early location work for Episode I was hit by severe freak weather. Following the third day of shooting in Tozeur, the location was struck by a severe sandstorm that wrecked many of the sets and destroyed props. Rapid rescheduling and some quick thinking enabled the shooting to continue and the crew departed on schedule. At the back of Lucas's mind was the faith that additional shooting and digital work could make up for any shortcomings, a luxury he did not have when making the original *Star Wars*.

Back at Leavesden, the second batch of studio photography closed out the summer of 1997. Another six weeks of shooting at the studio (and in the nearby forests) followed.

McCallum had purchased $60,000 of redundant military supplies and aircraft parts to build eighteen Podracer cockpits and engines, with the parts helping immensely in making each Podracer convincing as working machines. The illusion would be completed by a combination of digital effects and model work by ILM, enhancing and extending the physical sequences.

Also at Leavesden was a new creature shop under the supervision of Nick Dudman. He had been a trainee under Stuart Freeborn on *The Empire Strikes Back* and had helped in the creation of the first Yoda puppet, so it was fitting that he worked on the puppet of the younger Yoda. As with every *Star Wars* film, Episode I would feature a plethora of bizarre and weird alien creatures populating scenes.

Traditional make-up, creature suits, animatronics and more basic puppetry were all employed in bringing Episode I's menagerie of alien wonders to life. Dudman's approach was to adopt whatever technique worked best: if it was better for ILM to tackle something, he would gladly hand the task over (like the creation of Jar Jar Binks and most of the Podracer pilots). Dudman had a team of around fifty-five people working on the creation of hundreds of creatures, including the nasty Neimoidians, Nute Gunray and Rune Hakko. The Trade Federation villains were originally intended as CGI characters, but a late decision to create them with practical effects meant they fell to Dudman. Played by actors Silas Carson and Jerome Blake under heavy prosthetics, the Neimoidians had radio-controlled animatronics built in to allow movement in the eyes and mouths.

Key among returning characters were R2-D2 and C-3PO, much loved by *Star Wars* fans and general audiences alike. In bringing back the droids Lucas also gave them new back-stories. In Episode I, R2-D2 is one of several droids serving Queen Amidala, while C-3PO is a project undertaken by young Anakin Skywalker. Using technology unavailable in 1977, R2-D2 was a largely remote-controlled prop. Kenny Baker clambered back inside the dustbin-shaped droid shell for several key scenes to give R2-D2 a more 'human' feeling. Anthony Daniels's contribution to Episode I would be in voice-over only, as C-3PO was now a puppet. Daniels provided his dialogue from off-set for the benefit of the other actors. Other droids were built, such as ten battle droid figures, even though they would be largely digital creations.

The final day of principal live action photography on Episode I came on 30 September 1997. Among the final scenes to be shot were the climatic lightsaber battles between Darth Maul, Qui-Gon Jinn and Obi-Wan Kenobi. The three actors – Ray

Park, Liam Neeson and Ewan McGregor – were all tutored by stunt coordinator Nick Gillard in lightsaber technique. Lucas was intent on using lightsabers more often and in more imaginative ways. 'It's a wonderful weapon, because you can do almost anything with it,' said Lucas. 'For this movie, I wanted something that was lethal, but elegant and sophisticated.'

Lucas wanted a new take on the rather tame confrontations seen in the original trilogy: 'We'd never seen a Jedi in his prime. I wanted to do that with a fight that was faster and more dynamic, [but that was also] a kind of sword fighting reminiscent of the previous films.'

Like Dudman, Gillard had worked on the original movies – as Mark Hamill's stunt double. Now he was responsible for choreographing Lucas's 'faster and more intense' Jedi action. He put the actors, especially Neeson and McGregor, through a complex course of physical fighting lessons to prepare them for the lengthy lightsaber battle sequence. Each actor had to memorize a series of complex moves and be careful not to injure themselves or others. 'I had done some fighting at drama school, but never anything that physical,' said McGregor.

The result was a bravura sequence, played out to John Williams' new composition, 'Duel of the Fates', putting previous lightsaber fights in the shade. Using the multiple levels of the Naboo power complex to great advantage, Gillard put the three characters through their paces in a dynamic and visually impressive way. Maul's eventual defeat saw an intriguing character removed prematurely from the trilogy (although he would feature in the Extended Universe and eventually resurface in the fourth season of TV's *Star Wars: The Clone Wars*).

As a director Lucas appeared to have mellowed. He had been heavily criticized by some of the cast from the original trilogy for his lack of personal direction, simply leaving the acting up to the actors. It was something the director himself recognized and had come to terms with. 'There are two ways to approach working with actors,' he said. 'One is more "method", where you are involved with the actors on a personal level. I prefer the traditional way of working in Europe, [where] it isn't about trying to find the motivation for every moment. If an actor has a specific question, it is easy for me to give them a quick answer.'

Later, Ewan McGregor would look upon his work on *The Phantom Menace* with mixed feelings. 'Even though I've talked about how hard they are to make, it's still great being Obi-Wan Kenobi,' he told *Total Film*. 'It was the most heavily intense bluescreen [work]. I can act without anything being there – it's hard work, a skill, but I can do it.' Of the Jedi lightsaber battles, he noted: 'I think me and Ray Park set the standard when we go at it. It was so fast and furious they had to speed the camera up so that it would look slightly slower, 'cos it was too quick and they thought it looked speeded-up.'

By the side of George Lucas throughout the filming of Episode I was the quietly spoken and unassuming director of photography David Tattersall. Lucas relied on him as he was open to the use of new technology and techniques that were integral to the new production process in a way that a traditionalist like Lucas's original *Star Wars* cinematographer, Gil Taylor, hadn't been. Unfortunately, Tattersall didn't really know *Star Wars*, so prefaced his work with a crash-course viewing of the original trilogy. It was especially important given Episode I's return to Tatooine that Tattersall should bring continuity to the lighting and depiction of the planet as seen in *A New Hope* and *Return of the Jedi*.

Tattersall would also have to work closely with the technicians from ILM during Episode I's lengthy post-production period. Key to the process was ILM visual effects supervisor John Knoll, who was on set during the entire live-action shooting period to ensure that what was shot would work in conjunction with the planned effects.

Knoll had undergone his *Star Wars* apprenticeship on the *Special Editions*. It was his job to identify from the 3,000 storyboards which scenes would need visual effects, digital matte paintings or models. He worked closely with Lucas to ensure the raw footage would mesh seamlessly with the effects, with lighting references and 'match-move' data (where LED dots on the blue screen are used to synch up a moving digital background) proving invaluable. He also communicated regularly with Tattersall, especially in relation to the lighting of scenes on location and in the studio.

The technology used in the production and post-production of Episode I was groundbreaking, but it quickly became standard for Hollywood filmmaking. For Lucas, Tattersall and Knoll, it was all unknown territory and involved a fair amount of trial-and-error. Much of that would be in the hands of ILM, which had made huge strides in visual effects.

The challenge now was for ILM to match the vision in Lucas's screenplay. Of Episode I's 2,200 individual shots, 1,900 would require some form of digital enhancement – compared to almost 500 visual effects shots needed by James Cameron's *Titanic* (1997). Two additional visual effects supervisors joined Knoll on the project. While Knoll looked after the Podrace, space battles and Naboo's underwater sequence, ILM veteran Dennis Muren handled the climatic ground battle between the Gungans and the Trade Federation, and Scott Squires supervised the lightsabers and the final battle between the Jedi and Darth Maul. Director of Animation Rob Coleman took on the supervision of digital character animation – mainly focusing on Jar Jar Binks.

Initially, Binks was a cartoon-like character until Lucas made it clear he wanted as 'photorealistic' a creature as possible. He would have to stand next to real actors and function within real-world environments, so it was important that he not be an animated character pasted on top, as had been the case for Roger Rabbit in *Who Framed Roger Rabbit?* (1988). Using Best's performance, ILM animators had something with which to work. Observation of real faces – human and animal – were used to make Binks's expressions as convincing as possible. Once a library of expressions was built up, it was easier for each animator to bring the character to life. 'This movie had a dozen major digital characters', noted McCallum, 'one of which [Binks] would have ninety minutes of screen time. They all had to be seamlessly integrated into the movie – absolutely spectacularly and real.' The test was to make Binks look as real as Chewbacca had been in the earlier movies, a test the finished film failed in the eyes of many fans. The process, however, would pave the way for a host of new, digitally created characters starting with Gollum in Peter Jackson's The Lord of the Rings trilogy.

The key to integrating digitally animated characters with live action was in maintaining the lighting across both. If the digital character could be made to appear as though it was lit in the same way the real people were, an illusion of seamless integration could be achieved. The data captured during the live-action shooting was pivotal in this process, and its availability saved a huge amount of time.

Similarly, space battle sequences were achieved with a mix of tried-and-tested physical model work with newer digital creations: both had to appear in the same scenes. 'For each effect we used the technique that was most appropriate and best suited to the particular situation,' said Knoll. 'Certain effects were easier to achieve in one medium or the other – CG or models – and we went with the medium that made the most sense. We have found that [physical] models remain the best solution to some of our effects challenges.'

ILM faced a deadline, as in April 1997 the movie would enter the editing process. Editor Paul Martin Smith had come from *The Young Indiana Jones Chronicles* TV series, and was aware that he would be working for a director who had long considered his own forte to be editing. 'I came out of editing and I've worked as an editor,' explained Lucas. 'My whole focus on filmmaking is as an editor. The script is just a rough sketch of what I'm going to do. Filming is just gathering the materials. Editing is how I create the final draft.'

Digital editing techniques allowed flexibility in the director's manipulation of his footage. 'I could move things around, cut people out of one shot and put them in another, change sets or take a scene from one location and put it in another,' said Lucas. 'I could completely reconstruct and rewrite the story in the editing process.'

The ultimate aim was to produce a two-hour movie (although

The Phantom Menace, as the film was eventually controversially titled, would be two hours and thirteen minutes). By May 1998 a rough cut had been assembled. As with the original *Star Wars*, much of the material was still missing, including finished effects shots, and the whole thing was scored with temporary music. However, many of the missing story elements could be filled in with animatics that helped those seeing the movie for the first time to evaluate what worked and what didn't.

The result was a list of additional shots or scenes that were needed to make the film a better experience. With a full year until release, there was plenty of time for these pick-up elements to be created and inserted into the movie. Lucas often used the analogy of making a painting for the way he worked on the prequel trilogy. He could shape and reshape his materials using the full pallet of paints now available to him. It was a process that didn't have to have a definite end, as a painter could continually revise his work, painting out old elements in favour of new material. Following August 1998 pick-up shooting at Leavesden, the movie was further refined.

At the same time, work was progressing at Skywalker Ranch on the sound mix and score. John Williams returned to a *Star Wars* movie for the first time in sixteen years, using a mix of his now-classic *Star Wars* themes and a huge amount of new music. At the beginning of February 1999, Lucas, McCallum and Williams met at Abbey Road Studios in London to record the score, performed by the London Symphony Orchestra. That completed, the final sound mix took place in March and the last visual effects were locked in place in April. It had taken four years from the moment when George Lucas first put pencil to paper to write 'The Beginning', but Episode I was now complete and ready to be shown to an impatient worldwide audience.

The hype and anticipation for *Star Wars: Episode I – The Phantom Menace* was huge in the run up to the release date of 21 May 1999. When the title was announced to unbelieving fans in September 1998 it made major news bulletins. With many fans believing it to be a bogus title to fox would-be merchandise bootleggers (as with 'Blue Harvest' back in 1982), the 1930s serial-like title was actually a reference to Darth Sidious and his wider Sith plot, something that would only become clear when fans saw the movie.

Following the tradition of the previous *Star Wars* sequels, fans began lining up outside cinemas in advance. This time it was not for a few days, but an entire month. Encampments sprang up in major US cities and around the world, with many fans sleeping in tents raising money for charity through sponsorship. Fans had even queued up for the November 1998 trailer, often leaving the cinema after it and not staying to see the movie to which the trailer was attached. A few days later, the trailer became downloadable from the Lucasfilm website, a lengthy time-consuming process in pre-broadband days. The servers crashed repeatedly as eager fans attempted to view the trailer from their own homes.

On the day of release, up to 2.2 million full-time employees in the US reportedly skipped work to see the movie, according to a survey by Challenger, Gray and Christmas. This unauthorized absence was estimated to have cost the US economy $293 million. The *Wall Street Journal* reported that many companies dealt with the problem by closing down on opening day and giving staff the day off. In excess of $20 million was spent promoting the film, with a huge number of licensing deals resulting in images from the movie adorning Pepsi products and McDonald's meals, alongside a huge range of toys and a novelization by fantasy author Terry Brooks.

Critical reaction was mixed, with the comic character of Jar Jar Binks a lightning rod for complaints. Drew Grant, writing at Salon.com, wondered if 'perhaps the absolute creative freedom George Lucas enjoyed while dreaming up the flick's "comic" relief – with no studio execs and not many an independently minded actor involved – is a path to the dark side.' Most critics, like the *Chicago Sun-Times*' Roger Ebert, recognized the movie as 'an astonishing achievement in imaginative filmmaking'. Others complimented the performances of Liam Neeson and Ray Park and the full-blown Jedi action, with *Empire* magazine describing the climax as 'the saga's very best lightsaber battle'. Some of the critical comment was as much in reaction to the hype preceding the release as the actual movie. The *Seattle Post-Intelligencer* noted the hype had 'built expectations that can't possibly be matched and scuttled [the] element of storytelling surprise'.

None of that affected the film's box office, with records tumbling in rapid sequence. *The Phantom Menace* achieved the biggest single-day gross on its opening with $28 million, and was the fastest film to gross $100 million (in just five days). It was also fastest to $200 million and $300 million, becoming 1999's most successful movie. Total US box office was $431 million, with another $493 added around the world. The film's total worldwide total take was $924 million, making it the seventeenth highest grossing film of all time (and the highest placed *Star Wars* movie). While not regarded well critically, *The Phantom Menace* was an unqualified financial success.

'I don't think of myself as the best writer or director in the world,' said Lucas. 'I am always a little amazed when I do a movie and it is so well received. For every person who loves Episode I, there will be two or three who hate it, or who couldn't care less about the whole thing.' Within a month of the film's successful release, work would begin in earnest on the second *Star Wars* prequel.

Chapter 12

Cloning Success

Episode II has a certain melancholy about it ... It appears to be a nice movie with a somewhat happy ending, at least with Anakin and Padmé. It's only when you put it in the context of the bigger story that you see the handwriting on the wall. You notice the flaws in Anakin's personality that are going to sink him in the end.

George Lucas

George Lucas began writing Episode II before the first film in the prequel trilogy had even been released. He had a rough outline completed before production began on *The Phantom Menace*, but in June 1998 he started drafting the actual screenplay. 'I couldn't have done Episode I without knowing the complete story,' said Lucas. 'It was all mapped out – I just had to write specific scenes. It was still quite a challenge, because Episode II required that I write a love story in the middle of a *Star Wars* movie. It's a love story, with the Sith's relentless drive to take over the universe in the background. The challenge was to balance those two things.'

As ever, writing did not come easily to Lucas. By September 1999 (following a two-month European holiday after *The Phantom Menace*) Lucas had enough of the spine of the script ready to begin feeding material to the design department. 'I worked through the first draft as quickly as possible,' said Lucas, believing it was better to complete a swift draft rather than continually to rewrite the opening twenty or thirty pages. Much of the design work done for Episode I would carry over into the second movie, but there was almost as much again that would have to be created from scratch.

The Skywalker Ranch art department had started work on designing aspects of Episode II in June 1999, a mere month after the release of Episode I. It wasn't until December that year that they kicked into a higher gear thanks to a detailed scene breakdown from Lucas.

Producer Rick McCallum had set off on his initial location-scouting trip for the second prequel the day after the first opened in US cinemas. He and production designer Gavin Bocquet spent three months touring Tunisia, Italy, Portugal and Spain looking for easy-to-shoot locations that matched environments Lucas had described. McCallum had made several visits to Australia during the final year of production on Episode I to check out the Fox Studios facility in Sydney. The production of the next two *Star Wars* films would be based there, moving from Leavesden in the UK. The new deal would involve a lease that allowed core sets to be left standing for a substantial period of time – although the Fox facility was in increasing demand.

The biggest change, though, would come in the method of filming. Lucas had been experimenting for a while with the idea of shooting movies digitally, foregoing 35 mm film in favour of high definition (HD) video. This approach had several advantages, prime among them a simplification of the post-production process, especially in the integration of digital visual effects. The 24-P high definition digital camera developed by Sony and Panavision was selected as it was designed to record images at the traditional standard film rate of twenty-four frames per second. The tests convinced Lucas that the digital process retained the look and feel of film, finally deciding in April 2000 to commit. 'Every single shot we do has a digital effect in it,' noted McCallum. 'There's no point shooting on film [for us]. [Digital] is the way we want to go – it's just easier and more economical, and the results are fabulous.'

In November 1999 Robin Gurland returned to her role as casting director on the prequels. As shooting was to take place in Australia, she began by filling many of the smaller roles with local talent, drawing on actors from Sydney and Perth. Joel Edgerton (from Australian TV series *The Secret Life of Us*) was signed up as Owen Lars (a younger version of Luke's 'uncle' Owen, played by Phil Brown in Episode IV) and Bonnie Piesse as Beru Whitesun (again, a younger version of Luke's 'aunt' Beru, played by Shelagh Fraser). As they were playing characters already established within the *Star Wars* universe, Gurland was looking as much as possible for a physical match as well as for actors who had the skills to inhabit the roles.

Gurland also tapped actors from New Zealand. Episode II would delve into the back-story of one of the most enigmatic (and popular) *Star Wars* characters: bounty hunter Boba Fett (seen in Episode V and Episode VI previously). Temuera Morrison was cast as Boba's father, Jango Fett, while Daniel Logan played the younger version of Boba, shaped by tragedy into the character familiar to fans. They were joined by Leeanna Walsman as Zam Wesell, a bounty-hunter who stages an attempt on the life of Amidala.

While many of the key cast – among them Ewan McGregor, Natalie Portman and Ian McDiarmid – would be returning from *The Phantom Menace*, there was one major, challenging role to fill. Episode II was set a decade on from the first movie, so Anakin Skywalker was now in his late-teens, meaning Jake Lloyd could no longer play the role. The hunt was on for an actor who could take Anakin through the next two movies that would see pivotal changes in his character, primarily his fall to the dark side and his conversion into the formidable form of Darth Vader.

Finding the new Anakin was to be the biggest challenge for Gurland. The search had been ongoing while she filled the other key roles, with an open casting call bringing in around 1,500 submissions from young actors and their agents, all of whom knew the role could be career-making. Gurland viewed some

400 videotape tests, narrowing those down to a selection of around thirty actors whom she thought were serious contenders. At this point Lucas got involved, but neither the writer-director nor the casting director felt they saw the new Anakin among the selection – even though the actors who were auditioned included Ryan Phillippe, Colin Hanks (son of Tom Hanks), Jonathan Brandis (from TV series *seaQuest*, who would commit suicide in 2003, aged twenty-seven) and later *Fast and Furious* (2001) star Paul Walker. Lucas and Gurland even met with *Titanic* (1997) star Leonardo DiCaprio to discuss the role of Vader, but the actor proved 'unavailable'.

Time was running out and Gurland feared she would never find the right person when she came across Canadian actor Hayden Christensen. Initially struck by his physical presence, she then viewed his work, primarily the Canadian drama *Family Passions* (which Christensen appeared in when he was twelve) and several mid to late 1990s movies, including *The Virgin Suicides* (directed by Francis Ford Coppola's daughter Sofia). Of particular interest was his role in *Higher Ground* (2000), a Fox Family Channel TV drama in which he played a sexually molested teenager who turned to drug taking. 'Hayden Christensen convinced us all that not only was he good – he was bad,' said McCallum of the future Darth Vader. Christensen was officially announced as the new face of Anakin Skywalker in May 2000, just one month before filming was due to begin in Australia.

The new Fox Studios facility in Sydney had been converted from old show grounds at Moore Park into a state-of-the-art facility. The thirty-two-acre site would eventually encompass eight soundstages, production offices, workshops and a service community of up to sixty independent businesses. Several movies and TV series had used the facility before the *Star Wars* crew moved in, including *The Matrix* (1999) and the Ewan McGregor-starring musical *Moulin Rouge!* (2001). Here over sixty sets would be built for Episode II (many more than had been constructed for the previous movie – despite the fact that Lucas had promised his crew that Episode II would be a 'smaller' movie).

The administrative team for the film set up a central production coordination office in the hexagonal-shaped, low-level building in the middle of the complex. From here the comings and goings of cast and crew would be arranged, and each morning would begin with the issuing of that day's 'call sheets' showing who and what was required and which scenes were to be filmed. As always on a *Star Wars* movie, secrecy was of the utmost importance. Windows overlooking the soundstages from the next-door Fox Studios Tour (open to the public) were blacked out. That didn't stop some enterprising paparazzi gaining access to a next-door sports stadium that also overlooked the studio complex in the hope of grabbing a few shots of the new Darth Vader in action.

Although he had been working on it for a while, Lucas's final shooting script for the movie was incredibly late, much to the frustration of McCallum. Although much of the pre-production design work and set building had been possible based on story and scene outlines, Lucas's inability to finish the screenplay caused major problems. British screenwriter Jonathan Hales – who had written for British TV, American soap-opera *Dallas* and *The Young Indiana Jones Chronicles* – was drafted in to help wrap up the script for Episode II. The production draft was available less than a week before the start of filming, after the pair of writers spent May and June on further revisions: evidently the romance aspect of the storyline continued to give Lucas problems. 'I wanted to tell the love story in a style that was extremely old-fashioned, and frankly I didn't know if I was going to be able to pull it off,' admitted Lucas. 'In many ways, it is much more like a movie from the 1930s than any of the others had been, with a slightly over-the-top poetic style . . . I knew people might not buy it.'

The delays with the script were not allowed to slow the work on building sets needed by the production. 'At that stage,

[Episode II] felt like a "virtual film" because we got the script only days before we started shooting,' recalled McCallum. 'We had to build these sets to a script that didn't exist.' The screenplay would continue to be revised throughout production as Lucas reworked his dialogue.

McCallum was the one operating the clapperboard on the first day of principal photography on Episode II on 26 June 2000, exactly three years to the day since the start of filming on Episode I. For the next three months at Fox Studios and on locations around Europe and beyond, the *Star Wars* cast and crew would toil on the new movie. Even when they had finished shooting, a further year-and-a-half of detailed post-production work would follow. Much of the work completed on this first day of shooting would be cut from the final film (as on *Return of the Jedi*). Scenes featuring Ian McDiarmid as Chancellor Palpatine announcing the erroneous news of the assassination of Senator Amidala to the Republic Senate were shot, with Palpatine's podium against a vast blue screen.

Although he expected problems with the digital HD cameras, McCallum wasn't prepared for a power failure on the first day. Accepting the teething troubles, Lucas and McCallum decided to view the first few weeks of principal photography as an extended learning period as everyone figured out the best way to use the new technology. While the actors were nervous, especially McDiarmid, who had a lot of dialogue to deliver and no other actors to play against, the camera operators were particularly worried about how the brand new high definition cameras would perform. The decision to go digital was not without controversy (although the majority of major Hollywood movies now shoot this way). 'People asked, "Why are you doing this?"' recalled Lucas. 'The real question was "Why not?" It was vastly superior in every way, and it was cheaper. You'd have to be nuts not to shoot in this way. As far as I was concerned, we should have been shooting digital cinema twenty years ago.'

Coming to grips with older technology on that first day's shooting was Anthony Daniels, who suited up as C-3PO for the first time in thirteen years, having only voiced the incomplete skeletal C-3PO puppet in Episode I. Now the droid was kitted out in his familiar gold livery and working as a diplomatic aide to Amidala. Nothing had changed for the actor as he still faced hours confined in an uncomfortable, heavy, armoured suit in which he was virtually unable to walk. 'I'd forgotten how lonely it is in here,' admitted Daniels.

Although much of the film would be created digitally, the production of Episode II physically expanded to take up all available stage space at Fox Studios. 'We were trying to fit all the sets into every square inch of the studio,' said McCallum. '[It] was about half the size of Leavesden. We took over the entire studio, and still it was a tight fit.' The production's time at the studio was tightly scheduled into a period of nine weeks from June 2000. The majority of the studio filming would have to be completed during this period, as once the crew left to move on to shoot the locations, a return to Fox Studios would be impossible as other productions were booked to move in. Unlike on Episode I, where the crew were able to return to Leavesden to conduct more filming, any additional requirements for Episode II would have to be managed within the scheduled pick-up filming that would take place back in Britain (maintaining the traditional British connection to the *Star Wars* saga).

The second week of filming saw the shooting of the opening scene of the movie: the attempted assassination of Senator Amidala on the landing platform at Coruscant. This was one of Natalie Portman's first shots, working on a minimal set consisting of little more than the spaceship ramp and the immediate landing area, with the rest of the location to be created later digitally. Originally Lucas wanted to shoot the entire scene against blue screen, but was persuaded that having some 'real' elements within the scene would help sell the illusion, an important lesson that would go on to inform much of the approach to this movie and Episode III. 'George only builds what he needs,' said McCallum of his director's economical approach. Many of the Coruscant scenes were shot on non-existent or partially realized sets. This allowed for the creation of new scenes – such as the discussion between Anakin and Obi-Wan in an elevator (shot much later at Elstree in November 2001) or a meeting between assassin Zam Wesell and bounty-hunter Jango Fett (shot at Ealing in London in March 2001) – to be created and seamlessly added to earlier material.

An early set-piece sequence in Episode II illustrated this then-new approach to filmmaking. The speeder chase through the skies and skyscrapers of Coruscant, in which the two Jedi pursue Zam Wesell, was the latest indulgence by Lucas of his early days as a boy-racer back in Modesto. The speeders them-selves were even tricked out to look like futuristic versions of the 1950s or 1960s hotrods seen in *American Graffiti*. The script only loosely described the scene, omitting many details. It was more fully developed by the pre-production team working in pre-visualization at the Main House on Skywalker Ranch. Ben Burtt's 'videomatics' drew on the process Lucas had initially developed on the original *Star Wars* trilogy, using vintage movie clips, newsreels and stock footage, as well as specially shot models to create a primitive visualization of the action. 'It was a Saturday morning cartoon version of the speeder chase that illustrated what they needed to shoot on stage,' said Burtt. This in turn was used to create more sophisticated animated story-boards by pre-visualization and effects supervisor David Dozoretz and his four-strong team.

Two months before any live action footage was shot, director Lucas could view this action sequence in some detail and make adjustments. That meant that when it came time to film the live-action components of the scene over two-and-a-half days of blue-screen filming in Sydney, Lucas knew exactly what he needed to shoot. With the animatics available, McGregor and Christensen were also able to get a good idea of what the completed sequence would look like, allowing them to tailor their performances. McGregor noted that the usefulness of the process had progressed immensely. 'The animatics for the speeder chase were very well developed,' he said. 'On Episode I, they were just basic shapes that gave us a rough idea of what was going on, but the animatics for Episode II looked great.' In addition to the moving animatics, the cast and crew also had a detailed map of the chase worked up by the art department and a series of impressive, colourful concept paintings by artists Ryan Church and Erik Tiemens that showed the different districts (high rent, warehouse, old city and entertainment district) through which the chase would progress.

Shooting the scene in Sydney saw the actors clambering in and out of a full-scale yellow speeder prop mounted on a gimbal that gave them a series of realistic jolts, shocks and an ever-present rocking motion. 'It actually made us feel rather sick after a while,' noted McGregor, comparing the experience to spending days on a funfair ride. With the pre-visualization animatics and other illustrative material fresh in their minds, both actors were able to ignore the blue screen surrounding them and put themselves in the middle of the desperate chase through the skies of Coruscant.

Those few days of live-action shooting were not the end of work on that sequence. Pick-up shots filmed much later at Elstree saw McGregor perform the opening moments of the chase, as he leaps from Amidala's apartment window and clings to an assassin droid before dropping into the speeder piloted by Anakin. Months later again, the artists at ILM would take the edited footage and add in the digitally created backgrounds, other vehicles, creatures, people and all the other hundreds of individual elements needed to complete the scenes. Ben Burtt and Matthew Wood then added the soundscape, creating unique noises for the speeders, other traffic and various other atmosphere elements, before the music by John Williams helped to add further excitement to the chase. The sequence ends in a seedy entertainment district where the speeders crash and the Jedi finally catch up with Wesell. This was filmed on set, with around 150 extras wearing practical alien masks created the traditional way by creature supervisor Jason Baird. Some of the alien heads had even been pulled from the Lucasfilm archive, including a few seen in the infamous cantina scene in the original *Star Wars*.

This flexible, all-inclusive approach to filmmaking was developed by Lucas while making Episode I, refined on Episode II and perfected on Episode III. His mantra was to use whatever was most practical and economic for the scene, whether it be real-world, live-action monster masks, practical effects, well-understood simple techniques or the latest in computer-generated imagery developed by ILM. This one chase sequence involved all of those techniques and brought all of Lucas's skills as a filmmaker to bear on telling his story. Other locations – the water world of Kamino (with its 'Grey' alien-style inhabitants, where the clone troopers that prefigure the stormtroopers of Episode IV are created) and the desert planet of Geonosis (populated by insect-like creatures) among them – were realized this way. Since the early 2000s, when these films were in production, this approach to filmmaking has become the Hollywood standard, especially for big-budget, high-concept blockbusters.

As director, Lucas did much to keep the pace of filming brisk, hitting an average of thirty-six set-ups (individual shots) per day, an extraordinarily high amount for a film production, much more akin to that achieved in television. By the end of August the *Star Wars* crew had wrapped in Sydney and were on the move, taking in Lake Como in Italy (where Padmé's retreat at the Naboo lake was shot), the Plaza de España in Seville, Spain (where Anakin and Padmé touch down on Naboo) and a week in Tunisia where they returned to many iconic locations from Episode I and the original *Star Wars*.

The location shooting in Spain was completed in a just a few hours during a single day, even though it had taken ten weeks to set up. Watched by thousands of locals who had come to see the new *Star Wars* film in production, Portman and Christensen played out a relatively simple scene against a superb practical location (later augmented by digital additions). This was another example of Lucas's filmmaking approach in action – a visit to

Spain, however brief, gave the scene a sense of reality that all-digital environments lacked.

While Spain provided the Naboo exteriors, Italy's Palace of Caserta once more supplied the interiors of the Theed Palace. Following a day off after shooting in Spain, the cast and crew reassembled near Naples for another single day of shooting at the eighteenth-century palace. Then the *Star Wars* caravan moved on to Lake Como to film Amidala's home at Naboo's Lake Country. A popular retreat for aristocrats, the wealthy and movie stars, Lake Como has been occupied since Roman times and is the location of several extravagant villas. The Villa del Balbianello on the western shore was used as Amidala's retreat, the location of her clandestine wedding to Anakin that climaxes the film. Built in 1787 on the site of a Franciscan monastery, the building had been the final home of explorer Guido Monzino and now contained a museum dedicated to his work. It would later also be used as a location for the James Bond reboot movie, *Casino Royale* (2006). Lucas had visited there the previous year on his European holiday, so had written scenes with the location in mind. ILM altered the exterior of the building digitally, as usual, to make it fit better with the established architectural style of Naboo. As was seemingly traditional on *Star Wars* movies, location shooting was affected by unexpected, extreme weather – this time torrential rain around Lake Como caused a standby interior scene to be added to the schedule while the crew waited for the weather to clear up.

September 2000 saw the arrival of the *Star Wars* crew in Tunisia, shooting for a day and a half on the locations for Mos Espa, which remained more or less intact from their use on Episode I. A touch up of the paint and a quick refurbishment of the street and the scene was ready to be shot. That was followed by a more extensive trip to the iconic Chott el-Djerid location used for Luke Skywalker's home in the original *Star Wars*. As Episode II saw Anakin return to his home, these sets had to be recreated as nothing remained from the original shoot over twenty years before. Archived technical drawings (not always accurate compared with what had actually been built on location), photographs and even frame grabs from *A New Hope* were used to recreate the Skywalker homestead. It was important to Lucas – and to the fans of *Star Wars* – to get this right. 'It was wonderful trying to recreate that set,' said production designer Gavin Bocquet, well aware of its historic importance to many film fans. 'The homestead was at the very heart of *Star Wars*.' Only two people working on the current film – Lucas and Anthony Daniels – had been there in 1976 for the original, and the making of that film had not been as extensively chronicled as the later *Star Wars* movies. Their memories, alongside what material could be retrieved from the Lucasfilm archives, proved to be enough, along with locations that remained remarkably untouched, to recreate the Tatooine familiar to filmgoers and fans. Lucas found filming on these locations to be 'a very nostalgic experience. It was odd to be back in one of the places we shot the original movie, especially since it hadn't changed much. Last time I was there [in 1976] I was under a lot of pressure. I didn't have any idea of where my life was going or where this movie was going. This time, it was a much more mellow experience.'

The scheduled pick-up studio filming followed in September 2000 at Elstree Studios in Borehamwood, the traditional home of *Star Wars*. Although much diminished from its 1970s heyday, the studio still boasted the specially built George Lucas Stage and was regarded by the director as a lucky charm when it came to the *Star Wars* movies (he and Steven Spielberg had also filmed parts of the *Indiana Jones* trilogy there).

Principal photography on Episode II wrapped in the UK on 20 September 2000. The only actor present was Ewan McGregor, who shot the opening to the speeder chase. This final shot of the production saw McCallum wield the clapperboard once more, just as he had done for the first shot back in Australia. Thousands of miles of travel, journeys to five countries, sixty-one days of shooting and a year of pre-production had led to this moment. The task of making Episode II was not yet complete, though. The film would not be released to cinemas until May 2002, and an intense eighteen months of digital post-production remained.

The focus passed to the team at Industrial Light and Magic, who would take the raw footage Lucas had shot and work their digital magic on it. Digital special effects would be present in just about every aspect of the new *Star Wars* movie, sometimes obviously in huge space battles, but often invisibly as real-life sets were extended or little fixes made to troublesome live-action footage.

George Lucas was still at heart an editor. From his earliest days, the part of the process of filmmaking he had enjoyed the most was editing, in stark contrast to writing, the process he enjoyed the least. Lucas viewed shooting the film as 'gathering material' that was then endlessly malleable thanks to his development of new filmmaking technology. 'I like a film to be organic,' he said. 'I like to change it.'

Ben Burtt had initially assembled a very rough cut as production progressed, refining it as filming went on and more raw footage became available. Back at Skywalker Ranch after the shoot, Burtt and Lucas spent several months fine-tuning their first cut. That initial rough cut that ILM would start work on was completed in February 2001 and came in at two-and-a-half hours. This was a better outcome than the first cut of Episode I, which was almost three hours long, but still too long for a *Star Wars* movie (Lucas generally aimed for somewhere around the two-hour mark).

The first cut revealed the need for further additional shooting to clarify story points or improve on the visuals. 'My reaction to those first viewings is always disappointment,' admitted McCallum after he and Lucas first viewed the film in one sitting, rather than in bits and pieces as they had previously. 'All I see are things that are wrong, the lost opportunities: why didn't we do this or that?' Lucas agreed with McCallum's feeling, but the new way they were making films allowed for second (and third) chances to get things right. 'I began looking for anything that was unclear or needed to be amplified,' said Lucas. 'At that point, I wrote new scenes to fill in those spots.'

During the final week of March and the first week of April 2001 the *Star Wars* crew were shooting once again, this time at the venerable Ealing Studios in London (where Alec Guinness had shot such classics as *The Man in the White Suit* and *Kind Hearts and Coronets* in the late 1940s and early 1950s). This was the first of a total of three post-production pick-up filming sessions. Key actors were reunited, including McGregor, Christensen, Samuel L. Jackson, Christopher Lee, Natalie Portman and Anthony Daniels. Much of the new footage was shot against blue screen as it would be digitally integrated with the existing movie. 'Blue used to be my favourite colour,' said Daniels, 'but I think I've overdosed on it.'

Among the scenes shot at Ealing was an entirely new action sequence that sees C-3PO, R2-D2, Anakin and Padmé journey through a deadly droid factory on Geonosis. Lucas created the sequence to replace some rather static and talky scenes with one of action, replacing chat with excitement. There was another reason for the scene: 'The droid factory scene also got Artoo and Threepio out of the ship and more engaged in the final act of the movie,' admitted Lucas, who had always regarded the two droids as key to all six *Star Wars* movies.

This retooling of the film was an ongoing process for Lucas and his team from September 2000's wrap of principal photography through to the end of 2001. 'At that point ILM took over,' said Lucas. 'They created backgrounds and the final animation, but even then we were re-cutting and reassessing it all. I couldn't do a final cut on the whole of the last reel until I had all the material gathered, which wasn't until about March 2002. I couldn't really tell if something was working until I had the final visual effects shots.'

One of the major concerns on Episode II was the commitment to an all-digital Yoda, after the use of an unsatisfactory traditional puppet version on Episode I. Lucas had experimented with a CG Yoda for a final scene in *The Phantom Menace* that briefly saw the character walk, but was unconvinced the technology was well enough developed to pull off an all-digital Yoda, preferring instead to concentrate his efforts on Jar Jar Binks. With Yoda, noted Lucas, 'We weren't in a place where we could do it in close-up and make him look absolutely real. ILM probably could have done it, but I didn't want to lay that on them at that time.'

Now, on Episode II, the time was right and ILM were championing the idea of a fully CG Yoda. During the writing of the screenplay, Lucas had several conversations with animation director Rob Coleman and visual effects supervisor John Knoll. For Coleman, one of the attractions of working on Episode II was the chance to develop a digital version of such an important *Star Wars* character. To convince his director that it was possible and would be convincing, Coleman and his animation team carried out an experiment. They replaced the puppet Yoda in a few key scenes in *The Empire Strikes Back* with a digital Yoda and showed them to Lucas. Finally convinced that it would work, the writer-director took a new approach to writing for the character. 'I said, "OK, then, I'm going to treat Yoda in the script as if he were digital." It allowed me to write him in a very different way: he could walk around, he could fight with a lightsaber.'

That led to ILM's work on one of the most challenging sequences in the entire movie: the climatic lightsaber duel between Yoda and his old Jedi Master, Count Dooku. In something of a casting coup, Lucas had secured Hammer Horror star Christopher Lee to play Dooku, the rogue Jedi turned Sith Lord and right-hand man to the evil Palpatine. His casting connected the new films with the first, in which Lee's Hammer co-star Peter Cushing had played Grand Moff Tarkin, Vader's henchman. There was among those involved in the production huge concern about how this action sequence could be achieved: in private many disparagingly called it the 'fight between the frog and the old man', and they were worried about their ability to pull it off convincingly.

Lucas had recognized the difficulties in achieving his vision with a less-than-agile actor (Lee was then approaching his eighties) and a non-existent digital character. 'He's one of the most important characters in the pantheon of *Star Wars* characters,' said Coleman of Yoda, so he was determined to get him right. The other part of the equation was how to make Lee appear to be a convincing, agile swordsman. 'I didn't know how well it would work,' admitted Lucas. 'We set ourselves an impossible task and just hoped we could accomplish it.'

The aim was to show Yoda at the height of his powers as a capable, physical Jedi. Coleman, however, had long realized that there were other limitations to what could be done with Yoda: to stay true to the character as shown in the original *Star Wars* trilogy, the animators would have to recreate Frank Oz's Yoda, complete with his idiosyncratic movements that were actually the result of being a hand-operated puppet. 'It was difficult to visualize a fight between these two unlikely adversaries: an 80-year-old man who was about six foot five, and an 800-year-old creature who was three feet tall,' said Coleman.

A mix of techniques would be brought to bear on achieving a solution – some high-tech, some very low-tech. Lee was well trained in swordcraft, long a requirement of most classically trained British actors of a certain age (along with horse-riding skills). However, although he was fairly fit, there were some shots where a younger stunt double was required. In postproduction, the double's head was digitally replaced (not entirely successfully) with that of Lee. The CG Yoda was seen to leap around the spacecraft hangar in which the battle took place, making the height differential between the characters less of an issue. The scene was the biggest challenge for the animators at ILM, but was one they only achieved to 80 per cent of their satisfaction.

By January 2002 the film had gone through a total of around five major cuts and ILM had completed most of the effects work (with over 2,000 visual effects shots), allowing composer John Williams to work to an almost final version when recording his score with the London Symphony Orchestra at Abbey

Road Studios. Over a two-week period, the score was recorded, with a mix of new material and iconic *Star Wars* themes. 'The music is the glue that holds it altogether,' said McCallum of the finished movie.

The final shot completed by ILM was delivered on 8 April 2002, allowing Lucas to complete his final cut of the movie two days later. A preview screening for cast and crew was held at Skywalker Ranch's opulent Stag Theatre that same day, 10 April 2002. It was the first chance most involved had to see the finished film, complete with effects, music and sound effects. 'The original *Star Wars* was a joke, technically,' said Lucas looking back at the more primitive filmmaking methods available to him in the 1970s. 'I had to cut corners and cheat and make it kinda fuzzy so you couldn't see what was going on. Most of what we did on *Star Wars* had never been done before; it was all prototype stuff.' Technology Lucas had developed using his own time and money over twenty years now made it easier than ever before for him to complete his story. It was down to rebel filmmaker Lucas to show the rest of Hollywood the way forward.

In terms of storytelling, the intention of Lucas to replay and echo elements of the earlier films in the new ones became clearer. 'I've created scenes that were reminiscent of those in the first trilogy. Situations are the same, with slightly different circumstances. I compare it to a musical motif, where the same themes keep recurring.' This resulting middle instalment in the second *Star Wars* trilogy deepened and complicated the universe, showing the steps that would lead Anakin Skywalker to ultimate darkness in the third film, another production that Lucas knew would hold a host of brand new challenges – in storytelling, technology, filmmaking and in meeting audience and fan expectations.

Star Wars: Episode II – Attack of the Clones was the first ever theatrically released film to have been shot entirely digitally. Although Lucas and McCallum had been campaigning for cinemas to convert to digital projection in time for the release on 16 May 2002, only around 120 theatres in the United States were equipped to screen the film digitally (out of the 3,000 screens playing the movie). For the rest, traditional 35 mm film prints had to be supplied.

Despite the fan anticipation, Episode II failed to emulate the box-office success of its predecessor. By no means a financial disappointment, the film took over $310 million in the United States and a further $339 million across the world. However, it was the first *Star Wars* film not to be the biggest grossing film of its year of release. A trio of franchise movies out-grossed *Attack of the Clones* in the United States: *Spider-Man*, *Harry Potter and the Chamber of Secrets* and *The Lord of the Rings: The Two Towers*. Episode II would be the lowest performing of the six live action *Star Wars* feature films at the US box office (when figures are adjusted for inflation).

Critically, the film had a tough time, too. Hayden Christensen was widely criticized for his portrayal of Anakin Skywalker, although he would later win praise for other roles (such as journalist Stephen Glass in *Shattered Glass*, 2003). The problem may have been with the role he was being asked to portray – a whiny teenage Jedi, rather than the proto-Darth Vader many fans wanted to see. Roger Ebert identified the problem as being with the script rather than the film's impressive realization. 'As someone who admired the freshness and energy of the earlier films', he wrote in the *Chicago Sun-Times*, 'I was amazed at the end of Episode II to realize that I had not heard one quotable line of dialogue.' He also noted that the romantic relationship between Skywalker and Amidala had fallen flat on screen, whatever Lucas's stated intentions about recreating an 'old-fashioned' 1930s movie romance. 'There is not a romantic word they exchange that has not long been reduced to cliché,' wrote Ebert.

As with most of the previous *Star Wars* movies, *Attack of the Clones* won many technical awards including an Oscar nomination for Best Visual Effects. The controversial clash between 'the frog and the old man' won the film a Best Fight prize at the MTV Movie Awards. However, it was in the Golden Raspberry

Awards (dished out for the worst films of the year) that *Attack of the Clones* triumphed, with seven nominations and two wins, one for Lucas for Worst Screenplay and another for Christensen for Worst Supporting Actor.

George Lucas had made life difficult for himself in choosing to tell the story of the middle *Star Wars* prequel in the way he did, but he felt he had no choice as he was following a thirty-year-old template. *Attack of the Clones* was no *The Empire Strikes Back*, but it did offer many images and moments *Star Wars* fans had never seen before. It was also hugely successful in one vital aspect: it set the stage for the climatic events of Episode III.

Chapter 13

Revenge of the Rebel

*We're making a movie where the bad guys win, and everyone dies
– it's not destined to be the most successful movie of all time . . .*

George Lucas

Approaching what was intended as the final *Star Wars* movie, George Lucas was well aware there was one vital scene fans expected to see. The confrontation between Obi-Wan Kenobi and Anakin Skywalker on the rim of a volcano that results in the creation of Darth Vader had long been a core fan legend. Now, with Episode III concluding the saga, they would finally get to see that moment. First, Lucas had to write it.

One scene for Episode III had already been shot during the making of Episode II. Lucas already had a road map for the final instalment, and he knew a return to shoot a single scene on location in Tunisia was impractical. However, he wanted to feature scenes where Obi-Wan Kenobi hands over the Skywalker twins for safekeeping: Leia to Senator Organa on Alderaan, and Luke to Owen and Beru on Tatooine. Shot in Tunisia without Ewan McGregor, a hooded body double was used for Kenobi while actor Joel Edgerton played Owen Lars. The scene as filmed would not ultimately be used, but it was the first indication of where Lucas felt his six-movie saga might conclude.

As had become the necessary habit at Lucasfilm, the pre-production process on Episode III started without a completed script. The art department began development (mainly on several new planetary environments) following the briefest of outlines from Lucas. The final movie jumped three years forward from the second, opening with one of the final battles of the clone wars that had begun at the end of Episode II. Lucas offered several hooks to designers Erik Tiemens and Ryan Church to kick-start their work. The film would feature battles on seven unique planets, all with their own species. Boba Fett might be seen once more, this time as an angry fifteen-year-old. Alderaan (Leia's homeworld destroyed by Grand Moff Tarkin in *A New Hope*) would definitely appear in the movie, while the Wookiee homeworld of Kashyyyk might also feature (fulfilling a long-held Lucas ambition). One vital design note the director offered was that as the galactic war had taken its toll, the equipment and vehicles used should be moving towards the 'used universe' look of the original *Star Wars* – the universe was no longer in the grand state it was in the final days of the Republic. From that meeting in April 2002, the team would have until the end of the year to create concept art ready for the costume, prop and set-builders to use.

In the meantime, Lucas would continue to work on the draft script. His shooting schedule was set in stone, with all the elements of main photography and later pick-up shooting sessions already planned, as had been the case on Episode II. By the time of Episode III, Lucasfilm had the production of the new *Star Wars* movies so fine-tuned it was like an efficient machine at work. 'I'm shooting next summer [2003] for 60 days,' said Lucas while writing. 'I shoot the following March [2004] for 10 days, and I shoot that October for five days. It's all in the actors' contracts, it's in the budget. It's planned for. I started out as a documentary filmmaker, so I'm used to shooting, cutting material together, going out and shooting some more, [then] cutting it together. The actual story evolves.'

Although Lucas had a good idea of the outline of Episode III, many of the specific incidents had yet to be worked out. For his weekly meeting with the art department team, Lucas needed to have another aspect of his story fine-tuned to keep feeding them information so their work could continue. Some of their material was based on ideas discarded from previous films. Certain key elements of Episode III drew inspiration from original *Star Wars* concept artist Ralph McQuarrie's work completed in 1976 (his design aesthetic, as well as unused ideas, would provide further inspiration for the second *The Clone Wars* TV series).

Since the 1970s, Lucas had in mind the confrontation between Kenobi and Skywalker on the volcano world of 'Mufasta' (to become Mustafar in Episode III). He had spoken of it in interviews in the 1980s, and early design concepts of Vader's underground throne room had been published. At the time, Lucas had set the material aside, intending to use it at a later date. That time had now come and the new concepts for the volcano world were some of the first things the Episode III designers could work on in the sure knowledge that the scenes would be in the film.

The process of producing designs early fed back into the writing of this movie more than ever before. Ideas and concepts developed by the artists would inspire scenes or sequences in the evolving story, provide Lucas with characters and creatures to populate scenes he already had or give him new environments in which to set key moments. As always, the deadline for the production and the need for set building to begin in Sydney, Australia (where Episode III would shoot), loomed over both the writer-director and the concept artists. Many were also aware that as this was to be the final movie; it was their last chance to really push the limits of what *Star Wars* on the big screen could achieve.

Lucas's problems with writing and his unique production methods gave him some leeway in delivering a finished script for Episode III, but they also contributed to his own prevarication. Reluctant to commit to anything definitive, Lucas preferred the creative, open environment of the pre-production design department than the cold reality of putting words of dialogue and scene descriptions on paper. A visual communicator, Lucas found writing (as compared to simply imagining) limiting rather than freeing. Nonetheless, others were depending upon his words – the actors of Episode III most of all.

'The preliminary visuals serve as an inspiration for writing, more than anything else,' admitted producer Rick McCallum, despite the fact that he had to exert almost constant pressure on Lucas to progress the script. The date for principal photography at Fox Studios was fixed as 25 June 2003, and that would be the deadline to which Lucas would inevitably work. 'We're trying to do this for a price, but we're building backward, designing a twenty-five-floor skyscraper without foundations,' admitted McCallum.

By October of 2002 a great deal of conceptual work on Episode III had been completed. Much of it had passed final approval from Lucas, so production designer Gavin Bocquet and costume designer Trisha Biggar could begin actual creation of sets and costumes. Lucas had fine-tuned some of his story ideas, settling on several specific planets and providing the artists with a list complete with their prime environmental characteristics. Alderaan, for instance, was described as a planet of gleaming, futuristic cities set amid snow-topped mountain peaks, such as those of Switzerland. Lucas was also able to describe the climax of the movie, which would see Yoda go into exile on Dagobah (where he is discovered by Luke in *The Empire Strikes Back*) and Kenobi hand over the new-born Skywalker children following the lengthy battle with Anakin on the volcano world of Mustafar. Lucas also settled on a spectacular opening in which Anakin and Obi-Wan are caught up in the final major battle of the clone wars, fleeing from one cliffhanger situation to another (recalling his original inspiration of 1930s movie serials) in an effort to rescue the kidnapped Senator Palpatine. The sequence would climax with a confrontation between Anakin and Count Dooku. Lucas also confirmed the film's new villain would be a part-droid Separatist General, and that the long-awaited black-armoured form of Darth Vader would appear, albeit briefly, at the climax. The part-robot, part-organic Grievous was intended to prefigure the conversion of Anakin Skywalker into the 'more machine than man' Vader by the film's climax.

The challenge Lucas was facing was threefold: he had to tie-up all the loose ends from the previous two films in a satisfactory manner, while he also had to ensure the film connected to 1977's Episode IV to which it was essentially an immediate prequel. Finally, he also wanted to stay true to the original source material he had roughed out over thirty years before when he first conceived of 'The Star Wars'. As the end of the year drew closer, the writing process intensified and Lucas paid more attention to each of these goals – his biggest problem was including all the outstanding characters from the previous two films and introducing enough new ones to make the final film fresh in its own right.

Despite the lack of a finished screenplay, January 2003 saw many of the sets for the movie under construction in Sydney, with Biggar also continuing work on the costumes. By the end of the month, McCallum had managed to prise a rough draft fifty-five-page script from Lucas, and although it was not in a fit state to be shared with department heads, it gave the producer enough information to be more communicative with them about the film's actual requirements. The draft script gave a structure to the drama, confirmed the locations involved and offered a final list of significant characters. One major difference from the final film was the inclusion of a ten-year-old Han Solo who was to get involved with Yoda, an intriguing idea later abandoned. The draft also included an admission from Darth Sidious/Palpatine that he used his Sith powers to 'arrange' Anakin's conception through the midi-chlorians. This was intended to set up Sidious as an evil father figure for Anakin in the same way that Vader had been for Luke.

This draft script and the scenes it contained proved to be enough for storyboard artists to spend much of February designing some of the major sequences, while Lucas worked on expanding the screenplay.

Essentially, Lucas was directing the film on paper, instructing the storyboard artists on the dynamic way some of the scenes needed to be presented and expanding upon his intentions. Alfred Hitchcock approached filmmaking in a similar way, storyboarding the entire film to such an extent that he often declared the actual process of principal photography to be boring. The process of storyboarding, especially in working out action sequences, would be one more element that would feed back into his writing. They also allowed pre-visualization supervisor Dan Gregoire to begin creating videomatics of the dramatic opening space battle.

Lucas welcomed the input of Steven Spielberg in the creation of videomatics for two key sequences of Episode III. Spielberg was keen to get to grips with the tools of digital production, and saw Lucas's film as the ideal chance to get his feet wet. Spielberg 'directed' the sequence showing the pursuit and elimination of General Grievous by Obi-Wan Kenobi (although a much reduced version revised by Lucas was to make it into the film) and Yoda's duel with the Emperor in the Imperial Senate. Both of Spielberg's extensive animatics would feature on the complete *Star Wars* saga Blu-ray, allowing some comparison between his preliminary work and what Lucas eventually used in the movie.

In the weeks leading up to the start of principal photography, much of Episode III was created through pre-visualization. Entire sequences, mainly action-based, were put together (albeit crudely), subject to the input of Lucas. In this way, all involved had a solid idea of what much of the film would eventually look like, and enough of the story clearly to depict the emotional highs and lows of the saga's concluding chapter. It appeared that Lucas felt the only people who couldn't work without a complete script were the actors (who needed it for their dialogue), so he could put off committing to a final draft until everyone assembled in Australia.

Waiting patiently at Fox Studios in March 2003 was Rick McCallum, while work continued at the Skywalker Ranch. 'I'm a man without a script,' he told Jonathan Rinzler in *The Making of Revenge of the Sith.* 'Usually you get a script a year before production begins, and it's broken down, and storyboarded, costumes and sets are broken out; the actors are locked into dates – but we don't have that.' Nevertheless, construction on sets had begun at the start of the month, work on costumes was ongoing and creatures were being built.

Lucas showed a degree of self-knowledge of the frustration his script process caused others. 'I sit there with a page in front of me . . . Inertia. Procrastination,' he admitted. Despite keeping regular office hours for his writing (usually between 8.30 a.m. and 6 p.m.), he found the actual process as difficult as ever. 'I can be chained to my desk and I still can't write. I write five pages a day, but left to my own I'd probably write a page a day. I force myself – it becomes agonizing to get those other four pages . . .'

Lucas would finally finish his first draft script at the start of April. The story structure was in place along with many of the lines the actors would say, although as ever Lucas retained the right to change things. 'The last thing that will be dealt with [in revisions] is the dialogue,' the director admitted. 'You can change that on the set, or even afterwards. I'm not known for my dialogue . . . I think of it as a sound effect, a rhythm, a vocal chorus. Mostly, everything is visual.' At the end of that same month, Hayden Christensen arrived in Australia to begin physical training for his final turn as Anakin.

Around the same time, casting had begun for the new movie. Confirmed as reprising their roles alongside returning cast members Christensen, Ewan McGregor and Natalie Portman were Anthony Daniels and Kenny Baker as C-3PO and R2-D2, making them the only actors to feature in all six live-action *Star Wars* movies. For Episode III they would be joined by Peter Mayhew, returning as a younger version of Chewbacca, playing the character in a *Star Wars* movie for the first time since 1983.

Lucas arrived in Australia in mid-June 2003, just two weeks before the start of filming with a second draft screenplay in his hands. A non-stop schedule of seventy planned shooting days lay ahead, although Lucas was confident he could bring the film in faster, whittling the number of shooting days down to sixty-three by the end. The first shooting day, Monday, 30 June 2003, consisted of seven scenes featuring Anakin and Obi-Wan (and Lucas's good luck charm of R2-D2) battling their way through the Separatist cruiser. These scenes were all simple and straight-forward, the aim being to break in the actors and the crew gently. McCallum once more fulfilled his traditional role of operating the first clapperboard of the shoot, followed by Lucas's cry of 'Action!' on his final *Star Wars* movie. That day saw the completion of forty-eight individual set-ups, comprising two minutes and twenty-eight seconds of the final movie, with filming concluding at 7.10 p.m. The first day would set the pattern for the next three months in the studio as the film was efficiently created, minute-by-minute.

The first week featured the central cast – McGregor, Christensen, Portman, Daniels – in relatively simple scenes. During the second week new arrivals in Australia included Mayhew, Ian McDiarmid as the Emperor, Samuel Jackson as Jedi Mace Windu and Christopher Lee, briefly reprising his role of Count Dooku in the film's opening sequence. By the end of the second week, the key sequence when McDiarmid's Palpatine turns on a Jedi delegation and battles Mace Windu was shot. As with Dooku's fight with Yoda in Episode II, stunt doubles and digital trickery would be used to see the older Palpatine take on the younger Windu and defeat him, using the Emperor's Sith powers. The battle took around four days to shoot and culmi-nated in Palpatine renaming Anakin as Sith Lord Darth Vader.

One of the many links between Episode III and Episode IV – and certainly one of the most visual – was the recreation of the rebel blockade runner. It's within the blazing white corridors of this ship that the first *Star Wars* movie opened, introducing filmgoers to hero droids C-3PO and R2-D2. When the set was being constructed in Australia it attracted many onlookers among the cast and crew, the majority of whom were children when the first movie came out. Towards the end of July 2003 shooting began on a set that had seen the entrance of Darth Vader over twenty-six years before.

The scenes shot on this iconic ship mainly featured Jimmy Smits as Bail Organa, one of the originators of the rebellion chronicled in the original *Star Wars* trilogy. Organa's ordering of a 'mind wipe' for C-3PO explains why the protocol droid doesn't recall the events of the prequels in the original three movies. R2-D2 seems to escape such memory erasure, suggesting that he knows the full saga. This scene also gave the last line of dialogue in the film to the golden droid, making a neat link to the fact that the same character has the first lines in Episode IV.

The gruesome make-up devised for the burned Anakin Skywalker saw the final *Star Wars* film awarded a higher cinema age-restriction certificate than any of the previous movies. Devised by *Farscape*'s Dave Elsey, the 'burnt Anakin' make-up showed the injuries that resulted in him being placed within the Darth Vader life-support suit. Elsey had been encouraged by Lucas to put aside ratings concerns and go as far as he felt he needed to in creating the look for 'toasty Anakin'. The result was truly gruesome, and featured in an intense scene that climaxed the battle between Anakin and Obi-Wan. 'I feel like I've been researching this make-up since I was a kid and first saw *Return of the Jedi*,' said Elsey. 'This was a chance to do something fresh for *Star Wars*. We'd seen Vader without his helmet, but I always wanted to know how he'd got so badly scarred and had to wear the Vader suit. I had read that he'd fallen into volcanic lava, and in my mind I'd been creating a prosthetic make-up that demonstrated these devastating injuries.'

The start of September saw the shooting of the final scenes for Anakin Skywalker, with Hayden Christensen encased in Elsey's make-up and wearing blue stockings and a blue sleeve to allow for the digital removal of the limbs lost at the end of his fight with Obi-Wan. The final exchange of dialogue between McGregor and Christensen was filmed only after the pair worked on – and altered – Lucas's long-in-gestation dialogue.

As written, Obi-Wan lamented the fall of Anakin by saying, 'I love you. But I will not help you.' Between the actors and the writer-director, the lines were changed on the day to be delivered in the past tense, emphasizing the fact that Anakin is already dead to Obi-Wan. They became: 'I loved you. But I could not help you.' In that version, the lines also play up Obi-Wan's complicity in Anakin's longer-term fall to the dark side through his earlier failure to help him resist the temptations of the Sith. It proved a powerful climax, the culmination of all six films, although Christensen referred to the morning's filming as 'just another day playing in the dirt'.

That may have been because the actor had an even more momentous afternoon ahead when he would don the full Darth Vader regalia for the first time. On the original films Dave Prowse had played Vader in the suit (with James Earl Jones supplying the voice), but he was often supplanted by swordsman and stuntman Bob Anderson whenever Vader was required to engage in battle. Christensen had undergone several make-up tests for the 'burned Anakin' prosthetic back in July, while he had also been fitted for the full Vader armour during August. As with the rebel blockade runner, the first appearance of Vader on the set of Episode III drew a large crowd of interested onlookers from other areas of the production. More than twenty-five years had passed since his movie debut, but the pulling power of this cinematic icon had clearly not faded.

Christensen donned the newly built armour behind a series of curtains, emerging fully clad in black to applause on set. The scene to be shot had Vader revived by the Emperor, only to be informed of the death of Padmé. (Anakin's attraction to the dark side of the Force had been partly motivated by Palpatine/Sidious's implication that it was the only way he could save his wife from certain death.)

'The most special day of the shoot was when Hayden got into the Darth Vader suit,' recalled McCallum. 'Every single person in the studio was waiting outside the stage doors [to] get a glimpse of Hayden as Darth Vader.' For his part, the actor was thrilled to be making cinema history. 'I'd been looking forward to [it] since I found out I'd got the part,' he said. '[I was] hoping I'd get to don the dark helm[et].' Lucas was equally enthusiastic to see the completion of a vital scene that brought his saga to a satisfying close: 'Having [Anakin] finally make it into the suit completes the circle of the movies. There was this key missing piece, which everybody's always wanted to see – the return of Anakin Skywalker as Darth Vader.'

The following day Christensen shot the iconic scenes of the badly burned Anakin being put in the iconic suit, culminating in the iconic Vader facemask descending upon his scarred head. The blue stockings and arm coverings were again used so Christensen's limbs could be removed digitally in post-production. The day had begun with further work featuring Anakin's slide down the slope of the volcano, but the donning of the mask completed the character's story arc: the dramatic fall from hero to villain. In drawing on mythology for his inspirations, Lucas was touching on elements of Bible stories with Anakin's fall being modelled after that of Satan, from angel to devil, except the elder Skywalker is redeemed in a way the devil never can be . . .

The scenes of Anakin being put in the Vader suit had actually been started the week before, but would continue to be fine-tuned and filmed in the following days. Both McGregor and Christensen had been in training for the physically demanding battle they knew was coming. The fight sequences had been worked out in storyboards and animatics, revised by Lucas. Much more was shot than would eventually be used. Nonetheless, the finished film featured an epic conflict between the two accomplished Jedi across the lava fields of Mustafar.

Lucas had deliberately scheduled these fight scenes to follow the filming of the character-based, dialogue- and exposition-heavy scenes. So it wasn't until over forty days into the expected sixty-day filming schedule that McGregor and Christensen got to face off against each other with some lightsaber action. Each actor had to memorize a series of precise physical moves, while coping with filming largely against green screens and jumping from moving platforms. Lucas found the creation and filming of such scenes to be 'tedious', but he also knew that this was a dramatic moment for both characters where their building hostility finally bursts into the open – and neither will walk away from the conflict unchanged.

With minimal sets built amid a sea of green backdrops, the actors had to rely on their imaginations and the available concept art and animatics to understand what their characters were doing. The fight moved through several environments, from the Separatists conference room on Mustafar where Anakin kills the Separatist leaders, through a factory facility, and then down a river of lava. Swordmaster Nick Gillard (who had been a stuntman on *Return of the Jedi*) was responsible for choreographing all the lightsaber battles across the prequels. Now he faced the creation of the ultimate lightsaber fight, described by Lucas as 'one of the longest continuous sword-fights ever filmed'.

The last day of studio-based principal photography on Episode III saw the cast and crew shooting what would appropriately be the final scene of the movie: Vader, the Emperor and Governor Tarkin silently assemble on the bridge of an Imperial Star Destroyer to observe the construction of the Death Star. Under the prosthetic make-up of Tarkin was *Farscape* veteran Wayne Pygram, wearing a latex mask modelled after Peter Cushing, who had played the role in the first *Star Wars* movie – another connection uniting the saga.

Ewan McGregor had finished his role on the movie a few days earlier, replaying the scene in which he hands the baby Luke to the Lars family that had first been filmed without him three years previously in Tunisia during the filming of Episode II. In the interim Lucas has changed his mind about who should receive the new-born infant, preferring for the defeated Jedi hand to the child over to Beru rather than Owen, as had already been filmed. Australian Bonnie Piesse reprised her role as Beru, but due to the unavailability of Joel Edgerton, Owen was this time played by a stand-in (Edgerton would be shot against green screen in the summer of 2004 and added digitally).

For Christensen, it would be a few more days before he completed production, once more donning the Darth Vader armour for his final scene. Production wrapped on 17 September 2003, the fifty-eighth day of filming that saw Lucas beat his private target of sixty-three shooting days. With the completion of the final scene, five days ahead of schedule, an impromptu wrap party was held on the sound stage. McCallum and Lucas both delivered speeches thanking cast and crew for their dedication to the project and marking the bittersweet nature of the end of the final *Star Wars* movie. McCallum described the wrap as 'a very emotional moment', while Lucas admitted that Episode III had been 'the most fun film I've ever worked on. I think we've made a great movie.' It was a long way from the frustrated and defeated Lucas who had worked on the first *Star Wars* over twenty-five years earlier, and who had hated writing and directing, but felt compelled to make movies. Neither was it the end of the story, as the completion of principal photography was only the end of the second stage (following pre-production). Lucas had gathered his 'material' by mid-September 2003: now he had eighteen months or so to shape it into the final film he wanted audiences to see.

Even before the live action shooting, Industrial Light and Magic had started its work on Episode III. Back in May 2003 it had begun building computer models of spacecraft and vehicles and would work on the film non-stop right through until January 2005.

Lucas called his editing technique a form of 'orchestration' of the material he had collected during principal photography. He saw it as a form of creation equal to or even more important than writing the script or capturing the actors' performances. By Christmas 2003, Lucas and Ben Burtt along with editor Roger Barton had put together their first rough cut, using the live-action material and a host of temporary animatics and in-progress effects shots. The creation of the film continued as ILM moved forward with its work on the digital components, thought to make up almost 50 per cent of Episode III. 'A film used to have ten to fifty effects shots; we have at least 2,000,' said McCallum.

ILM animation director Rob Coleman once again supervised digital creature creation, but as on Episode II he took a special interest in the digital Yoda. As mentioned, as a warm-up exercise, Coleman had replaced the puppet Yoda featured in Episode I with a CG version (a revision that wasn't seen by fans until the 2011 release of the movie on Blu-ray). The first editorial task for Lucas was to compile the film's seven or so Yoda scenes in order to allow Coleman to get started on creating the digital Yoda, especially those sequences in which he fought with Emperor Palpatine in the Imperial Senate Chamber. Coleman saw Yoda as a character that was both technical- and performance-based. It was equally important that these scenes be adequately completed before voice-actor Frank Oz could record his dialogue.

The post-production period had grown across the three *Star Wars* prequels to become a form of virtual filmmaking in which the movie Lucas had envisaged – in his head, in his screenplay and on the sets in Australia – could be reshaped and reformatted.

As the weeks progressed, more footage was completed, either as finished shots or as low-resolution animatics that Lucas would approve before ILM developed them into final, full-resolution scenes. As each finished scene was completed, the overall film was built up, element by element. It was a painstaking process, but one that gave Lucas complete control over his material and one he knew would work successfully following Episode II. In editing, he was able to use digital tools to lift elements of an actor's performance from different takes and mix them together to achieve his desired effect. Characters could be digitally moved from one scene into another or from one location to another if Lucas felt it suited his evolving story. To Lucas, the tools might be different but the intention was the same as it ever was. 'I'm making movies,' he said. 'Some people do storyboards and intellectualize it – I prefer to do it this way. I just want to tell a story and make it work.'

The whole process was an attempt to keep the cost of making a blockbuster movie reasonable, as Lucas was paying for everything himself. McCallum had aimed to make Episode II for 10 per cent less than he had spent on Episode I. With Episode III, the plan was to make the movie for the same cost as the first in the prequel series. The movie cost around $60 million to shoot, with the same again being spent on digital post-production and visual effects, making the overall pre-release cost of Episode III in the $115 to $120 million range, a reasonable price for a contemporary franchise blockbuster, especially a third instalment.

By January 2004, the opening space battle sequence was in a near finished state, so was screened in a preview theatre for Lucas and the ILM producers. The biggest worry about this opening sequence was ensuring that it could be easily followed by the audience, given that it started in an area of space crowded with a host of conflicting spaceships. Lucas called this 'readability', and concluded that, 'It may be that some of these shots are a little fast.' While revisions of various sequences would continue for months to come, by the end of January the movie was over 75 per cent locked down. Given the amount of effects work and digital creations in the movie, Lucas admitted to Rob Coleman: 'You realize this is an animated movie?'

Lucas may have regarded Episode III as largely animated, but despite the presence of many digital characters he still could not make his films without actors (much as he may have liked to). To complete his vision for the final *Star Wars* movie, a series of pick-up shoots had been scheduled with the main cast members. The scenes to be shot would improve upon material already gathered, fill in story gaps shown up in the rough cut or bring to life new ideas and concepts Lucas had for the film since shooting in the summer of 2003 in Australia.

The intended first session of pick-ups scheduled for March

was pushed back to August 2004 as the rough cut and ILM's work on the film were taking longer than anticipated. This particular movie had been troubling for Lucas, and his difficulties in committing to the story for his final *Star Wars* movie had come out in his prevarication over finalizing the screenplay. 'As we've made this trio of films, this process of making things up as we go along has increased,' admitted editor Ben Burtt. 'I think it's satisfying for George to take the characters and the tools, and experiment with them, because he's developed it all, over many, many years.'

Reshaping the film in the digital realm had resulted in several near-finished scenes being dropped (much to the disappointment of many of those at ILM who had worked on them, as it put them behind schedule and that work would not be seen on the big screen). Characters' relationships and interactions changed in the editing, improving some scenes but leaving Lucas with a few narrative holes that the pick-up shoots could fill.

Additional shooting had taken place during April and May, with ILM working on model shots (varying in size from a few inches to almost life-size vehicles) and character inserts, such as the death of Jedi Aayla Secura during the haunting Order 66 sequence, in which the Jedi Order is all but eliminated by the Emperor's forces. By mid-May a larger unit was briefly back at Fox Studios in Australia shooting footage of a Wookiee army for battle scenes set on Kashyyyk. Animation director Rob Coleman directed these action scenes, rather than Lucas.

At the end of August and into the first week of September, the *Star Wars* crew were back in the UK shooting additional material at Shepperton Studios, just outside London. About two weeks of blue- and green-screen shooting were conducted with most of the principal actors present in various combinations across the shooting period. A handful of the scenes to be shot were brand new, while others were retakes or extensions of material already captured. Scenes shot included the Coruscant Opera scene in which Palpatine reveals to Anakin that he is a

Sith Lord, additional Mustafar scenes, additional Anakin/ Obi-Wan duel inserts and reaction shots, action scenes featuring Ian McDiarmid as Palpatine, and scenes on Utapau and from Amidala's funeral procession.

After further work by ILM, a new rough cut was completed by October, with a running time of two hours and twenty-five minutes – over the target length of two hours fifteen minutes. While the vast majority of the movie was shot in the studio and realized in the digital environment, real-world backgrounds shot in China, Thailand, Switzerland and Tunisia were used to provide planetary locations. A small crew even flew to Italy during the eruption of Sicily's Mount Etna in 2002 to capture footage of real-life lava for use in the Mustafar scenes. The end of January 2005 saw the final pick-ups completed at Elstree, with John Williams recording his Episode III score at Abbey Road in February.

Fittingly, the final shot captured for the movie featured Hayden Christensen as Anakin Skywalker running across a platform. This movie in particular, and the entire six-film *Star Wars* saga, had turned out to be the story of Anakin Skywalker, his rise and fall to the dark side. This final shot took place on Elstree's Stage 8, the same soundstage where Lucas had shot much of the first *Star Wars* movie back in 1976. Just as with the story within the films, the story of the making of the *Star Wars* films had come back to its beginning.

Following an out-of-competition screening at the prestigious Cannes Film Festival in France, *Star Wars: Episode III – Revenge of the Sith* opened in the United States on 19 May 2005, with a final running time of two hours and twenty minutes. As mentioned, the movie was given a more adult rating than the previous *Star Wars* movies, due to its 'intensity', especially in the scene that sees Anakin Skywalker burn on the edge of the volcano on Mustafar.

Episode III received a much more positive critical reaction than the previous two movies (especially Episode II). The *New*

York Times tagged the movie as 'the best of the four episodes Lucas has directed' (an interesting verdict, given that much of the 'direction' was not in the traditional areas of writing the script and working with the actors, but took place in building the movie in the digital realm). Negative criticism that was made revolved around the old targets of Lucas's occasionally inept dialogue and Hayden Christensen's performance (he was awarded a second Golden Raspberry for Worst Supporting Actor). Unusually, the film drew some political criticisms, with some conservative American viewers seeing it as an attack on the George W. Bush presidency and the conduct of the Iraq war. The *Seattle Times* claimed that 'Without naming Bush or the Patriot Act, it's all unmistakable no matter what your own politics may be.' Lucas claimed this was not the case, as his inspirations were the ancient history of the fall of the Roman Empire and the period of the Vietnam War he had lived through in his youth. However, he did comment that, 'The parallels between Vietnam and what we're doing now in Iraq are unbelievable.'

Episode III grossed almost $850 million worldwide following its release across 115 countries, making it the second highest grossing film of 2005 (behind *Harry Potter and the Goblet of Fire*). The midnight screenings held across the United States grossed $16.5 million alone, breaking the previews record held by *The Lord of the Rings: The Return of the King*. The $50 million opening day gross for the movie set a new record, surpassing the $40.4 million taken by *Spider-Man 2*, while the full single-day gross and Thursday gross broke records previously held by *Shrek 2* and *The Matrix Reloaded*, respectively. While some of these records were themselves later surpassed, the film was deemed to have set American records for the highest gross for all but two of its first twelve days on release. Across the first four days the film grossed $158.5 million, reaching the $200 million point within eight days, and hitting $300 million on its seventeenth day of release. On release in American cinemas until October 2005, Episode III's total US box office tally was $380.2 million, plus an international total of $469.8 million.

As always with the *Star Wars* movies, the awards the film won were not for writing or for acting, but largely technical. In a curious oversight, Episode III was the only *Star Wars* film not nominated for an Academy Award for Best Visual Effects. It was nominated for Best Make-up, but did not win. More populist awards, such as Favourite Film at the People's Choice Awards, Movie of the Year at the Hollywood Film Festival and various other science-fiction event and movie magazine awards, perhaps better reflected the sentiment of general film fans.

With the closing scenes of *Revenge of the Sith*, the *Star Wars* saga was now complete. George Lucas was simply happy to have succeeded in his aim of making the two *Star Wars* trilogies, but despite his oft-stated desire to leave *Star Wars* behind, the franchise wasn't about to let the creator go that easily.

Chapter 14

The Emperor

I like Star Wars, *but I certainly never expected it would take over my life . . . I find myself the head of a corporation; there's a certain irony there. I have become the very thing that I was trying to avoid. That is Darth Vader – he becomes the very thing he was trying to protect himself against.*

George Lucas

Star Wars didn't end with *Revenge of the Sith*, despite what all those involved – especially creator George Lucas – thought might happen. There was another movie unexpectedly released to cinemas, two animated TV series and an exponential growth of the Expanded Universe in books, comics, videogames and toys.

Generations had now grown up with *Star Wars*. Those who were children in 1977 when the first movie emerged to surprise them were now middle aged. While the 'dark times' between the trilogies attracted new fans to the saga (through re-releases in cinemas, on television, on video and on DVD), they often came to it through the Expanded Universe.

The next generation of *Star Wars* fans were children captivated by *The Phantom Menace* and the other prequels and regarded the original trilogy as 'old' movies. Even they were too old for the arrival of *Star Wars: The Clone Wars* on television, so yet another new generation was drawn to the saga through the ongoing animated series. For these kids, the 3D re-release of

The Phantom Menace in 2012 was their first chance to see their animated heroes in live-action form on the big screen. Those who were children when Episode I was first released in 1999 were by then into their twenties.

All this showed the apparently never-ending appeal of *Star Wars*, in all its multi-various forms. There are degrees of *Star Wars* fandom, from those who consume and collect everything, to those who simply enjoy the movies and have some old action figures from when they were kids. There have even been divisions between those who regard the Expanded Universe as legitimate *Star Wars* storytelling and those who only accept the movies (and some television material) – the so-called G-level canon (G for George Lucas created or approved) – as the 'real' deal.

Whatever level of interest and commitment viewers might have, there can be very few unaware of *Star Wars*. The world-wide reach and impact of the films – and everything associated with them – has been immense. *Star Wars* was seemingly everywhere as the second decade of the twenty-first century dawned. The thirtieth anniversary of the original movie came and went – with the United States Post Office issuing a series of celebratory postage stamps – and *Star Wars* spoofs seemed unending, from the movie *Fanboys* (2009) to dedicated episodes of *Family Guy* and *Robot Chicken*. Fans could view, read and play with *Star Wars* at their leisure, and the 2011 revamp of the venerable Star Tours ride (first launched in 1987) allowed them to become totally immersed in the Expanded Universe.

The first of the *Star Wars* animated TV series had appeared in 2003, between the cinema releases of Episode II and Episode III. Under the title *Star Wars: Clone Wars*, the series initially consisted of three-to-seven minute episodes chronicling battles and encounters between the forces of the Galactic Republic, represented by the Jedi Knights, and the Confederacy of Independent States, led by Count Dooku. Impressed by *Samurai Jack* and *Dexter's Laboratory*, Lucas invited animator Genndy Tartakovsky to create the series as a pump primer for

the release of Episode III. It was felt at Lucasfilm that something was needed to help keep *Star Wars* in the public eye in
advance of 2005's final instalment. It was also a relatively inex-
pensive way of exploring the possibilities for animated *Star
Wars* on television.

'We start the clone wars in one Episode and we end it in the
next Episode, but we never actually see the war,' admitted Lucas
of his films. 'So doing the animated series was a great opportunity to fill in some of the blanks in the middle where you get to
deal with the adventures of the war, because obviously that's a
very fertile ground for exciting storytelling.'

Tartakovsky was a Russian-born animator who had grown
up in the United States in the late 1970s, moving to the country
at the age of seven in the same year that *Star Wars* was released.
He spent time in Spain as an animator working on *Batman: The
Animated Series*, learning the nuts and bolts of American TV
animation. He had attended the California Institute of the Arts
and one of his student shorts formed the basis for the Cartoon
Network series *Dexter's Laboratory*.

Tartakovsky approached animating *Star Wars* in his distinctive style, adapting the already established characters to fit.
'George wanted our interpretation,' said Tartakovsky. '[It was]
important for him that we put our own signature on it. The
more we pushed things, the more they liked it.' He had pitched
the show as 'a clone wars-style story with a *Band of Brothers*-feel
to it – where it's episodes of different battles and strategies
during the clone wars'. He was a knowledgeable *Star Wars* fan
and brought this to his interpretation of some characters. For
example, he gave C-3PO more expressive and movable
animated eyes in the style of Nelvana, the animation house that
produced the Boba Fett sequence for the *Star Wars Holiday
Special* and the *Droids* cartoon.

The first group of ten episodes debuted in November 2003,
with a second batch following a year later. Although broken up
into short episodes, the story follows Obi-Wan Kenobi's assault
on the planet Muunilist, while Anakin Skywalker (still the

moody teenager of Episode II) provides air support in his distinctive Jedi starfighter. Meanwhile, Count Dooku trains a new Sith apprentice, Asajj Ventress. This popular character made her debut on the series, but was based upon concept art originally developed for Episode II depicting a female Sith. Ventress would enjoy a healthy ongoing life in the Expanded Universe, eventually becoming a key player in the follow-up animated series.

Dooku sends Ventress to assassinate Skywalker, who in turn pursues her to Yavin IV (site of the rebel alliance base in *Star Wars*). Engaging in a fierce lightsaber duel, Anakin emerges victorious, but only after giving in to his fear and anger (traits of the dark side of the Force and a hint of his future). Other episodes saw Kenobi battle the indomitable bounty-hunter Durge (from a species called the Gen'Dai, named for the show's animator); Kit Fisto leading an underwater assault (an idea later expanded upon in the fourth series of *Star Wars: The Clone Wars* in 2011); Mace Windu single-handedly taking down a seismic tank on Dantooine; Yoda and Amidala rescuing Jedi Luminara Unduli and her apprentice Barris Offe (characters from the climatic Geonosis arena battle in Episode II); and Ki-Adi-Mundi and other Jedi battling with General Grievous (a launching point for the main villain of Episode III).

The final batch of five episodes aired in March 2005 and each was longer in length at twelve to fifteen minutes. According to Lucas the intention was to supply 'a little background on what was going on right before Episode III'. The series jumps forward three years to the concluding stages of the clone wars. A more mature (and longer-haired) Anakin and Obi-Wan pursue Grievous to the planet Nelvaan (named after animation studio Nelvana), where they liberate the inhabitants who had been enslaved by the Techno Union. The show links directly into the opening moments of Episode III as Grievous launches an assault on Coruscant and kidnaps Chancellor Palpatine.

Lucasfilm regarded this *Clone Wars* series as a qualified success. As it was of limited duration, Lucas took to calling it a 'micro-series', claiming it as a pilot for later animated ventures. Widely welcomed by fans, most of whom complained about the short duration of the episodes, *Star Wars: Clone Wars* won two Emmy Awards for Outstanding Animated Programme in 2004 and 2005. The show broke new ground with a near-simultaneous release on television and on the internet via StarWars.com and Cartoon Network's own website (now standard in television). *Clone Wars* directly inspired a Dark Horse comic spin-off that adopted Tartakovsky's graphic style. A series of Hasbro action figures also adopted that distinctive look. The Japanese anime feel brought to the *Clone Wars* series was unique in *Star Wars*, attaching an in vogue style to a venerable franchise.

Many of the voice artists involved in *Star Wars: Clone Wars* would go on to work on the much more extensive follow-up series with the almost identical title *Star Wars: The Clone Wars*. These included Anthony Daniels, Corey Burton, James Arnold Taylor and Tom Kane (as Yoda). When announcing the second series in April 2005, Lucas called it 'a 3D continuation of the pilot series'. Pre-production began in July, once the final big-screen movie had been released. Lucasfilm established a dedicated animation facility in Singapore to facilitate production.

The new series was produced using 3D-style computer animation, but no attempt was made to make the characters photorealistic. Instead, they were modelled after marionettes featured in the 1960s puppet TV shows made by Britain's Gerry Anderson, including *Thunderbirds*. Designer Kilian Plunkett used Tartakovsky's 2D characters as a jumping off point, adapting them to the 3D CGI animation. He made the characters square-jawed with chunky hair that was mostly fixed in place (although this would loosen up in future).

Dave Filoni, an animation professional and huge *Star Wars* fan, was hired as the creative driver for the new show. His work for Nickelodeon on *Avatar: The Last Airbender* (2005–8) brought him to the attention of Lucasfilm. Animation screenwriter Henry Gilroy headed up the initial writing team, under the supervision of producer Catherine Winder – both departed after the first few years.

The big surprise for Filoni – and *Star Wars* fans – was how involved in the series Lucas became, given his oft-stated desire to step away from *Star Wars*. 'George saw what we were doing, the level of detail and what we can do visually, [and] he got more interested and came up with more story ideas of his own,' said Filoni. 'He's very involved with all the stories and coming up with ideas. It's turned out to be a really interesting collaboration.'

Late in the production process, Lucasfilm decided to convert the first three episodes into a movie and give the series a theatrical launch. Even though *Revenge of the Sith* was officially the 'final' *Star Wars* film, the first animated *Star Wars* movie hit cinemas in August 2008. Alongside Anthony Daniels as C-3PO, Samuel L. Jackson and Christopher Lee returned to voice their animated characters, but only Daniels would continue on the regular television series.

Following a spectacular battle on the planet Christophsis, the movie saw Anakin Skywalker and his new padawan Ahsoka Tano charged with the rescue of Jabba the Hutt's kidnapped son, Rotta. This is politically important to the Republic as it wants to keep the Hutt gangster clans on its side rather than that of the Separatists. It transpires that Jabba's uncle, Ziro (voiced in imitation of Truman Capote), orchestrated the kidnapping of his own nephew in league with Count Dooku in an attempt to force the Hutts to turn against the Republic. The revelation causes Jabba to cooperate, opening up his vital trade routes to the Republic's military and supply traffic.

Most reviewers were not kind to this unexpected extra *Star Wars* movie, with *Entertainment Weekly* being particularly scathing. Critic Owen Gleiberman wrote: 'It's hard to tell the droids from the Jedi drones in this robotic animated dud, in which the Lucas Empire Strikes Back – at the audience. What wears you out is Lucas's immersion in a *Star Wars* cosmology that has grown so obsessive-compulsively cluttered yet trivial that it's no longer escapism; it's something you want to escape from.'

The ninety-eight-minute movie had a budget of $8.5 million (almost the pre-release cost of the original *Star Wars* in 1977). Although not a failure, the worldwide box office of just $69 million ($35 million in the United States) was much lower than that usually expected for a *Star Wars* movie, although on a par with similar mid-budget animated films. DVD sales would add another $22.7 million in revenue. The income from the theatrical and DVD releases of *The Clone Wars* movie must have been helpful in financing the first series on television, in much the same way that the *Special Editions* had helped raise funds for the prequel trilogy. Lucas later described the cinema release of *The Clone Wars* as 'almost an afterthought.'

The TV series quickly followed, airing its first season from October 2008 with the introspective 'Ambush'. The episode focused on the relationship between Yoda and a squad of clone troopers without any of the main characters. It was immediately followed on the same night by a more action-packed instalment, 'Rising Malevolence'. The first of the 'Malevolence' trilogy, it was based around a Jedi assault on a secret Separatist super weapon. Just under four million viewers tuned in, making this one of the highest rated animated shows on American television, giving Cartoon Network its most-watched series premiere to that date.

Season one of *The Clone Wars* featured repeated appearances by *Revenge of the Sith*'s General Grievous, while other episodes followed the exploits of a rookie clone trooper squad, the adventures of R2-D2 (in episodes directed by *Revenge of the Sith*'s animation director Rob Coleman), and multiple episode story arcs dealing with the kidnapping of Count Dooku and the outbreak of a deadly virus. The twenty-two-episode season climaxed with 'Hostage Crisis', introducing a deadly new bounty-hunter named Cad Bane (modelled after Lee Van Cleef from *The Good, the Bad and the Ugly*, 1966). Ratings remained fairly steady, having fallen from that initial four million to between two-to-three million regularly.

Each subsequent season was a learning process for *The Clone*

Wars team, with refinements and improvements in animation techniques. The challenge came in filling in the story details of the three-year period between Episode II and Episode III, as everyone already knew the outcome. 'We get little pieces of the puzzle along the way that tell you more about Palpatine and tell you more about Anakin's relationship with him,' said Filoni. 'Things like that that help so that the next time you watch *Revenge of the Sith* you say, "Oh I see; now I understand even better why that occurred." We know how some of these stories come out, we know what happens to the Jedi and we know what happens to the clones. We know the Empire gets formed. But how do you create a series and suspend the interest knowing those facts?'

The big question mark was what would happen to major new characters that didn't feature in Episode III, primarily Anakin's new sidekick Ahsoka. Ashley Eckstein gave voice to the character for the show's run. 'That's definitely the number one question people always ask,' said Eckstein. 'I'm so emotionally attached to the character [that] the thought of anything bad happening to her makes me emotional. I trust [that] Dave Filoni and George Lucas are going to make the best decision for the overall storyline, and for Ahsoka. I'm fine with whatever her legacy turns out to be . . .'

The second season focused on bounty-hunters, building the character of Cad Bane into a recurring villain. 'Lightsaber Lost' – in which Ahsoka loses her vital Jedi weapon – riffed on the Akira Kurosawa film *Stray Dog* (1949) in which a detective loses his police-issued pistol and has to recover it. Episodes set around the planet Mandalore ('The Mandalore Plot', 'Voyage of Temptation', 'Duchess of Mandalore') not only reinvented the Mandalorian commandos that gave rise to the iconic Boba Fett armour, but also gave Obi-Wan Kenobi a romantic relationship. The season also reintroduced the revenge-obsessed young Boba Fett from Episode II (and he would reappear in the show's third season). A creature-feature B-movie double bill of 'The Zillo Beast' and 'The Zillo Beast Strikes Back' saw a giant lizard-like creature captured by the Jedi escape and terrorize Coruscant (a homage to *King Kong*, 1933). Ratings remained stable with individual instalments scoring between 2.5 and 3 million viewers.

The third season in 2010–11 featured not only a young Chewbacca in the season finale, 'Wookiee Hunt', but also Lucas himself in the form of Baron Papanoida. Lucas had originated the blue-faced character for a brief director cameo in *Revenge of the Sith*, but he was recreated in animated form for 'Sphere of Influence', co-written by his daughter Katie (as were several other episodes). The Citadel trilogy ('The Citadel', 'Counterattack', 'Citadel Rescue') not only played out as a reprise of the infiltration of the Death Star from *Star Wars*, but also introduced *The Clone Wars*' audience to a younger Grand Moff Tarkin. Here Captain Tarkin begins to develop an interesting relationship with Jedi Anakin Skywalker, sowing the seeds of the characters seen in *A New Hope*.

The first half of the third season was devoted to Republic politics (disappointing many fans keen to see clone wars action), reaching a creative low point with the episode 'Corruption'. The episode sees the foiling of a plot to import bootleg bottled tea (dubbed 'poison Snapple' by discontented fans) to Mandalore. Another low point was 'Evil Plans' in which C-3PO goes shopping (!), only to be captured by Cad Bane.

Things picked up dramatically in the season's second half. The surprising death of Ziro the Hutt (in 'Hunt for Ziro') was quickly followed by the Nightsisters trilogy ('Nightsisters', 'Monster', 'Witches of the Mist') and the mystical Mortis trilogy ('Overlords', 'Altar of Mortis', 'Ghosts of Mortis'). These six episodes showed the potential of *The Clone Wars* to go far beyond the movies, introducing more of the ever-growing Expanded Universe to younger *Star Wars* fans.

Introduced in the novel *The Courtship of Princess Leia* by Dave Wolverton, the Nightsisters were a Sith-style dark-side offshoot of the Dathomir Witches. Devoted fans would later 'ret-con' (meaning to make retroactive continuity links between stories) Siân Phillips's witch Charal from TV movie *Ewoks: The Battle for Endor* as a Nightsister. Various novels and even the Star Wars Galaxies trading card game had deepened the mythology of the Nightsisters, but this trio of episodes brought them more to the fore. The Nightsisters sent their super-powered assassin Savage Opress to be Count Dooku's new apprentice, while also secretly plotting Dooku's assassination. The trilogy ended with a hint of the return of Opress's 'brother', Darth Maul (picked up in the show's fourth season).

Previously described as an 'energy field' by Obi-Wan Kenobi and revealed to be propagated by midi-chlorians by Qui-Gon Jinn, the Mortis trilogy delved into the nature of the Force. These episodes introduced a new Force-powered 'family' located on the remote planet Mortis, itself a conduit for the mystical energy. The Father, Son and Daughter represent different aspects of the Force. Both Anakin and his padawan Ahsoka are subject to temptations and trials, with Anakin offered a glimpse of his ultimate fate as Darth Vader, and Kenobi seemingly encountering the Force-ghost of his dead Jedi Master, Qui-Gon Jinn. These fantasy-infused episodes looked superb, with atmospheric animation and wonderful characters. Together with the Nightsister episodes, they represented the highpoint of *The Clone Wars* and revealed the potential the series had yet to unlock. Ratings, however, fell slightly for the third season, ranging from a low of 1.5 million ('Citadel Rescue') to a high of 2.3 million (the Chewbacca-starring season finale, 'Wookiee Hunt').

By its fourth year, *The Clone Wars* was a known quantity both for those who made it and those who watched. Production techniques had improved, resulting in better animation and greater ambition as seen in the opening trio of Mon Calamari-set episodes ('Water War', 'Gungan Attack', 'Prisoners'). The action in these three adventures takes place almost entirely underwater, an unusual environment for *Star Wars* (touched upon in the Gungan city in *The Phantom Menace*). In a surprising throwback to the 1980s *Droids* TV series, a pair of episodes ('Mercy Mission', 'Nomad Droids') focused on the maverick adventures of C-3PO and R2-D2, whose picaresque antics spoofed various movies, including *The Wizard of Oz* and *Gulliver's Travels*. These episodes undoubtedly appealed to younger viewers, but also offered a direct connection to older fans' own childhood recollections of the animated 1980s *Droids* TV show.

The travails of war featured in the Umbara episodes ('Darkness on Umbara', 'The General', 'Plan of Dissent', 'Carnage of Krell'). A new Jedi General – Pong Krell – relieves Skywalker as the commander of the 501st Legion, only for his disdainful attitude to 'disposable' clones to put the squad in unnecessary dangers. Across the series many clone troopers had been given individual characters, but these episodes personalized their nature more than before. Walter Murch directed 'The General' using sound as much as visuals to bring the frantic world of galactic warfare alive (Murch had supplied the soundscape for Coppola's *Apocalypse Now*).

By the time Darth Maul appeared, following a series of episodes dealing with slavery and Anakin's personal feelings on the issues, on season four of *The Clone Wars*, Lucasfilm Animation in Singapore was well into production of the fifth season while in Lucasfilm's San Francisco HQ Supervising Director Dave Filoni was working on the scripts for a planned sixth season. Lucas had committed to 'at least 100 episodes' when launching the show, a run of at least five years.

The appearance of Darth Maul on the *Star Wars* television series was ideally timed for the character's reappearance in cinemas in the 2012 3D re-release of *Star Wars: Episode I – The Phantom Menace*. Since the resurgence of 3D movies in the twenty-first century and especially the success of James Cameron's *Avatar* (2009), George Lucas had been seriously investigating the possibility of converting the *Star Wars* movies for 3D presentation. Test work had been done and screened to theatre-owners using a portion of the original movie. Once he was satisfied with the results, Lucas decided to re-release the movies in 3D at the rate of one a year in numerical order beginning with Episode I. While that film featured many sequences enhanced in 3D – the Podrace, the Darth Maul duel – many fans were desperate to see the original trilogy in cinemas once more. This schedule would mean a wait until 2015 for *A New Hope*, with *The Empire Strikes Back* and *Return of the Jedi* following in 2016 and 2017. Even those releases were not guaranteed, as Lucasfilm announced that any 3D releases beyond Episode I would depend upon how well that movie performed at the box office. There seemed little doubt *The Phantom Menace* (re-released 'flat' at the same time) would be anything other than a box office success.

Beyond *Star Wars* in films and television, there was still much going on in the Expanded Universe. In June 2005, Lucasfilm had relocated Industrial Light and Magic, Lucasfilm Licensing and the LucasArts videogame company to the vacated Letterman Army Medical Centre in San Francisco's Presidio. Renamed the Letterman Digital Arts Centre, this new twenty-three-acre base (along with Marin County's Skywalker Ranch and the nearby Big Rock Ranch, and Lucas Animation in Singapore) was to be the headquarters of Lucas's consolidated empire.

The long-running 'New Jedi Order' novel series had been superseded by the 'Dark Nest' trilogy (from 2005), several Timothy Zahn novels (*Survivor's Quest*, *Outbound Flight*, *Allegiance*, *Choices of One*) and the nine-novel series 'Legacy of the Force' (starting with Aaron Allston's *Betrayal* in 2006 and concluding with Troy Denning's *Invincible* in 2008). A sequel series of another nine novels, under the umbrella title 'Fate of the Jedi', started in 2009 with Aaron Allston's *Outcast* and concluded in 2012 with Troy Denning's *Apocalypse*. All these books expanded upon the post-*Return of the Jedi* lives of the heroes from the original trilogy, with Luke, Leia and Han growing older and their children taking up the roles of the Jedi (and the Sith) in the post-Empire galaxy.

These ongoing series were interspersed by various standalone novels (notably titles like *Millennium Falcon*, charting the history of Han's ship; *Death Star*, covering the battle station's construction and destruction; and the pulp adventure *Luke Skywalker and the Shadows of Mindor*), and moves into new areas, like the horror novels *Death Troopers* and *Red Harvest*. Despite these varied titles, many fans of Expanded Universe storytelling were tired of the long-form novel series, feeling they often outstayed their welcome, with the 'Fate of the Jedi' series coming in for particular criticism. In the wake of long-term series editor Sue Rostoni's retirement in 2011, there was speculation of an Expanded Universe reboot, with a fresh start proposed for *Star Wars* spin-off fiction. While in some ways attractive (similar things had happened in movies with the James Bond and *Spider-Man* series), Lucasfilm and publisher Del Rey rejected the idea, preferring to continue filling gaps in the *Star Wars* universe timeline (counting back to the Old Republic era they had over 4,000 years to play with).

The world of *Star Wars* comics was similarly clogged with a proliferation of titles. The prequel era had resulted in a series of spin-offs (featuring Darth Maul, Qui-Gon and Obi-Wan, Jango Fett and Grievous), and some notable ongoing series (among them the continuity-busting *Infinities* [2001–4]; *Empire* [2002–6]; *Jedi* [2004–6]; and *Obsession* [2004–5]). The post-*Revenge of the Sith* titles looked back to the Old Republic era in *Knights of the Old Republic* (2006–2010); the original trilogy period in *Rebellion* (2006–8); and the future (set 137 years after *A New Hope*) in *Legacy* (2006–2010), featuring the adventures of Cade Skywalker, a descendant of Luke. The intermittent, although ongoing, *Dark Times* series (from 2006) continued to tell stories set during the original trilogy. A new title – *Dawn of the Jedi* – was launched in 2012 depicting the earliest days of the Jedi Order. Tie-ins with the videogame *The Force Unleashed* and *The Clone Wars* TV series were also put out by Dark Horse, although the company tried to restrict its individual titles to between three and four comics each month, believing that more than that meant fans had to make choices.

Besides the prequel movie spin-offs (which had also boosted

Hasbro's toy sales), *Star Wars* videogames were also flourishing. The aforementioned *The Force Unleashed* (2008) and its sequel was akin to the earlier *Shadows of the Empire* project, in that the game was part of a larger release programme (including a 'making-of' book, a novelization, a dedicated toy line and a comic book). *Star Wars* videogames were available in just about every genre, from flight simulators (the *Rogue Squadron* series), first-person shooters (*Republic Commando*), role-playing games (the epic *Knights of the Old Republic*) and online, massively interactive role-playing games (*The Old Republic*, from the end of 2011 onwards).

Fan activities continued unabated, with fan films, fiction and costuming proliferating – the charitable 501st Legion were celebrated in a documentary on the *Star Wars* Blu-ray release called *Star Warriors*. The Star Wars Celebration conventions had provided a new focus for fandom since 1999. The first notorious event (celebrating the release of *The Phantom Menace*) was held in Denver, Colorado, and was almost washed away by torrential rains (the event was held in a series of tents). A second (2002) and third (2005) Celebration followed in Indianapolis, Indiana, with attendance numbers building each time. Lucas attended Celebration III, announcing he was working on a live-action *Star Wars* television series and that the Disney *Star Wars* theme park ride, Star Tours, would be updated. In 2007, Celebration IV was relocated to Los Angeles and focused on the thirtieth anniversary of *Star Wars*: it was the biggest event to date, with 35,000 fans attending. That same year saw Celebration: Europe take place in London, with Celebration: Japan following in 2008 (celebrating thirty years since *Star Wars* was released there in 1978). A change of organizing company saw Celebration V relocated to Orlando, Florida, in 2010. The event was such a success that Celebration VI returned there for 2012. It seemed likely that Lucasfilm would maintain the Celebration events as long as attendance numbers held up.

When not at conventions or watching *The Clone Wars* (alongside rewatching the movies), fans were kept informed, up-to-date and entertained by such fan-produced media as the website TheForce.net and the popular audio podcast TheForceCast.

The *Star Wars* story grew and changed in the telling. The first movie relates to the rest of the expanded saga in the way that Tolkien's *The Hobbit* related to his epic *The Lord of the Rings*. The original *Star Wars* was a fairly light, standalone adventure pitching good against evil, with none of the elements that George Lucas later described as 'the Skywalker saga'. There is little in the publicly available material from Lucas's first attempts to work out the *Star Wars* story that suggests the family saga that resulted across the six movies. That element was drawn from his own life, as Lucas confronted his relationship with his own father.

The all-encompassing theme that runs through the entire *Star Wars* saga, though, is that of the mechanical versus the biological. The Empire represents 'technological terror' according to Vader's description of the Death Star, while the Empire's humanity-first policy marginalizes the diverse alien races that made up the Republic and largely populate the rebellion. Where the Empire (and its representatives, the Emperor and Vader) rely on technology, the Jedi put their faith in the Force. Yoda notes that 'a Jedi's strength flows from the Force', while Obi-Wan describes the Force as 'an energy field created by all living things. It surrounds us and penetrates us. It binds the galaxy together.'

The clearest depiction of these mechanical versus biological conflicts comes in the battles between the nascent Empire's battledroids and the organic Gungans (in *The Phantom Menace*) or the clone troopers (during the clone wars). *Return of the Jedi* pitches the mechanical forces of the Empire against the 'primitive', disorganized Ewoks. This is George Lucas reinventing his original take on *Apocalypse Now*, putting his 1970s view of the defeat of America at the hands of the Vietcong into action. He also brought his thoughts on the fall of republics to the prequel trilogy, again accessing his view of early-1970s American politics under Nixon and his reading of history (including the fall of the Roman Empire at the hands of more 'primitive' cultures, and the following Dark Ages – the equivalent of the 'dark times' mentioned by Obi-Wan).

Influences from mythology and religion are woven through the *Star Wars* saga, but it is perhaps the politics (in terms of wider society, as well at a personal level) that truly dominate. The prequel trilogy added a welcome layer of complexity to the simple good versus evil theme of the original trilogy. By depicting the evolution of the Republic into the Empire and the manipulations of the triple-identity of Palpatine/the Emperor/ Sidious, Lucas introduced moral ambiguity to his saga and brought some depth to his storytelling.

George Lucas was never a mystical guru or an eccentric recluse, despite the attempts of some commentators to portray him as such. While 'Jedi' has been listed as the religion of choice by many people in various countries' census forms (in 2001 there were 70,000 in Australia, 53,000 in New Zealand, 21,000 in Canada and over 400,000 in the UK), it has never been a real-world religion.

Lucas attributed the origins of the Force to a 1963 abstract film by Arthur Lipsett called *21-87* (Lipsett's sampling approach to video and audio influenced *THX 1138*). 'It had a very powerful effect on me [as] it was very much the kind of thing that I wanted to do. I was extremely influenced by that particular movie,' said Lucas. The short included a discussion between artificial intelligence pioneer Warren S. McCulloch and cinematographer Roman Kroitor (the developer of IMAX) about sources of intelligence. McCulloch argued that humans were simply complex machines, but Kroitor countered with his belief that 'Many people feel that in the contemplation of nature and in communication with other living things, they become aware of some kind of force behind this apparent mask which we see in front of us, and they call it God.'

Beyond this source, Lucas acknowledged that the idea of the Force was universal and drawn from a variety of worldwide religions and folklores, not to mention the 'flower-power' counter culture of California in the 1960s (of which Lucas was never really a part, but he was certainly aware of it even if only through Coppola).

'The Force evolved out of various developments of character and plot,' said Lucas. 'I wanted a concept of religion based on the premise that there is a God and there is good and evil. I began to distil the essence of all religions into what I thought was a basic idea common to all religions and common to primitive thinking. I wanted to develop something that was non-denominational but still had a kind of religious reality.'

Lucas lifted elements of Shinto, of Buddhism, of Taoism and of Celtic druidic lore. Hindu theology suggested a unifying Brahman energy that composes the universe and can be channelled for good or evil, as in the 'light side' and 'dark side' of the Force. The works of Carlos Castaneda, popular in the United States in the 1960s and 1970s, described humans as luminous 'eggs' connected with 'the force of nature' through 'lines of power'. This was echoed in Yoda's description of living beings as 'luminous' and not simply 'crude matter' in *The Empire Strikes Back*. In truth, Lucas amalgamated and simplified some of these influences into his notion of the Force, adding some spirituality and fantasy to his science-fiction epic.

John Baxter's 1999 biography of Lucas attempted to depict him as an isolated figure, surrounded by 'followers' who believed in the reality of the Force. Baxter described Skywalker Ranch as Lucas's 'home' (it is not; it's simply an office complex) and his entourage as 'people anxious to do whatever he ordered, agree with whatever he said' (McCallum – and others – will happily relate the many arguments they have had with Lucas). The biographer paints a picture of a Howard Hughes figure with a fear of physical contact and relationships, whose head is constantly in a fantasy world of his own creation rather than reality. While there may be some basic truths here, could such an isolated figure be not only a creative movie director, but also the builder of a business empire that employed thousands?

Watching Lucas at work on the sets of Episode II and Episode III in Australia and interviewing him on several occasions in London and at Skywalker Ranch, there was little sign of the non-communicative eccentric described by Baxter. He's certainly a man who guards his privacy, but he's also someone who set out to be a filmmaker but has found his destiny defined by just one film series. He's vacillated between resisting the pull of 'the force' of *Star Wars* and embracing it. In the mid-1980s to the mid-1990s, he tried to escape, but the pull of the Force was too strong, and Lucas gave in to the inevitable and embraced *Star Wars* once more.

What of the future? The *Star Wars* franchise was considered all-but-dead by the mid-1980s. Lucas, tired of his creation by this point, took a decade out from close involvement with *Star Wars*, attempting to expand his wider movie-making interests (not altogether successfully), while developing the filmmaking technology that would allow him to return to the universe of the Force. By the early 1990s, just a decade after wrapping *Return of the Jedi*, his thoughts had turned to actually making the prequel trilogy.

Following those three movies, which Lucas claimed concluded the Skywalker family saga (despite former promises of nine or even twelve *Star Wars* movies), this time he didn't walk away. Long-expressed thoughts of going off to create 'small, personal' movies that no one would want to see evaporated. Instead, Lucas got far more involved than he intended in the creation and supervision of *The Clone Wars* animated TV series, devoting himself to a deeper form of storytelling than his movies had allowed.

Following the conclusion of the movies in 2005, Lucas announced his intention to produce a live-action *Star Wars* television series, touted as being gritty and grown-up in the style of the popular Western show *Deadwood*. The series would be set in the twenty-year period between the rise of the Empire in *Star Wars: Episode III – Revenge of the Sith* and the rise of the rebellion in *Star Wars: Episode IV – A New Hope*. It would explore the underworld of crime lords, like Jabba the Hutt, and bounty-hunters, like Boba Fett. Off limits to the TV show would be the Skywalker saga: Lucas considered that story as having been concluded. Rick McCallum was set to produce the show, which he described as being 'like *The Godfather*, it's the Empire slowly building up its power base around the galaxy, what happens in Coruscant, and it's [about] a group of underground bosses who live there and control drugs, prostitution.'

Despite rumours of the production being based in Australia (as with the prequels) or in Czech Republic capital Prague (where Lucasfilm's 2012 movie *Red Tails* had shot), and that casting had begun, the project was still dormant in the second decade of the twenty-first century. While Lucas claimed to have over fifty scripts written, the cost of matching the movies' production values on television during an economic downturn was holding Lucasfilm back. Lucas stated to *TV Guide* that 'The Emperor and Darth Vader are heard about – people talk about them – but you never see them. There are stormtroopers, but there are no Jedi.'

Despite these ambitions, the conditions were just not right to launch the show. 'It sits on the shelf,' Lucas told *MovieWeb*. 'We are trying to figure out a different way of making movies. We are looking for a different technology that we can use, that will make it economically feasible to shoot the show. We have to figure out how to make it at about a tenth of the cost of the [*Star Wars*] features, because it's television. It's a very difficult process.' As always, Lucas was also wondering how his new technological developments could affect filmmaking generally beyond his own efforts. 'Obviously, when we do figure this problem out, it will dramatically affect features, because feature films cost $250 to $350 million. When we figure this out, they will be able to make a feature film for $50 million.'

The prospect of the live-action *Star Wars* television series seemed to rule out the idea that Lucas might continue the *Star Wars* story chronologically beyond *Return of the Jedi*. In 1983, interviewed in Denise Worrell's book *Icons: Intimate Portraits*,

Lucas had described his *Star Wars* ambitions beyond the initial three movies. 'The first trilogy is social and political [the prequels] . . . [the second trilogy] is more about personal growth and self realization [the original trilogy], and the third deals with moral and philosophical problems [the post-Jedi trilogy]. The sequel is about Jedi Knighthood, justice, confrontation and passing on what you have learned.' Despite being quoted early in his career as intending to make more than six *Star Wars* movies, by the time he embarked upon the prequel trilogy during the 1990s, he had begun to backtrack on whether he would ever complete the originally planned nine-film cycle. 'For the third trilogy, I don't know if I will still be alive when it comes time to make them,' he told the French edition of *Premiere* magazine in 1993. *Star Wars* producer Gary Kurtz confirmed in 1999 that Lucas did have rough ideas for a concluding trilogy. 'It was Luke's journey really up to becoming the premiere Jedi Knight in the Obi-Wan Kenobi mould and his ultimate confrontation with the Emperor,' reported fan site TheForce. Net of his address to a convention audience. The planned confrontation with the Emperor was used in *Return of the Jedi* (as was the notion that Luke had an unknown sister, originally part of the sequel trilogy, but a role given to Leia instead).

By 2001, Lucas was quite emphatic: the long-rumoured final *Star Wars* trilogy would not be happening. 'Each time I do a trilogy it's ten years out of my life. I'll finish Episode III and I'll be sixty. The next twenty years after that I want to spend doing something other than *Star Wars*. If at eighty I'm still lively and having a good time and think I can work hard for another ten years between eighty and ninety, I might consider it. But don't count on it.' He later told *Entertainment Weekly*, 'The saga itself, the story of the Skywalker family, is over!'

Fans, however, could never let go of the idea of a final *Star Wars* trilogy, especially after the mixed reception that met the prequels. Where the first films had been about the son (Luke Skywalker) and the second trilogy of prequels focused on the father (Anakin Skywalker), many hoped the third post-*Return of the Jedi* trilogy might feature the daughter (Leia Organa). As with Luke, Leia was also powerful in the Force (explored to a degree in spin-off novels, although her character follows a more diplomatic career in rebuilding the galactic Republic). A third series of films could be built around Carrie Fisher's Leia, passing on the knowledge of the Force to a younger cohort of would-be Jedi. Fisher's 2011 dramatic weight loss fuelled speculation she was preparing to return to movies, and what could be more suitable than acting as the Alec Guinness figure in a brand new *Star Wars* trilogy? There was no reason Mark Hamill could not play an older Luke (the actor had long claimed that Lucas had told him he would want him back thirty years after the first movies to play an older Luke), while even the *Star Wars*-hating Harrison Ford might be persuaded to perform a cameo.

With the annual 3D re-releases of all six *Star Wars* scheduled to run until 2017, there would be plenty of time to create and produce a third trilogy of films for immediate release thereafter. Such movies could also provide the ideal launch platform for the long-delayed live-action television series. Whether Lucas himself would write and direct a third trilogy or not is unclear. Like the first trilogy, he may be happier to hand over the films to others. There is definitely interest among some directors who would love to get involved. Director Joe Johnston (*The Rocketeer,* 1991) used the release of his *Captain America* (2011) movie to publicly tout for a Boba Fett-focused film that he could direct. Johnston had originally been involved in the creation of the character for *The Empire Strikes Back* and was keen to explore Fett further. Little came of his suggestion, but it did prove that successful filmmakers other than Lucas might be willing to carry on the *Star Wars* saga beyond what the creator had intended for it.

As Lucas approaches seventy, it is uncertain whether he is giving thoughts to how the *Star Wars* legacy can continue without his involvement, but fans certainly are. Despite the fact that Lucas could easily enjoy another twenty years of good health and creative involvement with the franchise, there have been signs that others are being groomed to take over. The slightly younger McCallum (sixty in 2012) would in all probability continue to be his facilitator. McCallum once told of a nightmare he'd had featuring both him and Lucas in their eighties. In the dream, the aged Lucas calls McCallum telling him to pull the *Star Wars* movies out again, as the creator had just come up with another idea to change them again and make them 'perfect'.

However, others have been more involved in the ongoing creative storytelling work of *Star Wars* than McCallum. Both Dave Filoni and Lucas's adopted daughter Katie were heavily involved in *The Clone Wars* series and could be seen as inheritors of the legacy. It would be more likely for either of those (or both) to step in as the lead creative forces on *Star Wars* than anyone from the Expanded Universe worlds of novels, comics or videogames. Both Filoni and Katie Lucas worked very closely with Lucas in the creation of storylines for *The Clone Wars*, alongside a team of other writers. It seemed the creator was using the animated television series, and Filoni, to explore the wider implications of his creation beyond the scope offered by the movies and the saga of the Skywalker family.

George Lucas has long been an admirer of Walt Disney, who launched a theme park and merchandising empire on the back of his animated cartoons. Disney's iconic characters of Mickey Mouse and Donald Duck had gone on to entertain generations long after Disney's death in 1966. Lucas had even been among the first visitors to Disneyland in 1955, aged just eleven. He worked directly with the Disney company on the *Captain EO* theme park film and the two versions of the Star Tours ride. The Disney company had eventually gone on to buy animation studio Pixar, which had begun as the graphics department of Lucasfilm.

Lucas is the nearest thing the movie world has produced to a second Walt Disney. His timeless creations have entertained millions, and have been lucratively spun-off into every conceivable format. They have attracted a dedicated and devoted fan base as well as appealing widely to general audiences. In heroes like Luke Skywalker, Han Solo, Princess Leia and Obi-Wan Kenobi, and in tragic figures like Anakin Skywalker, Boba Fett and Darth Maul, Lucas created cinematic icons. He had started out wanting to make simple films to entertain audiences, but had inadvertently created a classic movie mythology and built a filmmaking empire.

The most successful star to come out of the *Star Wars* movies, Harrison Ford, recognized a great drive and a surprising amount of autobiography in Lucas's telling of the *Star Wars* saga. 'It is amazing what you can do when you have a vision', Ford said, 'when you can bend other people's will to your desire. Despite the enormous difficulties of the production of *Star Wars*, the thing that kept it focused and directed towards the ambition was George's vision and passion for the idea. I always thought the character of Luke Skywalker was George; George growing up, George facing conflict and the need to prove himself – and he did, powerfully. So you'd see the character of Luke Skywalker change from one film to the next in much the same way that George was developing.'

In the original *Star Wars* Luke gives up his guidance computer and trusts his instincts and the Force to guide him in destroying the Death Star. In creating *Star Wars*, Lucas had unleashed a monster that came to dominate his life. After the initial trilogy he tried to resist the lure of his creation and branch out in new directions. Instead, his immersion in filmmaking technology brought him back to *Star Wars* and he created a new trilogy that somehow lacked the heart of the original, despite all the digital innovation. Perhaps, like Luke, Lucas should have given up his computers and trusted to the Force within himself. He started out as a rebellious filmmaker, aiming to buck the Hollywood system. Instead, he'd built an empire he could not escape.

Over thirty-five years *Star Wars* grew from a little-regarded space movie to an all-conquering multi-media franchise. Behind it all had been a natural born rebel who refused to do things the established way. From making comic books, novels and toys central to his launch strategy for the original *Star Wars*, to spending his own fortune in developing technology that changed the way movies were made, George Lucas had created a unique world that future generations would continue to play within. It appears that the Force will be with us . . . always!

Appendix

Acknowledgments

During my decade as editor and managing editor of the UK *Official Star Wars Magazine* and the US *Star Wars Insider*, I had the great privilege of meeting and interviewing several of those involved in the creation of the original *Star Wars* saga, and the cast and crews of Episode II and Episode III. I wouldn't have believed it as a ten-year-old captivated by the original *Star Wars* that I would not only meet these folks, but also visit Skywalker Ranch (several times!) and the *Star Wars* studios in Australia. Thanks are due to everyone who made that young kid's dream come true. Also thanks to Paul Simpson for reading (and re-reading!) the manuscript in draft and pointing out the inevitable howlers . . .

Works consulted include:

Author interviews with George Lucas, Mark Hamill, Anthony Daniels, John Mollo (costumes), Charles Lippincott (marketing), John Williams, and the cast and crews of Episode II and Episode III, including Rick McCallum, Ben Burtt, John Knoll, Rob Coleman, Trisha Biggar and Robin Gurland.

Alan Arnold. *Once Upon a Galaxy: A Journal of the Making of Star Wars: The Empire Strikes Back* (New York: Del Rey, 1980).

John Baxter, *George Lucas: A Biography* (London: Harper Collins, 1999).

Peter Biskind, *Easy Riders, Raging Bulls* (London: Bloomsbury, 1998).

Laurent Bouzereau (ed.), *Star Wars: The Annotated Screenplays* (New York: Del Rey, 1997).

Laurent Bouzereau and Jody Duncan, *The Making of the Phantom Menace* (London: Ebury Press, 1999).

Charles Champlin, *George Lucas: The Creative Impulse* (London: Virgin Books, 1997).

Jody Duncan, *Mythmaking: Behind the Scenes of Attack of the Clones* (New York: Del Rey, 2002).

Garry Jenkins, *Empire Building: The Remarkable Real Life Story of Star Wars* (London: Simon & Shuster, 1997).

Sally Kline (ed.), *George Lucas: Interviews* (Mississippi: University Press of Mississippi, 1999).

Marcus Hearn, *Attack of the Clones: The Illustrated Companion* (London: Ebury Press, 2002).

The Official Star Wars Magazine.

John Philip Peecher (ed.), *The Making of Star Wars: Return of the Jedi* (New York: Del Rey, 1983).

Dale Pollock, *Skywalking: The Life and Films of George Lucas* (Hollywood: Samuel French, 1990).

J. W. Rinzler, *The Making of Star Wars: Revenge of the Sith* (London: Ebury Press, 2005).

J. W. Rinzler, *The Making of Star Wars: Revenge of the Sith – The Final Chapter* (online supplement) (New York: Del Rey, 2005).

Jim Smith, *Virgin Film: George Lucas* (London: Virgin Books, 2003).

Star Wars Insider.

Ryder Windham, *Star Wars: Year by Year – A Visual Chronicle* (London: Dorling Kindersley, 2010).

Resources

The *Star Wars* movies (and spin-offs) have been available to buy on VHS, LaserDisc, DVD and Blu-ray Disc.

starwars.com is the official Lucasfilm web site and a good resource for information and video.

theforce.net is the best fan-run news site, updated daily with all things *Star Wars*.

forcecast.net is the home of the best *Star Wars* podcast, The ForceCast, professionally presented by Jason Swank and Jimmy 'Mac' McInerney.

rebelscum.com is the home of *Star Wars* collecting.

jedinews.co.uk is the prime UK-based *Star Wars* news and information fan site

ralphmcquarrie.com is the official home for the art of *Star Wars* concept artist Ralph McQuarrie.

Index

The initials GL refer to George Lucas